KEY CONCEPTS IN CRIMINOLOGY

Palgrave Key Concepts provide an accessible and comprehensive range of subject glossaries at undergraduate level. Ideal companions to a standard textbook, they are invaluable reading for students throughout their course of study and especially effective as a revision aid.

Key Concepts in Accounting and Finance
Key Concepts in Business and Management Research Methods
Key Concepts in Business Practice
Key Concepts in Criminology and Criminal Justice
Key Concepts in Cultural Studies
Key Concepts in Drama and Performance (second edition)
Key Concepts in e-Commerce
Key Concepts in Human Resource Management
Key Concepts in Information and Communication Technology
Key Concepts in Innovation
Key Concepts in International Business
Key Concepts in Innovation
Key Concepts in Language and Linguistics (second edition)
Key Concepts in Law (second edition)
Key Concepts in Leisure
Key Concepts in Management
Key Concepts in Marketing
Key Concepts in Operations Management
Key Concepts in Philosophy
Key Concepts in Politics
Key Concepts in Public Relations
Key Concepts in Psychology
Key Concepts in Social Research Methods
Key Concepts in Sociology
Key Concepts in Strategic Management
Key Concepts in Tourism

Palgrave Key Concepts: Literature
General Editors: John Peck and Martin Coyle

Key Concepts in Contemporary Literature
Key Concepts in Creative Writing
Key Concepts in Crime Fiction
Key Concepts in Medieval Literature
Key Concepts in Modernist Literature
Key Concepts in Postcolonial Literature
Key Concepts in Renaissance Literature
Key Concepts in Romantic Literature
Key Concepts in Victorian Literature
Literary Terms and Criticism (third edition)

Further titles are in preparation

www.palgravekeyconcepts.com

Palgrave Key Concepts
Series Standing Order
ISBN 978–1–4039–3210–5
(outside North America only)

You can receive future titles in this series as they are published by placing a standing order. Please contact your bookseller or, in the case of difficulty, write to us at the address below with your name and address, the title of the series and the ISBN quoted above.

Customer Services Department, Macmillan Distribution Ltd
Houndmills, Basingstoke, Hampshire RG21 6XS, England

Key Concepts in Criminology and Criminal Justice

Helena McFarquhar
Visiting Lecturer at the College of Law, London, having previously taught at the universities of Cambridge and Anglian Ruskin

palgrave
macmillan

First published 2011 by
PALGRAVE MACMILLAN

Palgrave Macmillan in the UK is an imprint of Macmillan Publishers Limited, registered in England, company number 785998, of Houndmills, Basingstoke, Hampshire RG21 6XS.

Palgrave Macmillan in the US is a division of St Martin's Press LLC, 175 Fifth Avenue, New York, NY 10010.

Palgrave Macmillan is the global academic imprint of the above companies and has companies and representatives throughout the world.

Palgrave® and Macmillan® are registered trademarks in the United States, the United Kingdom, Europe and other countries.

ISBN 978-0-230-51698-4   ISBN 978-0-230-34557-7 (eBook)

DOI 10.1007/978-0-230-34557-7

This book is printed on paper suitable for recycling and made from fully managed and sustained forest sources. Logging, pulping and manufacturing processes are expected to conform to the environmental regulations of the country of origin.

A catalogue record for this book is available from the British Library.

10   9   8   7   6   5   4   3   2   1
20   19   18   17   16   15   14   13   12   11

Contents

Introduction

Although Criminology and Criminal Justice studies have long featured in university degree programmes, they have become particularly popular with students in recent years – no doubt influenced by crime fiction and media crime dramas which have captured the public's imagination, such as *Cracker* or *Kavanagh QC*.

Criminology is concerned with crime and the ways in which society deals, or should deal, with it. It is a multidisciplinary subject, deriving from philosophy, psychology, geography, sociology, biology, medicine and law, to name but a few disciplines!

Crime impacts significantly on people's lives, on citizens, offenders and criminal justice personnel, and the work of criminologists gives rise to or supports policies and practices adopted by government and its institutions.

Crime is not static or fixed but is constantly changing as attitudes, values and circumstances alter through time in society. Activities which were once not illegal may become so, such as paedophile grooming of potential victims in Internet chat rooms or stalking of celebrities. Similarly, conduct which was illegal may be decriminalized, adult homosexuality and suicide being obvious examples.

Public opinion undoubtedly impacts on this process as do powerful groups, especially the media and politicians. However, there is little universal consensus regarding definitions and concepts in these matters. Thus students need to be aware of the dynamic nature of their studies in choosing Criminology and Criminal Justice as their focus.

The selection of entries in this book tries to reflect this dynamic nature of crime and its study and development, and every attempt has been made to include relevant key concepts from both disciplines. However, these two areas are very diverse and, inevitably, I have had to be selective in my choice of entries.

One of the greatest difficulties initially facing students studying Criminology, Criminal Justice and legal subjects is the terminology used that can be rather daunting. This book is written especially for readers studying these areas for the first time; and it aims to explain key terms and concepts to make understanding easier and to provide a basic introduction to both Criminology and the Criminal Justice System. I have tried to provide explanations rather than technical dictionary-style definitions which can often be more confusing than helpful for readers new to a subject unless very self-explanatory. It is therefore likely to be useful for A and A/S level students and especially for first-year undergraduates in Criminology, Criminal Justice and Law or combinations thereof. It may also appeal to professionals working as criminal justice personnel or indeed anyone who would appreciate criminal jargon to be demystified!

In terms of structure, I have used underlining to indicate cross-references in the entries which should assist readers to find related concepts and italics to indicate further reading references to facilitate follow-up research if required. These include book and journal references, cases where appropriate and websites which may help readers who want to further explore concepts. I have retained the alphabetical presentation for speed and ease of access and included some Latin terms which are still in common usage in cases and textbooks. Diagrams, figures and tables are sometimes provided to simplify or summarize concepts in the text, and some entries contain a critical component to enable readers to evaluate the concept, especially if it is an innovative development.

This book seeks to help those new to these areas of study and are looking to understand basic terms and concepts. It is not intended to replace textbooks, journals or specialized materials but to complement them and make the students' journey easier, less stressful and, therefore, more fun. There may be no need to read it from cover to cover but instead it can be used as a point of reference and clarification as concepts are encountered.

Finally, turning to acknowledgements, I would like to thank Suzannah Burywood of Palgrave Macmillan for her immense patience, support and understanding of the setbacks encountered during the initial stages of the preparation of this book which meant the writing took far longer than envisaged. I would also like to thank the reviewers who provided me with invaluable feedback which I have endeavoured to incorporate in the text.

I hope this book provokes an interest in the world of Criminology and Criminal Justice that has held me, for one, fascinated for decades.

Table of Statutes

Abortion

The termination of pregnancy.

Prior to 1967 abortion was generally illegal in the UK but was legalized by the Abortion Act 1967, provided

- it is carried out by a registered medical practitioner;
- the pregnancy is under 24 weeks;
- two medical practitioners certify that it is necessary because *either* the continuation of the pregnancy would create a risk to the life, physical or mental health of the woman (or her existing children) greater than the risk of termination *or* there is a substantial risk that the child would be born with a serious physical or mental disability.

A medical practitioner can conscientiously object to performing an abortion.

Absolute Discharge

The release of a convicted offender without imposition of a punishment.

It may be unconditional or conditional upon the defendant not reoffending within a period set by the court (3 years maximum). If he/she is convicted within that time they may be sentenced for the original offence as well.

Abolitionism

A branch of contemporary critical criminology, originating in Norway (Thomas Mathiesen 1974, Nils Christie 1976). It is based on notions that

- criminal justice and its agencies have a vested interest in ensuring that crime remains out of control,
- punishment is merely power justified,
- social control should not be about imposing pain (via punishment) but reducing it.

This school advocates the decentralization ('abolition') of the processes and institutions of the criminal justice system which, it argues, would eliminate the problems generated by the system itself, for example, labelling, stigmatization, discrimination, social exclusion, moral panics and the proliferation of anti-social behaviour.

This, in turn, would allow alternative forms of conflict-resolution, based on restorative justice, to develop and to be funded, for example, community justice, conciliation, rehabilitation and other social inclusionary measures.

Analysis of the relationship between imprisonment and recidivism, it argues, shows that the almost continual recycling of the same individuals/groups creates a dangerous and self-perpetuating process.

Penal institutions should therefore be dismantled with their emphasis on punishment and be replaced by community controls and treatment.

Further Reading

Mathiesen, T. (2005). Prisons on Trial. Waterside Press.

Sim, J. (1994). The Abolitionist Approach; A British Perspective, in A. Duff et al. (eds). Penal Theory and Practice. Marcel Dekker Inc.

Acceptable Behaviour Contracts (ABC)

A relatively recent development to deal with anti-social behaviour, along with Anti-Social Behaviour Orders (ASBOs).

They are informal, voluntary, written agreements between anti-social behaviour offenders and the local police aimed at reducing such offending.

Being informal they are flexible as regards content and format but can have enforcement problems unlike ASBOs which are statutory and have legal effect.

ABCs were originally introduced for young offenders (10–17 years) but are now also applicable to adults.

They seem to have been quite effective as a means of encouraging young persons, adults and parents to take more responsibility and have improved quality of life in local communities.

Accused

A person charged with a criminal offence, more commonly known as a defendant.

Accomplice

A person who aids or abets another in the commission of a crime and who is subject to the same punishment as the principal offender.

Acquisitive Crime

A term used to categorise economically motivated crime, for example, where articles are stolen (theft and burglary).

Acquaintance Rape

Rape perpetrated by a person known to the victim as opposed to a stranger.

Acquittal

A finding by a criminal court that a defendant is not guilty of the offence for which he/she was tried resulting in release by the court.

A

Acquittal was an absolute bar to a further <u>prosecution</u> for that <u>offence</u> (<u>autrefois acquit</u>) until this <u>double jeopardy</u> rule was modified for trials on <u>indictment</u> where new and compelling <u>evidence</u> becomes available [Criminal Justice Act 2003].

Act of Parliament

<u>Legislation</u> enacted by <u>Parliament</u>, also known as a <u>statute</u>.

To become law, <u>Bills</u> are usually passed by both Houses and then receive the Royal Assent. Today the <u>House of Lords</u> can only delay a Bill (1 year or 6 months in the case of a money Bill) passed by the <u>House of Commons</u> unless it is a Bill to extend the duration of <u>Parliament</u> beyond 5 years which may be vetoed.

There are different types of Acts:

- **Public Acts** apply to the public as a whole.
- **Private Acts** are applicable to a limited group for specific purposes.
- **Amending Acts** alter existing <u>statutes</u> which may then be incorporated into a **Consolidating Act**.

Actuarial Justice

Deriving from the word 'actuary', this refers to a system of criminal justice based on risk calculation, using statistical data to predict risk and the likelihood of future events (e.g., offending/reoffending) and to identify and classify dangerous groups (e.g., sex offenders).

It is a concept taken from accountancy and business studies and applied by criminologists.

Further Reading

Feeley, M. and Simon, J. (1994). Actuarial Criminal Justice: The Emerging New Criminal Law. In D. Nelken (ed.). The Future of Criminology. Sage.

Kernshall, H. (2003). Understanding Risk in Criminal Justice. In M. Maguire (ed.). Crime and Justice. Open University Press.

Bruinsma, G. et al. (eds) (2004). Punishment, Places and Perpetrators: Developments in Criminology and Criminal Justice Research. Willan Publishing.

A

Actus Reus (guilty act)

The Latin term for an essential element of a crime which must be proved in order to obtain a criminal <u>conviction</u> – as distinct from the mental element (<u>mens rea</u>) which generally must be proved also.

The actus reus varies with the crime and may be an act (e.g., appropriation of property or a blow to the body – as in theft and <u>battery</u>) or an omission (e.g., failure to take care or to perform a legal duty) or even a set of circumstances (e.g., goods having been stolen – as in the crime of <u>handling stolen goods</u>).

Adjournment

The postponement of a court case until a future date (fixed or indefinite), usually at the <u>discretion</u> of the <u>court</u>.

Administrative Court

The High Court which has jurisdiction over judicial review cases.

Admission

A statement by a defendant/suspect admitting the commission of a criminal offence.

An informal admission is called a confession while a formal admission is usually a guilty plea in court.

Admissibility (evidence)

The decision as to whether evidence maybe received by a court. To be admissible, evidence must be relevant; but even relevant evidence maybe ruled inadmissible if it falls within the exclusionary rules of evidence (e.g., hearsay or illegally obtained evidence).

Adoption Studies

Studies used by biological criminologists to support genetic theories of predisposition to crime. These look at whether children adopted at birth carry their birth parents' criminality.

If biological predispositions are involved in criminality, the children of convicted offenders would be more likely to have criminal records.

Some research seems to support this showing 15 per cent of boys with criminal records where their adoptive parent(s) had records but their natural parents did not as compared with 20 per cent having records where the biological parents had records but adoptive parents did not (Medrick et al. 1987).

However, critics have identified the following problems which may undermine these results:

- Selective placement
  Adoption agencies may tend to match adoptive and natural families in terms of social class and physical characteristics.
- Pre-adoption influences
  Since a large percentage of adoptees spend time with their biological parent(s) and foster families before adoption, it may be difficult to exclude the effects of early parenting.
- Institutional factors
  Children who spend more time in institutions show a higher level of criminality in later life.

Adrenalin

A natural hormone stimulant made in the adrenalin gland of the kidneys.

There have been suggestions that it maybe linked with criminality.

A low level of it has been found in some persons with habitual aggressive tendencies and those who are easily bored, quickly disinterested, craving excitement and less likely to learn from unpleasant experiences, including punishment.

Adversarial System/Adversarialism

The system of court procedure adopted in England and Wales (as distinct from the Continental inquisitorial system) in which criminal trials take the form of contests between the parties, dominated by their lawyers who present their evidence, witnesses and submissions to the court. The judge does not actively attempt to determine facts but, effectively, acts as an umpire until the parties have presented their cases and a verdict is required from the judge or jury.

Traditionally emphasis is placed on testimony of witnesses.

The judge plays a much more dominant role in inquisitorial procedure in which direct questioning of the lawyers by the judge is more usual.

There is, however, evidence that the two systems are borrowing from each other and the differences are now more blurred than in the past, probably under the influence of the European courts.

Adverse Inference

A finding of fact that is unfavourable to a party in criminal proceedings. If a suspect fails to mention something at the time of his arrest which is later relied on in his defence or if a defendant refuses to give evidence or answer questions without good reason, a court may allow adverse inferences to be drawn by the prosecution.

This controversial modification of the rights to silence and non-self-incrimination was introduced by The Criminal Justice and Public Order Act 1994.

Advocate

See Barrister.

Aetiology

The study of the causes of behaviour.

Affidavit

A sworn statement used as evidence in court proceedings.

Affirmation

Testimony given, usually in open court, under a solemn declaration equivalent to an oath by a person who objects to taking an oath [Oaths Act 1988].

Age of Consent

The age at which a person can legally consent to sexual intercourse. This is now 16 years for both heterosexuals and homosexuals.

A

Further Reading
See Table 4.

Agencies

See Criminal Justice Agencies.

Age of Criminal Responsibility

The age at which a person can be deemed legally able to commit a crime, which is 10 years in England and Wales. This is, apart from Scotland, the lowest criminal age in Europe.

This age varies from country to country as shown in the Table 1 below.

Table 1   Ages of criminal responsibility

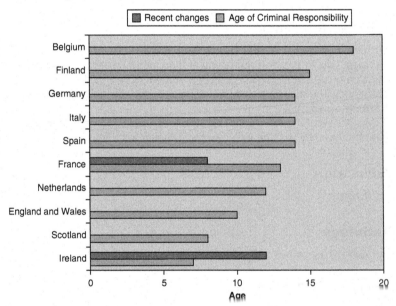

Agent Provocateur

A person who actively encourages someone to commit a crime for the purposes of securing a <u>conviction</u>. The agent is treated as an <u>accomplice</u> in such a situation.

If committed by the <u>police</u>, it is called <u>entrapment</u>.

Aggravating Factors

Factors determining the gravity of an offence for the purposes of sentencing, for example, use of violence or perversion, age of the victim or premeditation.

Ageism

Discrimination based on age (actual or presumed).

Alias

An assumed name ('alius dictus').

Alibi

A defence to a criminal charge whereby the defendant claims to have been elsewhere at the time of the alleged offence and therefore could not be responsible for it.

Advance notice (seven days) must normally be given to the prosecution if this defence is to be raised in a criminal trial.

Alienation

The process by which persons become isolated from others and estranged which may lead them to reject general social values or aspirations, show lack of concern for fellow humans and generally be in conflict with society.

In turn this may mean that criminal activity is seen as acceptable and even attractive.

Altruism

The principle of putting other's interests and welfare before one's own.

There is a perspective in criminological theory called social altruism (also known as social support) which indicates that social support is inversely and significantly related to the rate of violent crime; social support prevents crime in society.

Social support maybe defined as the delivery (actual/perceived) of assistance by the community in meeting the needs of individuals or groups (Cullen and Vander).

This theory has it that, in order to reduce crime and to rehabilitate offenders, society needs to increase the sources and levels of social support.

Further Reading

Chamlin, B. and Cochran, J. K. (1997). Social Altruism. In Journal of Criminology, vol. 35(2), 203.
Calvin, H. et al. (2002). Coercion, Social Support and Crime: An Emerging Theoretical Consensus. Journal of Criminology, vol. 40(1), Feb., 19.

A

Anarchism

A theory of crime, sometimes called 'anti-authoritarian justice', which considers that crime is caused by organizational structures and institutional power.

Rather than analysing how this occurs, the focus of this theory is on the need to replace these structures.

It has its roots in nineteenth-century writings which argued that centralized authority in any form (including government), is oppressive because it is based on inequality.

All forms of hierarchy should be dismantled because the most successful societies are those founded on mutual co-operation.

Criminal justice systems should therefore be replaced by decentralized structures of collective negotiation in which all members of society could participate and share in problem-solving.

The underlying aim should be to get offenders to accept responsibility for their behaviour by associating them with other members of society.

Anti-authoritarian Justice

See Anarchism.

Amentia

A type of mental defect meaning literally 'lack of mind' and describing a person *born* with limited intellect.

It is contrasted with dementia, the term used for a person who has *lost* mental capacity because of illness, deterioration or accident.

Amnesty

A pardon by which crimes committed up to a certain date are condoned so that persons cannot be charged with them.

Amnesty International

The international, non-governmental, independent organization that works to protect human rights worldwide and campaigns against inhumane treatment and punishments.

Founded in London in 1961, it is the longest-standing human rights organization and received the Nobel Prize in 1977 for its campaign against torture. Historically, its attention has focused on the rights of women and children, refugees, prisoners of conscience and protection of human dignity. The effects of globalization and September 11 have seen its scope extend to include economic, social and cultural rights. It operates via research and as a pressure group mobilizing public opinion on these issues.

Further Reading

www.amnesty.org

A

'Angry Lawns Syndrome'

See Fear of Crime.

Animus

The intention with which an act is done.

Anomie

A lack of regard for generally accepted social or moral standards in an individual or group. This is a criminological theory deriving from the work of Emile Durkheim.

It emphasizes the influence of social factors on criminal behaviour and describes the concept of a state of lawlessness (normlessness) often brought about by rapid social change where shared norms and values come under threat, leading to increased levels of <u>deviance</u>.

Anomie is thus a form of social disorganization which is most acute during transitional periods in society.

The transition from agriculture to industrialization in the nineteenth century, for example, resulted in profound social disorganization and lack of moral direction during which more deviance was discernible.

Further Reading

Downes, D. and Rock, P. (2003). Anomie, Chapter 5, in Understanding Deviance, Oxford University Press.
www.durkheim.itgg.com/anomie
www.sad.ch/forschung/anoiresearch.

Anti-social Behaviour (ASB)

A loose concept encompassing a wide range of conduct ranging from relatively minor inconveniences to major crime. Legally it is defined as 'acting in a manner that caused or is likely to cause harassment, alarm or distress to one or more persons not of the same household' [Crime and Disorder Act 1998].

In the past it focused on aggressive, criminal behaviour but would now include activities such as noisy neighbours, loud parties, teenagers hanging around in groups, vandalism, graffiti, littering and abandonment of vehicles.

It has been a growing concern for governments in the last decade, highlighted by the introduction of legislation which provided for

- the establishment of the Anti-social Behaviour Unit in the Home Office and its Action Plan in 2003 which aimed at disseminating ideas of good practice in <u>anti-social behaviour</u> strategies;
- allowing the dispersal of teenage groups from streets (<u>dispersal orders</u>), naming and shaming persons in receipt of <u>ASBOs</u>;
- the ASB Academy to train the <u>police</u>, local authorities and court staff to deal with <u>anti-social behaviour</u>;
- A national telephone advice line explaining these new powers.

[Anti-social Behaviour Act 2004]

A

This concern has become more profound as a result of recent suicides, specifically Fiona Pilkington who set herself and her disabled daughter alight in her car because of distress and frustration caused by prolonged abuse from anti-social gangs and families in her neighbourhood. Despite more than 30 calls for help to the <u>police</u> and local authority and a public meeting discussion of the anti-social activities in the area, nothing was done to prevent the harassment and intimidation of her family, with tragic results.

The inquest <u>jury</u> found that this collective failure by state agencies contributed to the deaths.

A number of problems have been identified in the context of <u>anti-social behaviour</u>, including

1. the costs of dealing with it (estimated at £3.5 billion per annum in England and Wales in 2003),

2. the ambiguities and subjectivity of its definitions now that it has been extended beyond the criminal law,
3. the apparent contradictory government approaches as regards young persons.

Initially legislation reflected concern for the poverty and neglect of young persons but measures are increasingly being used to target and to criminalize them rather than to address their problems.

Further Reading

www.homeoffice.gov.uk/antisocial-behaviour

Anti-social Behaviour Order (ASBO)

The civil response to anti-social behaviour introduced in 1998 as a preventative measure. It may be used against anyone over 10 years who is proved, on a balance of probability (civil standard of proof), to be behaving anti-socially and it may impose conditions on the individual restricting his/her activity.

These orders have been used to control behaviours including prostitution, racial abuse, vandalism, nuisance, begging, assaults, batteries and vehicle crime.

ASBOs may be imposed on persons who have not committed a crime and yet it is a criminal offence to breach such an order, punishable by imprisonment.

There has been much criticism of these orders in that they are seen as undermining individuals' due process protections under PACE and as using the civil law as a crime reduction tool.

Further Reading

Crime and Disorder Act 1998
Squires, P. (ed.) (2008). ASBO Nation: The Criminalization of Nuisance. Policy Press UK.
www.homeoffice.gov.uk/antisocial-behaviour

Anthropological Criminology

Criminologists (e.g., Darwin, Lombroso) who advocate that criminality can be explained by physical appearance, genes and physiological factors.

Appeal

An application to a superior court challenging a conviction and/or sentence delivered in a lower court.

Appeals (other than to the Supreme Court or by case stated) lie on matters of fact or law or both.

In criminal cases appeals lie from

- Magistrates' Courts to the
  (1) Crown Court against conviction and/or sentence (by the defence only)
  (2) High Court (QB Divisional Court) by means of an appeal by case stated on a point of law only (by the prosecution or defence).

A

A further appeal may lie to the Supreme Court on a point of law of general public importance with permission.
- Crown Court to the Court of Appeal (Criminal Division) by the defendant and with permission.

A further appeal may lie to the Supreme Court on the same grounds.

While the prosecution cannot appeal against acquittal or sentence, the Attorney-General may refer unduly lenient sentences to the Court of Appeal which may then confirm, increase, decrease or vary the sentence.

Prosecution rights of appeal have been increased by the Criminal Justice Act 2003 so that the prosecution can now appeal to the Court of Appeal against judicial decisions to terminate a trial on indictment in the Crown Court, on admissibility of evidence and grants of bail.

The appeal process must be distinguished from the process of judicial review which is a challenge to the legality or fairness of a decision of a public body rather than the merits of that decision.

Further Reading

See Courts diagram.
The Criminal Justice Act 2003 s 18, 57, 62

Appellant

A person who appeals against a court decision.

Appropriate Adult

An independent, responsible third party called in by the police to give special assistance to a vulnerable suspect during a police interview.

Their role is to advise the suspect, to observe whether or not an interview is conducted fairly and to facilitate communication with the interviewee.

Arraignment

The calling of a defendant to the bar of the court in order to answer a charge on indictment which is read out to him/her and to which he/she is asked to plead guilty or not guilty.

A

Arrest

The formal apprehension of a person for a criminal offence.

Powers of arrest are governed by the Police and Criminal Evidence Act 1984 (PACE).

Typically an arrest is made by a police officer after a warrant had been issued by a magistrate. Arrest without warrant is available if a police officer has reasonable grounds to believe that an offence has been, is being or is about to be committed.

An arrest may also be made without a warrant by a private citizen on similar grounds.

Arson [Criminal Damage Act 1971]

Intentionally or recklessly causing destruction or criminal damage to property by fire, without lawful excuse.

Assassination

The murder of a (prominent) person by targeted attack by an assassin usually hired to carry out the killing and often for political, religious, military or ideological purposes.

The murders of Abraham Lincoln, J. F. Kennedy, Gandhis, Bhutto, Aquino and Rabin are just a few of the international assassinations that could be mentioned.

Assisted Suicide [Suicide Act 1961]

A suicide which involves another person helping the deceased to kill him/herself.

Although suicide is no longer a crime, assisting another to do so is in the UK unlike some other countries, for example Switzerland.

This has resulted in over a hundred Britons travelling abroad to euthanasia clinics (e.g., Dignitas) in order to be assisted in their suicides.

As a result of campaigns by seriously ill patients for a change in the law, most recently, Debbie Purdy, the House of Lords called for clarification of the law in an unprecedented ruling in 2009.

Draft guidelines, effective immediately, were issued by the DPP to help persons travelling abroad to assist others in their suicides to determine if they will face criminal prosecution on their return. A final policy is expected soon.

The guidelines do not decriminalize assisted suicide nor give guarantees against prosecution but make it clearer in what circumstances a prosecution may or may not be brought in respect of compassionate assistance.

A range of factors will be taken into account including how the decision to die was taken, whether there might have been financial motivations or emotional pressures and whether the suicidal person was competent and had demonstrated a clear and settled wish to die.

Further Reading

Suicide Act 1961

www.assistedsuicide.org

www.dignitas.ch

A

Assault [Offences against the Person Act 1861]

Intentionally or recklessly causing a person to apprehend fear of immediate, unlawful personal violence.

Actual physical contact is not required so that pointing a gun or brandishing a knife may also be assaults.

Common assaults are summary offences while aggravated assaults constitute more serious offences such as assaults with intent to resist arrest or commit robbery.

In everyday language the term 'assault' is often used to include the application of actual physical violence which is technically a battery.

Association of Chief Police Officers (ACPO)

An independent strategic body which leads and co-ordinates the direction and development of the police service and, in times of national emergencies, co-ordinates the national police response.

Further Reading
www.acpo.police/uk

Asylum

A place where a person can take refuge.

To seek political asylum means to seek permission to stay in a country so as to avoid persecution or harassment abroad (asylum seeker).

Atavism

A term used by Lombroso who suggested that while most individuals evolve, some devolve and become primitive (atavistic) and represent the most violent criminals in society. According to this theory criminals are hereditary throwbacks to more primitive evolutionary forms.

Lombroso claimed to have discovered the secret of crime during the postmortem examination of a bandit.

This is a somewhat discredited theory today.

At Her Majesty's Pleasure

The legal phrase meaning indefinite detention until it is decided by the authorities that it is safe to release the detainee.

A person who is found not guilty by reason of insanity by a court may be ordered to be detained in a mental institution at Her Majesty's Pleasure.

Attempt

An act which is preparatory to the commission of a crime and which is, itself, a crime.

A

Attention Deficit Disorder (ADD)

Commonly known as hyperactivity, this syndrome has been associated as a possible factor in criminality.

Inability to concentrate and hyperactive or impulsive behaviour may reduce the ability of children to do well in mainstream activities, especially school, and lead them to seek success in alternative ways. The fact that they tend to have less educational skills and, therefore limited employment opportunities, may add to their problems.

Critics of this view argue that ADD is simply a device to justify medication intervention to control unruly children and maintain classroom order (Box 1977).

Attorney-General (A-G)

The head of the <u>Bar</u> and chief legal adviser to the government who also represents the <u>Crown</u> in judicial proceedings.

He/she is also responsible for conducting <u>prosecutions</u> involving the public interest (e.g., <u>treason</u>) and whose consent is required for certain prosecutions (e.g., <u>incest</u>, official secrets). He/she has the power to terminate any criminal prosecution by entering a <u>nolle prosequi</u>.

The A-G is usually an MP holding ministerial office.

Audience (right of)

The right of a lawyer to represent a client in court.

Audi Alterem Partem Rule

See Natural Justice.

Automatism

Involuntary conduct which may be pleaded as a criminal <u>defence</u>.

> 'The mind does not go with what is being done'.
>
> (Bratty v A-G for NI 1963)

It must be caused by an external factor (e.g., blow to the head) and not an internal factor (e.g., epileptic fit).

The defendant may be semiconscious (e.g., reflex action, spasm, post-traumatic stress) or unconscious (e.g., sleepwalking, trance) at the time of the alleged offence.

Self-induced automatism (e.g., intoxication) and irresistible impulse are not defences.

The burden lies on the prosecution to disprove automatism once the defendant raises some evidence of the defence.

Generally the defendant's own assertion will be insufficient and expert medical evidence is needed in support.

It takes two forms:

- Insane automatism which is treated as <u>insanity.</u>
- Non-insane automatism as described above.

If successfully pleaded, automatism will result in <u>acquittal</u>.

Autonomic Nervous System (ANS)

The part of the nervous system that controls emotions.

Biological criminologists have argued that individuals who are not easily aroused tend to be less responsive to conditioning (e.g., punishments, rewards) and consequently resist socialization and are more likely to commit crime without fear of consequences (Eynsenck 1964, Mednick 1977).

The evidence for this is inconclusive, however.

Autonomy

The capacity of individuals for deciding issues which affect themselves, sometimes referred to as the right of self-determination.

It is central to the relationship between law and morality; should the law enforce private morality or is this a matter for the individual in the absence of harm or threatened harm to others?

The fact that suicide [Suicide Act 1961] and homosexuality [Sex Offences Act 1967] were decriminalized shows the current respect that the criminal law has for autonomy.

The opposite is heteronomy: the authority of the law is placed above the individual.

The facts that soliciting for prostitution is criminal and consent to serious bodily harm is no defence to criminal assault reflect this principle.

Autopsy

Examination of a body after death in order to determine the cause of death.

Autrefois Acquit ['previously acquitted']

See Double Jeopardy.

Autrefois Convict ['previously convicted']

A special plea that a defendant has previously been convicted of the same, or substantially the same, offence as presently charged with.

If successful, it bars further criminal trial proceedings.

A

'Bad Apple Argument'

An attitude associated with some police cultures, often discriminatory, reflected in the view that the solution to crime control is to identify and remove delinquents ('bad apples') from a troubled location and then prevent any more from getting into it.

This argument has, at times, been used to excuse criticism of institutions such as racism in some police forces.

Bail

The release of a suspect or defendant from legal custody pending trial or appeal against a criminal conviction.

Bail may be granted by the police prior to charge (e.g., if time is required to gather evidence) or an arrest warrant, may be 'backed for bail' directing the police to release an arrestee on bail to attend court at a future date.

Generally there is a presumption in favour of bail unless the prosecution proves it should not be granted.

It may justifiably be denied if

1. The offence is punishable by imprisonment and there are reasonable grounds to believe that the defendant would:
   - fail to attend court ('jump bail')
   - commit further offences
   - interfere with witnesses
   - be at personal risk
   - appear to be under the influence of class A drugs
2. The charge is murder, manslaughter, rape (or attempts thereof) for which the defendant has previous conviction(s).

Bail may be unconditional or conditional [e.g., passport surrender, reporting to a police station, sureties and surviving may be required to act as financial guarantors of the defendant's attendance at court.

Failure to attend is itself a criminal offence.

Both the defence and the prosecution can appeal bail decisions, and recent concerns about dangerous offenders committing crimes while on bail have resulted in increased powers for the Crown Prosecution Service to appeal against Magistrates' bail decisions.

The Criminal Justice Act 2003 made a number of changes to the law of bail including the introduction of two new types of bail:

- Conditional bail which allows the police to attach conditions to bail granted to suspects pending a decision as to charge and prosecution and

- Street bail which allows the police to instruct suspects to attend at a police station at a later date, rather than immediately.

Further Reading
Criminal Justice Act 2003 s 13–19

Balance of Probability

The standard of proof in civil law which is also applicable in criminal law where, exceptionally, the onus of proof shifts to the defendant, for example, to raise evidence of the defences of insanity or diminished responsibility.

This standard requires proof that it is more likely than not that there is liability and it is therefore a lighter burden than the usual criminal burden of beyond reasonable doubt.

Ballistics

The science of shooting; the functioning and impact of firearms and ammunition.

Wound ballistics specifically deals with the medical implications of trauma caused by bullets.

Bar

A term used in several senses:

- collective term for barristers;
- place where lawyers stand in court when representing clients and where defendants stand to be tried in court;
- legal impediment as a bar to, for example, marriage (close blood relationship) or, example, to bringing a legal action (expiry of the limitation period).

Bar Council

The governing body of the Bar, responsible for education, training, regulation and complaints against barristers.

Barrister

See Legal Profession.

Basic Intent Crime

See Intention.

Battered (Women) Syndrome

A psychological syndrome suffered by a person, usually a woman, as a result of prolonged, extensive physical or mental abuse by a partner.

It has been used as a partial <u>defence</u> to <u>murder</u> where the woman has killed her partner. Typically she may have attacked him while he was asleep which would make it difficult to establish <u>self-defence</u> which requires proof that violence was imminent and the force used in self-defence was proportionate.

If successful, the charge is reduced to <u>manslaughter</u>.

Battery [Criminal Justice Act 1988]

Intentional or reckless application of unlawful force (however trivial) to a person without their <u>consent</u>.

There is no requirement for an <u>assault</u>; thus an unsuspecting or unconscious person can be the victim of a battery.

BB Gun

An imitation gun which discharges plastic pellets.

Beccaria, Cesare 1738–94

An Italian aristocrat and philosopher regarded as the founder of <u>classical criminology</u> in the eighteenth century that represented enlightenment and humanitarian thinking as opposed to the spiritual and religious ideas of earlier times.

His text 'On Crimes and Punishments' (1764) was essentially a critique of Italy's punitive criminal justice system which he perceived as inconsistent and arbitrary.

According to him punishments need to make offending unattractive by extracting losses greater than the possible benefits of offending.

His model therefore rests on the assumption that offenders are rational and calculating which may often be questionable.

Becker, Howard

See Labelling Theory.

Further Reading
Becker, H. (1963). Outsiders. The Free Press.

Behaviourism

A scientific approach that stresses that the only proper subject-matter for scientific study in psychology is directly observable behaviour.

Bench

The collective term for <u>judges and magistrates</u> sitting in a courtroom.

Benchers

The governing officers (senior members) of the <u>Inns of Court</u>.

B

Bentham, Jeremy (1748–1832)

Another classical criminologist, regarded as the founder of utilitarianism which, essentially, argues that actions are moral only if they are useful. Thus punishment can be morally justified only if the harm and suffering that it prevents is greater than that which it inflicts on offenders; and unless punishment reduces future crime then it adds to, rather than reduces, human suffering.

He proposed that punishment should be rationally based, fair and used to achieve some greater good for society, for example, crime reduction.

He viewed the individual as a rational being with free choice who could be deterred by anticipated future punishment.

Effectively he thought that there were a number of ways in which deterrence could be achieved and recidivism reduced:

- removing the ability to offend (incapacitation)
- removing the desire to offend (reform/rehabilitation)
- making the offender afraid to offend (deterrence)

His panopticon prison designs, based on observability and inspection, became a model for much many Victorian prison buildings.

Further Reading
Bowring, J. (1962). The Collected Works of Jeremy Bentham. New York.

Bently, Derek

The 19-year old (with a mental age of 11 years) who was convicted, along with his younger accomplice, of the murder of a policeman and hanged in 1953 after the Home Secretary rejected a plea for clemency despite the recommendation of the jury at his trial. The gun had been fired by his accomplice who escaped the death penalty because he was a minor; he was detained At Her Majesty's Pleasure and released after 10 years.

After a determined campaign by his family, Bently was eventually pardoned posthumously and had his name cleared by the Court of Appeal in 1998.

It is generally recognized that this is one of the worst miscarriages of justice cases in UK history.

Further Reading
Montgomery Hyde, H. (ed.) (1954). The Trial of Craig and Bentley. William Hodge & Co.
www.derekbentley.com

B

Beyond Reasonable Doubt

The normal standard of proof in criminal law which requires the prosecution to prove the defendant's guilt. This is a high standard which complements the presumption of innocence.

Bias

See Natural Justice.

Biggs, Ronnie

One of the famous Great Train Robbers of the 1960s who escaped from prison and absconded to South America where he remained for many years until he was returned and spent the rest of his prison term in an English prison. He was finally released on health grounds in 2009.

His high-profile escape, along with others put prison security high on the prison agenda and led to the Mountbatten Report 1966. This highlighted the weaknesses in prison security and set up a new categorization of prisoners based on their security risk. This system which determines where prisoners will serve their sentences remains in place today.

Further Reading

Gray, M. (2009). Ronnie Biggs: The Inside Story. Apex Publishing Ltd.

Bifurcation

A sentencing policy related to cost-effectiveness under which tougher sentences are reserved for the most serious offences while less serious and low-risk offenders are diverted from the criminal justice system at various stages.

The increased use of police cautions and victim-offender mediation schemes illustrate this approach.

This is seen by some critics as conflicting with other sentencing aims, for example, just-deserts and denunciation.

Bigamy [Offences Against the Person Act 1861]

The crime of knowingly marrying a person when already married to another. It is punishable by up to 7 years imprisonment.

There is a special defence if the defendant's spouse has been missing for 7 years (minimum) and is therefore presumed dead.

Biochemical Theory of Crime

A component of biological criminology which posits that there is a connexion between biochemical factors, behaviour and personality.

It developed at the end of the nineteenth with the discovery of hormones and their possible effects on behaviour, particularly criminal behaviour.

In the 1960s and 1970s much theorising was more and influential and the dominant view among criminologists was that, at best, hormones may have only an indirect link with behaviour; they may act as a catalyst for behaviour complementing other causal factors.

Sex hormone imbalances (e.g., PMT) have sometimes been accepted as mitigating factors in sentencing offenders.

The crime of infanticide would also seem to be recognition of the connexion.

The difficulty is how to establish this possible link and to determine whether anti-social behaviour is caused by biochemical factors or vice versa, or indeed if both are related to other causes.

Until this is determined, policies based on such theories, such as forcible drugs administration or psycho-surgery, remain controversial and problematic

B

from the point of view of human rights. This is why policymakers have tended to shy away from them. They may, however have a limited role provided they do not involve the use of force, intimidation or serious side effects.

Further Reading

Dabbs, J. M. and Dabbs, M. G. (2000). Heroes, Rogues and Lovers: Testosterone and Behaviour. McGraw Hill Companies.

Fishbein, D. (2001). Behavioural Perspectives in Criminology. Wadsworth Publishers.

http://crime-times.org

Biological Criminology

See Criminological Theories.

Biological Causes of Crime Theory

The theory that crime may be caused by biological factors.

Although biological criminology became discredited, it was re-invigorated by genetic explanations of crime (geneticism) which identified certain biological traits as potential causes of crime.

That is not to say that there is a 'crime gene' solely responsible for criminality but it may be that a combination of hereditary and environmental factors can lead to crime.

> 'Behaviour, criminal or otherwise, is not inherited; what is inherited is the way in which an individual responds to the environment. It provides an orientation, predisposition or tendency to behave in a certain fashion'.
> (Fishbein 1997)

This approach does not abandon the idea of free will but prefers a form of conditional free will in which various factors may affect an individual's exercise of free-will choices – including criminality.

Further Reading

See Table 2

The criminal justice model associated with this theory is the medical model which takes the view that if there are biological predispositions towards crime, then criminal justice policy should focus on the identification of individuals having such traits and treating rather than punishing them. Thus indeterminate sentences allowing for individual offender needs are seen as most appropriate measures.

These might include incapacitation, drug-therapy, surgery and counselling, some of which raise ethical issues and remain controversial.

Further Reading

Taylor, L. (1984). Born to Crime: The Genetic Causes of Criminal Behaviour. Greenwood Press.

Bill

A draft Act of Parliament which must usually pass through both Houses and receive Royal Assent in order to become law.

Table 2   Biology and crime

Disposition	Criminality
Defective genes	Defective genes may result in, for example, low emotional arousal, impulsiveness which, under certain conditions, may make criminality more likely.
XYY Chromosomes	Extra male chromosomes may produce 'alfa-males' who tend to be more violent and aggressive, and crime-prone.
Low IQ learning disabilities	
Attention deficit disorder	Hyperactivity may undermine ability to learn with consequent lack of skills development which may limit employment potential and lead to crime.
Hormone Imbalances	High levels of testosterone are linked with aggression in males; pre-menstrual tension caused by changes in women's hormone levels produce anger and irritability. These states are sometimes associated with criminal behaviour.
Brain chemistry disorders	
Neurotransmitter imbalances	Persons suffering from such conditions often need greater stimuli which may be obtained through the adrenalin of crime, drug-taking or other risk-inducing activities. Persons with low serotonin are prone to violence.

Bill of Rights

A formal document containing declarations of the rights and freedoms of citizens.

The original Bill of Rights 1689 which established Parliament's supremacy over the king is still in force today, complemented by the European Convention of Human Rights and the Human Rights Act 1998.

Binding Over

An order to a person to agree, under penalty, to do something (e.g., appear in court) or abstain from doing something (e.g., committing a breach of the peace).

Binge Drinking

Consumption of large amounts of alcohol in a single drinking session.

Recently this has been associated with crime and disorder problems especially with young people in public places.

Government proposals to deal with it include, for example, raising the cost of alcho-pops, cider, beer and tightening up of age identification requirements.

B

Further Reading
Hayward, K. and Hobbs, D. (2007). Beyond the Binge in Booze. British Journal of Sociology, 58:3, 438.

Birmingham 6

The six catholic men wrongly convicted of the murder of 21 people in the Mulberry Bush pub bombing in Birmingham in 1974. They served more than 16 years in prison before the Court of Appeal quashed their convictions in 2002 on the grounds of discredited forensic evidence and police corruption.

Further Reading
Blom-Cooper, L. (1997). The Birmingham 6 and Other Cases. Duckworth & Co.
www.birmingham6.com

Blackmail [Theft Act 1968]

An unwarranted demand with menaces made with a view to financial gain for the blackmailer or financial loss to another.

The term derives from the old English word 'mail' meaning payments made in kind, such as work, goods, crops or base metal (black).

A demand will be regarded as unwarranted unless the defendant proves that he/she thought it was reasonable.

There is a paradox with blackmail: if a person asks a victim for money or threatens to tell their spouse that they are having an affair, there is no crime; but if they threaten to give this information unless paid, the crime of blackmail is committed.

Blackmail may overlap with theft (forcing a victim to hand over property by threats) or robbery (obtaining property by immediate force).

Black Sheep Effect

A term used in the context of jury decision-making meaning the tendency for social perceptions to influence decisions.

Social identity theory has it that people view their own groups ('in-groups') more favourably than 'out-groups' and tend to discriminate between them.

Thus, it is argued, juries maybe more lenient towards defendants with whom they can identify (Kerr et al., 1975).

However the counter hypothesis is the 'black sheep' effect which occurs when an 'in-group' member is seen as a threat to the collective self-image by other members of that group and therefore viewed even more negatively than a defendant from an 'out-group' (Marques 1990).

B

Blake, George

The notorious British spy who, while employed by MI6 in Berlin, spied for the Soviet Union.

In 1961 he was sentenced to 42 years' imprisonment, the longest determinate sentence imposed in Britain. 5 years later he escaped to East Berlin.

Blue-collar Crime

Mainstream crime as opposed to white-collar crime committed by business, professionals and corporations.

Board of Visitors

See Independent Monitoring Boards.

Bona fides

The Latin term meaning to act in good faith, honestly, without fraud or deceit.

Boomerang Effect

See Nine-Steps Approach.

Boot Camp

A hard-line sentencing regime, originating in USA and associated with very punitive and zero-tolerance policies, encapsulated in New Labour's 1997 slogan 'Tough on Crime – Tough on the Causes of Crime'.

The camps are run on military lines with rigorous daily routines, physical training and tough punishments for misbehaviour.

They are controversial and critics argue that they may actually increase anti-social behaviour and recidivism and undermine therapeutic treatment programmes.

Despite this, in 2008, the new Mayor of London revealed plans to introduce about one hundred weekend boot camps across the capital for misbehaving youths.

'Born Criminal'

The theory that 'crime is in the genes' (hereditary) is the hallmark of biological criminology which has it that some humans have physical features which, under some conditions or environments, may predispose them to commit crime.

The features identified include body and head shape, genes, eyes and physiological imbalances.

Advocates of this theory include Darwin and Lombroso.

Further Reading

Taylor, L. (1984). Born to Crime: The Genetic Causes of Criminal Behaviour. Greenwood Press.

Bow Street Runners

Early British court officials, founded in 1749, whose duty was to pursue and arrest suspected criminals on behalf of magistrates.

B

They were formally attached to Bow Street magistrates' office and were funded by central government.

These were the forerunners of the British police force.

Brady, Ian

See Moors Murderers.

Breach of the Peace

A disturbance of the public peace. It is not an offence, as such, but a court can bind a person over not to breach the peace in the future.

It must relate to violence and might include harm or threatened harm to a person or property, unruly demonstrations, picketing, neighbour disputes, intimidation and street brawls.

The possibility of breach must be real and immediate.

Bribery

An inducement for the performance or non-performance of an obligation or duty.

Bribery is a corrupt practice in election law as is corruptly obtaining a grant of honours.

Bridgewater 3

The three men convicted of the murder of the 13-year-old newspaper boy, Carl Bridgewater, who were freed in 1997 after the Court of Appeal was told that police had probably fabricated evidence. They served 18 years of their sentence before their convictions were quashed in 1997 as an acknowledged miscarriage of justice.

The men had always protested their innocence but it took six police inquiries and three full appeals before their convictions were declared unsafe.

In 1998 the Crown Prosecution Service (CPS) decided not to prosecute the four ex-police officers involved in the original investigation due to lack of evidence.

No one has subsequently been convicted of the murder.

Further Reading

Foot, P. (1986). Murder at the Farm. Penguin Books.

B

Brief

The document containing details of a client's case which a solicitor gives to a barrister when he/she instructs him/her to represent the client in court.

British Crime Survey

See Statistics.

British Society of Criminology

The international society, established some 50 years ago, which aims to further knowledge and interest in criminology for academics, professionals, researchers and others engaged in the study of crime and criminal behaviour.

Further Reading

www.britsoccrim.org

British Society of Criminology Code of Ethics

See Ethics.

Broken Britain

The current description by some politicians (e.g., David Cameron) of the state of anti-social Britain, characterized by family breakdown, deep social deprivation, high levels of substance abuse and welfare benefit dependency.

Broken Windows Theory (Wilson and Kelling 1982)

The theory that a great deal of crime is a response to visible signs of disorder or neglect; broken windows in a building are a statement that nobody cares and are, in effect, an invitation to vandalism.

By analogy, street drug dealing, discarded needles, graffiti and litter send out a message that it is a neighbourhood where criminal activity can be carried out, relatively freely, without detection.

It is associated with zero-tolerance policing.

Bulger (James) Case

The horrific murder case in which two 10-year-olds, Jon Venables and Robert Thompson, killed a toddler, James Bulger, whom they abducted from a shopping centre in Kirkby in 1993. His mutilated body was found on a railway line.

They were convicted and ordered to be detained At Her Majesty's Pleasure with a recommendation that they serve 10 years (minimum).

As a result of a successful newspaper-led campaign and petition, this was increased by the Home Secretary to 15 years (minimum) in 1995.

In 1997 The House of Lords ruled that this tariff decision was unlawful because the Home Secretary had given too much consideration to public opinion.

Subsequently the European Court of Human Rights held that it is the responsibility of the trial judge and not a politician to set minimum tariffs.

They served 8 years and were released on life licence in 2001 after a parole hearing decided that the public would not be at risk by their release.

Public outrage, threats and fear of reprisals, however, caused them to be given new identities, moved to a secret location and a life-time injunction against reporting of their new details to be issued by the courts.

One of them was returned to prison for new offences in 2010.

B

Further Reading
Smith, D. J. (1995). The Sleep of Reason: The James Bulger Case. London Arrow.

Burden of Proof

The onus on a party in legal proceedings to prove fact(s) at issue.

Generally it lies on the prosecution in a criminal case to discharge this burden beyond reasonable doubt in order to secure a conviction. Exceptionally, it lies on the defendant to raise evidence (on a balance of probability) supporting certain defences, for example, self-defence, insanity and diminished responsibility.

Bureaucratic Model

See Models of Criminal Justice.

Burglary [Theft Act 1968]

A crime which takes two forms:

- Entering a building/part thereof as a trespasser with *intent* to commit theft, grievous bodily harm or criminal damage.
- Having entered a building/part thereof as a trespasser *actually* stealing/ attempting to steal or committing grievous bodily harm or attempting to do so.

A burglar who carries a firearm, weapon or explosives commits aggravated burglary.

B

Cab-rank Rule

The requirement that a practising barrister take on a <u>brief</u> within their area of expertise if he/she is not otherwise engaged on a case.

Cadaver

A dead body of a human being, especially one intended or used for medical dissection.

'Cafeteria Style' Sentencing

A term adopted (Ashworth 2002) to describe a <u>sentencing</u> system, which does not have a single aim, in which sentencers can choose from a range of sentences as they think appropriate; a type of 'self-service, pick and mix' arrangement not unlike a cafeteria menu.

Further Reading

Ashworth, A. (2002). Sentencing, in Maguire et al. (eds). The Oxford Handbook of Criminology. Oxford University Press.

Cambridge Institute of Criminology

The first <u>criminology</u> institute in Europe, established in 1959 by the University of Cambridge. It has a worldwide reputation for academic excellence and has had a strong influence on the development of <u>criminology</u> as a discipline.

The Radzinowicz Library, named after its first Director and Wolfson Professor of Criminology (1959–73) holds one of the world's largest collection of criminology publications.

Cannabis

The botanical name for the plant from which marijuana comes.

It may be smoked or eaten, producing euphoria.

It is illegal in most countries but also has medical uses in the palliative care of cancer, AIDS and other illnesses.

Canteen Culture

A term used to describe an excessively sexist or macho institutional environment (e.g., police) characterized by coarse language, sexist/racist teasing and joking, macho posturing and sometimes heavy drinking.

The alleged clannishness of some police forces is said to inhibit reporting of harassment, bullying, corruption, assault and racist practices among its members.

Further Reading

Waddington, P.A.J. (1999). Police (Canteen) Subculture: An Appreciation. The British Journal of Criminology, 39, 287.

Capital Punishment

A sentence of death imposed by a court as punishment for a crime. In the UK it was generally abolished in 1965 with some exceptions but was totally abolished when the UK ratified Protocol 6 (ECHR) except in wartime (see Table 3).

Table 3   List of countries retaining capital punishment

Afghanistan	Guinea	St. Kitts and Nevis
Antigua and Barbuda	Guyana	St. Lucia
Bahamas	India	St. Vincent & the Grenadines
Bahrain	Indonesia	Saudi Arabia
Bangladesh	Iran	Sierra Leone
Barbados	Iraq	Singapore
Belarus	Jamaica	Somalia
Belize	Japan	Sudan
Botswana	Jordan	Swaziland
Burundi	Korea, North	Syria
Cameroon	Korea, South	Taiwan
Chad	Kuwait	Tajikistan
China	Laos	Tanzania
Comoros	Lebanon	Thailand
Cuba	Lesotho	Trinidad and Tobago
Dem. Republic of Congo	Libya	Uganda
Dominica	Malawi	United Arab Emirates
Egypt	Malaysia	United States
Equatorial Guinea	Mongolia	Vietnam
Eritrea	Nigeria	Yemen
Ethiopia	Oman	Zambia
Gabon	Pakistan	Zimbabwe
Ghana	Palestinian Authority	
Guatemala	Qatar	

C

Case

A court action which, in criminal law, involves a prosecution of a defendant by the State and, perhaps, an appeal in relation to such a matter.

Case Law

Law developed by the courts as distinct from legislation enacted by Parliament.

Case Stated

A criminal appeal (by the defence/prosecution) from the Magistrates' or Crown Courts on a point of law, certified as suitable for appeal to the High Court (QBD).

Causation

An element which must be proved to establish criminal liability.

For example, the prosecution must establish an unbroken chain of causation between the defendant's actus reus (e.g., use of a weapon) and the criminal consequences (e.g., death) to secure a murder conviction.

This is usually approached in two stages; establishing that the defendant's act or omission was both the factual and legal cause of the unlawful consequences.

- Causation in fact: courts apply the 'but for' test and ask if the unlawful consequences would not have occurred but for the defendant's unlawful conduct. If the consequences would have occurred in any event they cannot be said to be caused by the defendant.
- Causation in law: courts require the defendant's conduct be a legally operative cause and that it made a significant, though not necessarily sole, contribution to the unlawful consequences.

A defendant will be taken to have caused all reasonably foreseeable consequences. If, however, an event or an action of a third party breaks the chain of causation and its effect is so potent that it renders the defendant's contribution negligible, it will be regarded as a new intervening act (novus actus interveniens) and absolve him/her of liability.

Caution

A formal police warning which can take two forms:

- Warning to an arrestee or suspect to the effect that 'you do not have to say anything but it may harm your defence if you do not mention when questioned something which you later rely on in court. Anything you do say may be given in evidence'.
- A diversionary mechanism available to the police whereby a senior police officer informs a suspect that a prosecution is not intended for the alleged

offence, but that if he/she is reported subsequently for another offence, the first offence may be taken into account.

This should only follow an admission of guilt and should normally be given at a police station with the consent of the suspect.

A caution given for a suspected sex offence results in the suspect being placed on the Sex Offenders' Register (Sex Offenders Act 2003).

A new form of conditional caution is now available for adults against whom the Crown Prosecution Service (CPS) decides there is sufficient evidence of guilt and who make an admission of guilt. Conditions will often relate to reparation or participation in rehabilitation programmes.

An offence is deemed detected if a formal caution has been given.

This is to be distinguished from an informal police warning given at the scene of an incident (e.g., motorists) when the suspect is not taken to the police station at all.

There has been a huge increase in the use of diversionary police cautions, and their use for crimes of violence and burglary has been criticized by the Metropolitan Police Commissioner as undermining public confidence in the criminal justice system. In 2008 nearly 39,000 offenders received cautions for aggravated bodily harm, a charge which could carry a term of imprisonment of up to 5 years.

CCTV

Closed circuit television (video cameras) used as a surveillance technique.

This is particularly common in the UK where, it is said, there are more cameras per person than in any country in the world. This has increased concerns about the balance between security and privacy and the coalition government is pledged to redress this imbalance and restrict the use of surveillance.

Further Reading

www.crimereduction.homeoffice.gov.uk/cctv/index

Cavadino, P.

A writer of the reductivist school of punishment, concerned with reducing future crime by reforming or deterring re-offending.

He was an influential penal reformer.

Censure Theory

A theory of crime which perceives crime as a social censure (adverse moral judgement) (Sumner 1990, 1994).

In this theory there is no implication that conduct labelled as criminal is inherently bad or harmful but is deemed to be so because members of the public condemn such conduct; crime is a product of social censure.

Further Reading

Sumner, C. (ed.) (1997). Violence, Culture and Censure. Taylor and Francis.

Chain-fighting

The modern term for illegal dog-fighting (also called 'rolling').

Challenge

An objection to the selection of a juror for a particular trial in the Crown Court.

Today this is usually 'for cause' which means that reasons must be given. A successful challenge results in the person being excluded from the jury in the particular case.

Chambers

A term with various meanings:

- room of a judge in a court where applications and enquiries incidental to a case may be considered, usually in private,
- offices of practising barristers.

Chancery Division (High Court)

One of the three Divisions of the High Court whose jurisdiction includes the administration of deceased's estates, partnerships, companies trusts and bankruptcy matters.

Chaos Theory

See Criminological Theories.

Charge

A formal accusation of a crime, usually after police investigation and interrogation.

Charismatic Authority

A form of authority or power based on commitment and loyalty to a leader because of his/her's exceptional qualities.

It is seen by some as potentially unstable as it depends on the leader retaining support and loyalty which may not always be possible.

Chicago School

The School of Sociology developed in USA in the 1920s concerned with qualitative research on the sociology of deviance, relying on ethnography. This involved the systematic and prolonged study of groups in their natural setting doing ordinary daily activities. Studies included were homelessness, delinquency, gangs and subcultures. This School began to influence British criminological research in the 1950s particularly in the areas of youth <u>delinquency</u> and <u>cultural criminology</u>.

Chief Constable

The head of a constabulary police force.

Child Abuse

Any form of behaviour which, intentionally or otherwise, causes harm to a child.

Four possible types have been identified (Kempe and Kempe 1981):

(1) physical violence
(2) physical and emotional neglect
(3) emotional abuse, for example, long-term terrorization, deprivation or neglect
(4) sexual abuse

It is an area that has long been ignored or tolerated, but high-profile, tragic and horrific cases such as those of the <u>Moors Murderers</u> (1960s), The Wests (1980s), Victoria Climbie and Baby Peter (2000s) have heightened awareness and concerns about its prevalence in society.

Research shows that two out of three victims are known to the authorities.

This is of particular current concern as a result of the findings of the official watch-dog, Ofsted, in October 2009. It studied 173 serious case reviews involving death or serious injury to children where abuse was known or suspected from April 2008–March 2009, and found that 34 per cent of case reviews were inadequate.

The causes identified were lack of co-ordinated teamwork between agencies, poor management, failure to focus on the needs of the child, insufficient staff expertise and poor identification of ethnic and social issues.

Child Destruction [Infant Life (Preservation) Act 1929]

Wilfully killing an unborn child which is capable of being born alive unless it is necessary to preserve the mother's life.

C

Child Safety Order (CSO)

An <u>Anti-Social Behaviour Order (ASBO)</u> for children of the age of 10 years and under.

It is put into place when there are no other means available of trying to prevent criminal behaviour by a child and where there is sufficient concern as to the behaviour of a child in the care of his/her family. If there is reason to suspect that the child's behaviour is a direct result of problems within the family unit, a CSO may be issued by the Family Proceedings Court in order to allow for the intervention and supervision of either local authority and/or <u>Youth Offending Service</u>.

Unfortunately as the child under the supervision of a CSO is not of prosecutable age, he or she is not liable to any criminal proceedings if they break the conditions of the CSO. However given specific circumstances, the local authority involved may seek a <u>Parenting Order</u> which, in turn, makes the parents responsible for the behaviour of the child.

Child Sex Abuse

See Sexual Abuse.

Child Witness

A young person who gives evidence as a <u>witness</u>.

Until 1990 criminal courts considered children under 6 years as not competent to give evidence in court, but then the <u>Court of Appeal</u> ruled that a child of any age could do so if the judge regarded them as competent. This was enacted into legislation by the Criminal Justice Act 1991 which also made provision for video recorded interviews with children to be routinely admissible if a judge considers it appropriate.

In 2008 more than one thousand child witnesses were listed for court and a 4-year-old girl became the youngest witness in a rape trial which was controversial as she was cross-examined by four barristers. There is provision for an intermediary to put questions to child witnesses but a research report in 2008 found that 70 per cent could have benefited from this procedure whereas only about 1 per cent in fact did so.

NSPCC research published in 2004 revealed that child witnesses in sex abuse and violence cases faced excessive delays of, on average, 13 months from reporting the offence and the trial in the <u>Crown Court.</u>

Suggestibility is seen as a problem with child witnesses; their memories may be more easily manipulated by misinformation, leading questions or other interviewing practices. There is some research evidence indicating that once a child has been subjected to a suggestive interview, it is very difficult to later distinguish accurate from inaccurate reporting, even on cross-examination (Bruck et al. 2002).

Further Reading

Plotnikoff, K. and Woolfson, R. (2009). Measuring Up: Evaluating Implementation of Government Commitments to Young Witnesses in Criminal Proceedings. NSPCC Research. www.nspcc.org.uk/measuringup

Chivalry Thesis

The theory that holds that women are advantaged in the criminal justice system because of beliefs about female weakness and vulnerability.

Thus patterns of female criminality are viewed as the product of the benign selectivity of <u>criminal justice agencies</u> based on sexist assumptions and perceptions.

The thesis has it that in the past women have featured less in <u>criminal statistics –</u> not necessarily because they are less criminal but because of chivalry and sympathetic treatment from the <u>criminal justice agencies,</u> including the courts.

Arguments against this theory relate to the fact that, despite the low criminality of women, they are accelerated through the criminal justice system rather than treated leniently.

Christie, Nils

A Norwegian critical criminologist who has written extensively on punishment, imprisonment, dangerous offenders and criminal justice in Norway. His particular concern is that crime control has grown into an industry, dominated by multinational interests, potentially as dangerous as crime itself.

Chromosomes

Structures in both plant and animal cells which govern the individual characteristics of the organism.

It has been argued that anti-social or criminal behaviour can be connected to chromosomal (genetic) abnormality; and extra Y chromosome may be associated with greater aggression and violence and seems to be over-represented among prisoners in maximum security institutions. There is, however, considerable criticism of this view by others who argue that there is insufficient evidence of genetic transmission of violent or anti-social tendencies.

CIA

The Central Intelligence Agency, the US government bureau responsible for intelligence, counter-intelligence and espionage activities abroad in the national interest.

CID

The Criminal investigation Department, established in 1878, which is the branch of the British and many Commonwealth police forces to which plain clothes detectives are attached, thus distinguishing it from Uniformed and Special Branches.

Circuit Judge

A judge in the County or High Court and, exceptionally, the Crown Court.

Circumstantial Evidence

See Evidence.

Citation

A term meaning

- The method of quoting legal cases as authorities in court proceedings, for example, R (Daly) v Secretary of State for Home Department [2001] 2 WLR 1622.
- A summons to a person to appear in court.

Citizen's Arrest

An arrest by a private person who is not a law enforcement officer.
A citizen's arrest may be made where a person

* is committing or has committed an indictable offence
* is reasonably suspected to be committing an indictable offence
* is reasonably suspected of being guilty of an indictable offence which has been committed.

In addition, in order to be lawful

1. it must not be reasonably practicable for a police officer to make the arrest and
2. the citizen must have reasonable grounds to believe that the arrest is necessary to prevent the arrestee from committing one of the following:
   * suffering physical injury
   * causing physical injury to himself/herself or to others
   * causing loss or damage to property
   * absconding before the police can arrest him/her

A citizen's arrest may not be made in connexion with a polling station offence nor for an offence involving stirring up racial or religious hatred.
The power of citizen's arrest is narrower than that of a police officer; in that a citizen cannot make an arrest of a person who is, or is reasonably suspected to, (a) *about to* commit an offence *nor* is reasonably suspected of (b) being guilty of an offence if that offence has *not been* committed.
Thus a person anticipating making a citizen's arrest should be cautious as it may expose them to an action for wrongful arrest or false imprisonment if the grounds are unjustified.

Further Reading
Police and Criminal Evidence Act 1984 s24.

Civil Law

Private law which deals with relationships and disputes between individual parties (e.g., law of contract) as distinct from public law (e.g criminal law) and which is dealt with in the civil courts.

Clark, Sally

The victim of a miscarriage of justice as a result of her convictions for the murders of her two baby sons in 1999. She served 3 years of her life sentences before her convictions were quashed, largely on the grounds of discredited medical evidence.
Tragically she was found dead in her home in 2007.

Further Reading
Batt, J. (2004). Stolen Innocence: The Story of Sally Clark. Ebury Press.
www.sallyclark.org.uk

Classicalism

See Criminological Theories.

Clear-up Rate

The term for crimes solved which includes those prosecuted, formally cautioned or taken into consideration at a time where an offender is being sentenced for a specific offence and for which he/she admits responsibility.

It is much higher for offences against the person than for offences against property.

Claimant

The party bringing a legal claim (suing) in civil law proceedings, previously called the plaintiff.

Clerk to the Justices

A legal adviser to lay Justices of the Peace (JPs) in Magistrates' Courts.

'Coasting'

A recent term used by politicians to describe complacency among politicians and criminal justice agencies towards the control of anti-social behaviour.

Code(s) of Practice

Professional guidelines and standards which are not legally binding but breach of which might result in disciplinary action.

The most important criminal codes include those under PACE, namely,

- Code A and B (Search and Seizure)
- Code C (Detention, Treatment and Questioning)
- Code D (Identification)
- Codes E and F (Recording of Interviews)
- Code G (Arrest)
- Code H (Terrorism)

Code for Crown Prosecutors

The code issued by the DPP which lays down a two-stage test for prosecution decisions:

- Evidential sufficiency
    There must be admissible, substantial and reliable evidence that the accused committed the offence and a realistic prospect of conviction.
- Public interest
    Prosecution must be in the public interest as determined by reference to specific criteria, including

C

- does the likely penalty justify the time and cost of proceedings?
- was the offence motivated by discrimination against the victim?
- was the offence committed more than 3 years prior to the likely trial date?
- is a caution an appropriate alternative to prosecution?
- is the offender mentally ill?
- what is the attitude of the victim or the local community?
- was the offender only peripherally involved in the crime?

Cognition

The term encompassing the concepts of memory, intelligence, reasoning and imagination.

Cognitive Behavioural Therapies (CBT)

A group of psychotherapeutic approaches that are based upon the assumption that people's emotions and behaviour are heavily influenced by the way they reason about their experiences. By giving people insights into their (dysfunctional) thought patterns they may be able to change their behaviour and eliminate their problems and change how they think ('cognitive') and what they do ('behaviour').

CBT has been effective for the treatment of a range of problems including clinical depression, anxiety, eating disorders, substance abuse, psychosis and post-traumatic stress conditions.

These therapies have also become key theories behind offender management programmes today.

Further Reading

Cooper, M. (2008). Essential Research Findings in Counselling and Psychotherapy: The Facts are Friendly. SAGE Publications.

Yochelson, S. and Samenow, S. (1976). The Criminal Personality: A Profile for Change. NY: J. Aronson.

www.nice.org.uk

www.babcp.com

Cognitive Development

The development of attitudes and beliefs that a person holds about the world.

Cognitive Theories

Theories of moral development which focus on how mental thought processes are used to interpret, evaluate and determine people's actions and how they develop in stages from childhood to adulthood.

These were identified as

(1) pre-moral stage: decisions are influenced by outside authority
(2) conventional stage: decisions are based on the expectations of others
(3) social awareness stage: decisions are based on subjective perceptions

These theories were founded on the ideas of the Swiss child psychologist, Jean Piaget (1896–1980).

Criminologists applied these theories by saying that crime is associated with the way a person thinks; criminal thinking is very different from an early age.

Generally criminals think concretely rather than abstractly, are impulsive, irresponsible, self-centred and are motivated by fear and anger.

Cohen, Albert

A main contributor to subculture theory who wrote about male juvenile delinquency, especially gangs, in the 1950s.

He theorized that lack of male role models for boys resulted in anxiety and low self-esteem which became resolved by delinquent subcultures (e.g., gang membership), operating on different value systems and which, in turn, contributed to anti-social attitudes and activities.

Cohen, Stanley

One of the several proponents of the view that media presentation of crime can distort and manipulate public perceptions and create a misleading picture of crime in society.

He popularized the notion of 'folk-devil' in his book *Folk Devils and Moral Panics* (1972).

'Societies seem to be subject, every now and again, to periods of moral panics (when) a condition, episode, person or group of persons emerges to be defined as a threat to societal values and interests'.

(Cohen 1972/2002)

They are then subject to strong criticism and calls for social reaction, often fuelled by over-sensationalized stories in the media.

He argued that, especially at times of social unrest or rapid change, folk-devils and moral panics serve to create a sense of social control over these events, groups or individuals who appear to threaten societal norms.

In recent years young persons' involvement in public disorder and crime has been the focus of such moral panics so that muggers, hoodies and football hooligans, for example, have tended to be demonized.

Further Reading
Cohen, S. (1972/2002). Folk Devils and Moral Panics. Routledge.

Cohort Studies

Longitudinal studies, used in the social sciences, of a group of persons who share common characteristics or experiences. Typically, the participants are regularly surveyed about the crimes they commit or their victimization.

Their value depends on the ability of researchers to stay in touch with subjects over a long period and are therefore time-consuming and expensive.

Collective Conscience

Associated with Durkheim, this refers to the shared moral values and sense of belonging which members of society have.

'College Boys'

See 'Corner Boys'.

Commissioner of the Police of the Metropolis

See Metropolitan Police Service.

Commission for Victims and Survivors

The body responsible for promoting the interests of the victims of crime.

Committal

Referral of a case by a Magistrates' Court for trial or sentence to the Crown Court, following its preliminary investigation or trial.

Common Law

This phrase has a number of meanings, including

- Common Law as law not embodied in a statute but pronounced by judges in individual cases and applied by the doctrine of precedent.
- Common Law System of the UK, developed from Anglo-Saxon customs and characterized by adversarial procedures as distinguished from the inquisitorial system on the continent which is strongly based on Roman law.

Community Justice (Programme)

A programme designed to raise awareness of the impact of crime and to enable local people to become involved in dealing with anti-social behaviour in their area, for example, drug-dealing, grafitti and vandalism.

It is aimed at improving local quality of life by allowing people affected by such behaviour to have a say in how it is dealt with and to promote ideas which might reduce it.

Various criminal justice agencies (Courts, Police, Probation and Youth Offending Services and CPS) are involved in community justice teams working together with local residents to tackle these issues.

Further Reading
www.community.justice@hmcourts-service.gsi.uk

Community Notification

The process of allowing communities to have information about a sex offender who has moved into the community and which originated from Megan's Law in the US and Sarah's Law in the UK.

Colloquially referred to as 'naming and shaming', the perceived level of risk posed by the offender usually determines the amount of information given and the extent of its dissemination.

The aim is to increase the public's ability to protect itself and reduce sexual recidivism.

These schemes are controversial and raise a large number of issues in that they

- clearly prioritize the right of the public to be protected above the offender's right to privacy, potentially indefinitely;
- imply that the end of a sentence is not the end of punishment and risk being disproportionate;
- raise difficulties in the risk assessment of dangerousness;
- may not be very efficient;
- make for a high administrative burden especially as cumulative numbers increase over the years;
- create labelling and stigmatization effects which may be very difficult to lose;
- encourage offenders to go underground, thus making victims less safe;
- have the difficulty of keeping track of offenders who relocate;
- focus on a relatively small number of convicted offenders which may detract attention from unconvicted persons who may present a greater risk, often within the family network;
- create the danger of vigilantism;
- cause victimization of the families of offenders.

Community Order

The generic order which has replaced the various community sentences which used to be available for adult offenders (e.g., community punishment order).

For crimes committed after April 2005, courts are now able to choose a Community Order with a range of possible requirements to suit the particular offender and the crime(s) committed.

The range of requirements available with a generic community sentence or Community Order are

- compulsory (unpaid) work in the local community (300 hours maximum);
- participation in specified activities, for example, education and learning, day-centre activities, skills assessment and training (60 days maximum);
- programmes (individual/group) aimed at changing offending behaviour, for example, general, violent, sexual, substance abuse;
- prohibition from certain activities on day(s) or for a specified time;
- curfew requiring the offender to stay indoors, usually at home (2–12 hours per day) for the curfew period, monitored by electronic tagging;
- exclusion from certain areas for a specified period (2 years maximum);
- residence at an approved hostel or private address;
- mental health treatment (with the consent of the offender);
- attendance centre over a set period of time (12–36 hours);
- supervision under an Offender Manager from the Probation Service;
- attendance at drug or alcohol rehabilitation programme(s) (with the consent of the offender).

Further Reading

Criminal Justice Act 2003
www.cjsonline.gov.uk/offender/community_sentencing
See Probation.

Community Policing

A policing strategy based on the idea that community interaction and support can help control crime, social disorder and fear.

The police try to become more involved with members of the public, going out into the community rather that waiting for citizens to come to them.

Communities are encouraged to engage by reporting incidents, identifying and even detaining suspects.

It allows the police and the public to get together and discuss ideas and develop programmes that will help solve community problems.

The overall aim is to reduce crime and make neighbourhoods safer; thus it is sometimes also referred to as neighbourhood policing.

There are three main elements in this strategy:

- Community partnerships: between members of the public, social and business organizations, the media and law enforcement agencies aiming to increase trust and find solutions.
- Organizational reform: which seeks to move away from traditional reactive law enforcement practices (e.g., response time and arrest rates) and towards proactive practices involving the police actively trying to improve problems by addressing the factors causing or contributing to them.
- Problem solving: by identifying, examining and prioritizing issues and evaluating solutions.

Further Reading

Fielding, N. (1995). Community Policing. Oxford University Press.
Brogden, M. and Nijhal, P. (2005). Community Policing. Willan Publishing.
www.communitypolicingawards.org.uk

Community Safety

A generic term used to cover <u>crime prevention</u> and reduction in the context of crime in the local community.

It has been defined as

'An aspect of quality of life in which people, individually and collectively, are protected as far as possible form hazards or threats that result from the criminal or anti-social behaviour of others and are equipped or helped to cope with those they do experience'.

(Home Office: Community Safety Advisory Service, Community Safety and Crime Reduction, 2007)

It aims at early intervention to prevent or resolve <u>anti-social behaviour</u> issues which pose a threat to individuals or groups in the community.

There is a National Community Safety Plan which outlines community safety objectives which include

- Tackling serious violence
- Improving flexibility so that local partners can focus on local priorities

- Increasing community confidence in neighbourhood safety
- Addressing the threat to communities from violent extremists

Further Reading

Policing in 21st Century: Reconnecting Police and the People. (consultation document). www.homeoffice.gov.uk/publications/consultations/policing-21-century

Community Safety Partnerships

Partnerships, comprising representatives from local agencies (police, health, probation_and local authorities), established by the Crime and Disorder Act 1998 (and replacing Crime and Disorder Reduction Partnerships) to provide strategies for reducing crime in their area.

Under the Act every 3 years they are required to

- conduct and publish an audit of local crime and disorder problems, taking into account the views of those who live and work in the area,
- determine priorities for action,
- devise and publish a strategy which tackles these priority problems,
- monitor progress of the strategy.

Further Reading

Hughes, G. (2002). Crime and Disorder Partnerships: The Future of Community Safety, in G. Hughes et al. (eds). Crime Prevention and Community Safety.

Community Sentence

See Community Order.

Compensation Order

An award of financial compensation ordered by a court, payable by a convicted offender to the victim, based on ability to pay.

An offender, wrongly convicted, may also apply to the Home Secretary for compensation.

Competence

The legal capacity of a person to give evidence as a witness.

Generally any person of sound mind and understanding is competent although there are some exceptions; children under 14 years cannot give sworn evidence and other young persons can only give it if they understand the nature of an oath.

Complainant

A person who claims a crime has been committed against them.

A complainant alleging rape has a statutory right to remain anonymous and evidence of their sexual history may not normally be given except at the court's discretion.

Computer Misuse [Computer Misuse Act 1990]

The criminal offence of knowingly securing unauthorized access to a computer programme or data.

Concurrent (Sentences)

A number of sentences (e.g., imprisonment) which a judge orders to be served simultaneously as opposed to consecutively.

Concentric Zone Theory (Ernest Burgess)

An ecologic theory associated with the Chicago School explaining the causes of crime.

Ernest Burgess identified five concentric zones (two miles wide) in Chicago, within which there were specific defined neighbourhoods with their own social and economic identity (Afro-American, German, Polish, Irish, Chinese, Italian etc.).

These zones were

- Zone I: at the heart of the city, comprising the commercial district, with valuable resources, for example, transport, water).
- Zone II: the transitional zone, comprising formerly desirable residences devalued by commerce and industrialization. These had often degenerated into slums, run by landlords unwilling to invest in maintenance, and so attracted low income tenants, typically new immigrants.
- Zone III: comprising workers' homes, often second or third generation immigrant escapees from Zone II.
- Zone IV: comprising residential suburbia with more expensive homes and apartments.
- Zone V: often called the commuter zone, comprising highly priced residences, populated by the white upper and middle classes, representative of mainstream culture and values.

Essentially this theory had it that city growth was generated by pressure from the city centre, expanding outwards. This expansion threatened to encroach on the surrounding areas in concentric circles. These concentrations became progressively less intense with greater distance from the centre which had the highest density of occupation.

Social order was said to be more stable in the settled zones; thus these theorists saw the impoverished, transient Zone II as likely to have higher levels of criminality, drug-abuse, illness and mortality.

Conditional Bail

See Bail.

Conditional Caution

See Caution.

Conditional Discharge

See Discharge.

Conditioning

A learning theory which posits that individuals' past experiences or associations influence their present or future actions.

Crime can thus be seen as the outcome of learning that, under certain circumstances, behaviour will be rewarded.

The classic exponent of this approach was Pavlov (1906) who argued that stimuli will consistently produce a given effect; a dog will salivate when presented with meat.

Central to this theory is reinforcement which may be positive or negative; a company wins a lucrative contract by undercutting costs by manufacturing defective products (crime is rewarded) or breach of health and safety regulations enables a company to reverse its declining productivity (crime avoids negativity).

Confait Affair

A miscarriage of justice case which led to the Royal Commission on Criminal Procedure 1981 which, in turn, resulted in two of the most significant pieces of legislation which restructured the pre-trial process in England and Wales and re-positioned the police role in it.

The Police and Criminal Evidence Act (PACE) 1984 laid the basis for police power and its limits and The Prosecution of Offences Act 1985 established the (CPS).

In 1972 three boys were convicted of the killing of Maxwell Confait and the arson of his house, largely on the basis of their confessions.

In 1975 their convictions were quashed and the Fisher Inquiry in 1979 found that police had fabricated evidence to fit around these confessions.

Confession

An admission of guilt by a suspect or defendant.

To be admissible as evidence, a confession must be voluntary, that is, not obtained by oppression or inducement.

Ideally, there should be corroboration of confession evidence and juries are warned of the dangers of convicting on confession evidence alone.

The 1990s saw considerable concern about false confessions and there were a series of notorious miscarriages of justice cases during this time where convictions were set aside because of unreliable confessions obtained by police intimidation and fabrication.

Confiscation Order

A court (Crown) order authorizing the confiscation of assets gained from crime and now administered by the Serious Organized Crime Agency which is empowered to use civil court procedures to recover the proceeds of unlawful activity by way of an action in the High Court.

Confiscation targets are increased year by year and the 4,743 target for confiscation orders was exceeded in 2009, netting £116 million for the criminal justice agencies.

It has been revealed that CPS lawyers are receiving personal bonuses linked to their success in confiscating criminal assets.

Solicitors, accountants and insolvency practitioners who suspect their clients of tax evasion now have a statutory duty to report them to the authorities without telling the clients.

Further Reading
Proceeds of Crime Act 2002.
Serious Crime Act 2007.

Conflict Theory

See Criminological Theories.

Consent

A defence available to some criminal offences (e.g., minor batteries) whereby it is claimed that the victim genuinely consented to the criminal activity.

It is no defence to murder, serious batteries, incest or non-medical drugs administration.

* A person cannot consent to serious sadomasochism (R v Brown 1993).
* Submission is not consent.
* Consent obtained when the victim is intoxicated is invalid.
* Consent may be express or implied.

The courts have held that there is no implied consent where a person, unaware of the fact that an accused is infected with a disease (e.g., AIDS, HIV) has unprotected intercourse with that person. If, however they were aware of the accused's condition, consent would be a defence (Dica 2004).

Consent will also negate liability for rape, in that lack of consent is a definitive element of the offence which must be proved; a person commits rape if he intentionally penetrates the victim without his/her consent and without reasonable belief in consent.

A person under the age of 16 years cannot give valid consent to sexual activity in the UK.

Further Reading
R v Brown [1993] 2 WLR 556.

Consensus Theory

The theory that states that shared norms and values are the basis of laws and social order.

Consolidation Act

An Act of Parliament which repeals and re-enacts, with amendments, a number of previous Acts.

Conspiracy [Criminal Law Act 1977]

A statutory crime comprising an agreement between two or more persons to carry out a crime.

For example, two people agree that one of them shall steal from a safe while the other drives the getaway van.

The agreement itself is the crime and it is usually punished in the same way as the offence agreed upon even if the full offence is not, in fact, carried out.

There can be no conspiracy where the only other person(s) to the agreement is/are an intended victim or spouse/civil partner.

Since 1981, a person can be convicted of conspiracy even if it is impossible to commit the full offence, for example, the safe is empty.

Particular forms of common law criminal conspiracy include conspiracy to defraud, to outrage public decency and to corrupt public morals

Further Reading
Criminal Law Act 1977 s 1
Criminal Attempts Act 1981

Containment

The hard-line sentencing strategy which maintains that the humane and moral aspects of offending should be ignored and that indefinite containment is the only option for certain categories of offenders in order to protect the public.

Contempt of Court [Contempt of Court Act 1981]

A criminal offence comprising conduct that obstructs the administration of justice and/or interferes or prejudices the outcome of legal proceedings.

This might include bribery or intimidation of witnesses, judges or jurors, disturbances in court, disclosing jury deliberations or publishing material which could prejudice the outcome of court proceedings.

Further Reading
Contempt of Court Act 1981

C

Controlled Drugs

Drugs which are subject to criminal control.

It is an offence to have unlawful possession or to deal in controlled drugs.

These are classified according to the degree of harm attributed to them and classification affects the penalties available:

• Class A are the most dangerous, for example, opium, heroin, morphine, cocaine, LSD, ecstasy, crystal meth and magic mushrooms.

Penalties include an unlimited fine and/or up to 7 years imprisonment (possession) and up to life imprisonment and/or unlimited fine (dealing).
- Class B are medium dangerous, for example, amphetamines, Ritalin and cannabis (as of 2009).

Penalties include an unlimited fine and/or up to 5 years imprisonment (possession) and 14 years imprisonment and/or unlimited fine (dealing).
- Class C are the least dangerous, for example anabolic steroids, ketamine and some anti-depressants, pain-killers and tranquilisers.

Penalties include up to 2 years imprisonment and/or unlimited fine (possession) and up to 14 years imprisonment and/or unlimited fine.

There is an automatic 7-year (minimum) sentence for third-time dealers in Class A drugs unless the court thinks this would be unjust in the particular circumstances.

The Drugs Act 2005 introduced new powers for the police and courts in respect of Class A drugs including

- A new civil 'intervention order' which may be attached to an ASBO for adults to tackle drugs-related anti-social behaviour, requiring them to attend counselling.
- Powers for the courts to remand a person who swallows drugs' evidence in police custody (192 hours maximum) in order to increase the chances of recovery of such evidence.
- Allowing police to test suspected drug offenders at the point of arrest rather than charge, as previously.
- Requiring a person with a positive test to undergo assessment by a drugs professional.
- Allowing adverse inferences to be drawn where a person refuses, without good cause, to undergo a test, body search, x-ray or ultra-sound scan.
- Creating a presumption of intent to supply where a defendant is found in possession of a certain quantity of controlled drugs.
- Permitting police to enter premises to issue a drugs' closure notice.
- Classifying magic mushrooms as Class A drugs.
- Requiring sentences to take into account aggravating factors, for example, dealing near a school.

Further Reading

Misuse of Drugs Act 1971
Misuse of Drugs Order 2001
Drugs Act 2005
ACMD@homeoffice.qsi.gov.uk

Control Orders

An anti-terrorist measure, introduced under The Prevention of Terrorism Act 2005 to restrict the liberty of individuals (foreigners and British citizens) in the interest of public protection.

They were brought in after the House of Lords held that the detention of foreign suspects without trial was discriminatory and incompatible with human rights.

The order is made by the <u>Home Secretary</u> which may take one of two forms:

1. an order lasting 12 months with strict conditions attaching to it including <u>curfews</u>, passport surrender, <u>electronic tagging</u>, daily reporting to the police, restrictions on mosque attendance and internet access or
2. an order lasting only 6 months with severe restriction on the controlee's movement which, effectively, involves derogating from human rights' protections in order to protect the public in a potential terrorist emergency situation.

The <u>Home Secretary</u> is required to make a statement to Parliament every 3 months reporting on the exercise of these powers.

The Act contains very limited rights of <u>appeal,</u> and the absence of <u>double jeopardy</u> protections means that even if a recipient wins an appeal, the Home Secretary could simply re-apply a similar order.

There have been a number of cases where the courts have criticized or annulled control orders for incompatibility with the <u>ECHR</u>.

Further Reading
Prevention of Terrorism Act 2005 s1-4
Secretary of State for the Home Department v. MB (FC) (Appellant) [2007] UKHL 46

Convention Rights

See Human Rights Act.

Conviction

A finding of guilt by a criminal court, resulting in a <u>sentence</u> imposed by the judge.

The conviction finding is the decision of the <u>jury</u> in the <u>Crown Court</u> and of the judge(s) in the <u>Magistrates' Courts</u>.

It forms part of the criminal <u>record</u> of the convicted person.

Cop Culture

The colloquial term for police culture which refers to the values, attitudes, beliefs and reactions of police officers and their institutions.

It is sometimes identified as a negative feature of the police service (most ostensibly among rank and file officers) especially in its most serious traits (racism, sexism and discrimination).

'Corner Boys'

A concept of <u>Albert Cohen's</u> which held that, as well as the delinquent subculture, there were two other identifiable subculture groups:

1. 'College boys': whose members strive, against all odds, to achieve conventional success.

2. 'Corner boys': whose members, recognizing that they are unlikely to succeed conventionally, join with others for support and engage in deviancy.

Coroner

An officer responsible for holding an <u>inquest</u> in a coroner's court, usually with a jury, in order to investigate suspicious deaths because they were sudden, violent, unnatural or occurring in prison.

Coroners are usually lawyers or medical practitioners.

A National Coroner Service was created by statute in 2009.

Further Reading

Coroners and Justice Act 2009

Coroner's Court

See Coroner.

Corporal Punishment

Punishment of a physical nature, for example, caning, flogging, beating and branding.

Historically, most forms of punishment were corporal and remain so in some cultures today, especially in Islamic legal systems.

The main types are

- Parental, for example, smacking children
- Educational, for example, caning students
- Judicial, for example, flogging convicted criminals

It was banned in UK state schools in 1987 and in the private sector in 1999 although there have been numerous demands to reinstate it.

As of May 2009 the only European countries to permit it in both the home and the school are France and the Czech Republic.

Corporate Crime

Crime committed by a corporation rather than by an individual(s) which is often referred to as white collar crime.

Further Reading

Simpson, S. (2002). Corporate Crime, Law and Social Control. Cambridge University Press.
Tombs, S. and Whyte, D. (2003). Unmasking Crimes of the Powerful. Springer Netherlands.
Clinard, M. B. and Yeager, P. C. (2006). Corporate Crime. Transaction Publishers.
www.corporateaccountability.org
www.SeriousCrime.co.uk/corporate.
www.corporatecrimereporter.com

Corporate Manslaughter

<u>Manslaughter</u> committed by a corporation rather than an individual.

This offence was finally recognized in the UK after the disaster in which the Herald of Free Enterprize sank in Zebrugge owing to the negligence of the employees of the P & O Ferries Company.

It was not until 1994, however, that the first company was actually convicted and fined £60,000 (Lyme Bay canoe tragedy).

The Corporate Manslaughter and Homicide Act 2007 introduced a new offence throughout the UK making it possible for corporations, partnerships and government departments to be tried for manslaughter provided it is proved that death resulted from gross failure of health and safety duties and that there was a substantial connexion between that failure and senior management. The maximum sentence is an unlimited fine, and a convicted organization can be required to publicize its conviction and remedy the state of affairs that caused the fatality.

The first prosecution took place in 2009 when a company was charged and convicted of manslaughter of an employee who died as a result of its gross negligence. It was fined £200,000.

Further Reading

Ministry of Justice (2007). A Guide to the Corporate Manslaughter and Homicide Act 2007. www.nio.gov.uk/guide_to_the_cmch_act

Corroboration

Evidence given in support of other (primary) evidence.

It is not required for most types of evidence except for confessions, accomplice and some opinion evidence and in cases of perjury and treason.

Counsel

A barrister or solicitor representing a client in court.

Count

A paragraph in an indictment containing particulars of a criminal charge against a defendant.

Counting Rules

Instructions issued by the Home Office on how the police should count and classify criminal offences.

Court(s)

The bodies responsible for the enforcement of criminal law by hearing prosecutions and appeals.

There exists a hierarchy of courts in England and Wales in which the courts are arranged in order of importance.

The criminal hierarchy is set out below in Figure 1

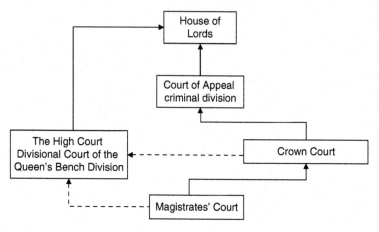

Figure 1   Criminal proceedings

———— appeal by way of case stated

Further Reading

www.courtservice.gov.uk

Court of Appeal (Criminal Division)

The court which hears appeals against <u>conviction</u> and/or <u>sentence</u> from the <u>Crown</u> and <u>Magistrates' Courts</u>. Its judges are called <u>Lords Justices of Appeal</u>.

It also considers cases referred by the <u>Attorney-General</u> or <u>Criminal Cases Review Commission</u> where there are concerns that the sentence is too lenient or there is a <u>miscarriage of justice</u>.

Cracked Trial

A trial in which a last minute <u>guilty plea</u> is entered, the <u>defendant</u> having previously indicated an intention to plead not guilty.

This may occur because the <u>defence</u> is 'playing the system' but more likely because the CPS only agrees to reduce the <u>charge</u> at the last minute.

Crime

There is no single definition of crime but it is usually described as an act or omission which is a <u>public law</u> <u>offence</u> (cf <u>private law</u>) prosecuted by the state in criminal proceedings against the <u>defendant</u>.

Crimes maybe classified as offences against the person, property or the state.

The most serious crimes (<u>indictable</u>) are tried in the <u>Crown Court</u> while <u>Magistrates' Courts</u> try the least serious (<u>summary</u>) and the hybrid category (<u>triable-either-way</u>) may be tried in either court.

Crime is the core focus for criminological investigation involving a complex interaction of many social, political, theoretical and economic forces which include

- the creation of the concept of crime
- the identification of events as crime
- the response to crime
- the establishment and punishment of crime

These interactions occur in the context of time and place and so it is important to understand the dynamic nature of crime.

Further Reading

Tierney, J. (2005). Criminology: Theory and Context. Longman.

Crime and Disorder Reduction Partnerships (CDRPs)

See Community Safety Partnerships.

Crime Control Model

See Models of Criminal Justice.

Crime Flux

A concept that defines the crime rate as a product of the prevalence of victims in the population and the frequency with which they are victimized.

Crime Prevention

The term applied to attempts to deter and reduce crime and victimization, enforce the law and maintain criminal justice.

It applies to government and criminal justice agencies' policies and practices.

Criminologists (e.g., Farrington, Gottfredson, Mckenzie) have been very instrumental in identifying and researching what works in preventing crime.

Three key elements have been identified in the commission of crime:

- criminal motivation
- skills and tools for the commission of the crime
- opportunity

Prevention has to focus on these key elements.

It is said that there are two levels of crime prevention:

(1) Primary prevention which addresses individual and family factors correlated with criminal activity, for example, truancy from school, parenting skills and police response to domestic-violence situations (Sherman 1993).

(2) Secondary prevention which focuses on risk situations, for example, school dropouts, gang membership. It employs social programmes (e.g., youth at risk programmes) and law enforcement strategies in areas where crime rates are high.

There is an International Centre for the Prevention of Crime, created in 1994, which promotes crime prevention, encourages the development of innovative policies and practices and facilitates the exchange of experiences between criminal justice systems across countries.

In criminology there is also a Crime Prevention Theory which says that crime is often committed through the accident of opportunity, for example, an unlocked car.

Therefore it focuses on reducing crime by increasing the associated risks and difficulties and reducing the potential rewards.

Routine Activity Theory is associated with this theory.

Further Reading

Farrington, D. et al. (eds) (2006). Preventing Crime: What Works for Children, Offenders, Victims and Places. Springer.

www.crime-prevention-int.org

Crime Prevention Theory

See Crime Prevention.

Crime Rate

The measure that gives an index of crime occurring (overall or specific categories) in an area for a specific period of time.

For example, rate of burglary per 100,000 population in Cambridge in 2010.

Crime Reduction Programme (CRP)

A £250 million programme that ran for 3 years from April 1999 taking an evidence-based approach to reducing crime in England and Wales.

The CRP had three goals:

1. To achieve a sustained reduction in crime
2. To improve and mainstream knowledge of best practice
3. To maximize the implementation of cost-effective crime reduction activity

To achieve these, the CRP worked through an array of 20 separate but linked crime reduction initiatives which were to be primarily delivered at the local level through Crime and Disorder Reduction Partnerships (CDRP).

Ultimately few projects were implemented and it ended prematurely in 2002.

Further Reading

www.crimereduction.homeoffice.gov.uk

Crime Scene

A location where a crime occurs and from which <u>forensic evidence</u> may be recovered by the police, forensic scientists or crime scene investigators.

Crime Trend(s)

The measure of the <u>crime rate</u> over a period of time (usually plotted on a graph) and linked to population ratios; essentially the crime rate per unit of the population.

It is necessary to calculate by reference to population ratios in a given area to ensure that crime counts do not decrease or increase solely as a result of population changes over the years.

The crime trend in England and Wales is upwards; from a low of about 430,000 in 1954, recorded offences increased to over 6 million in 2003.

Some of the possible causes have been identified (Loder and Sparks 2007) as

- the shift from economies based on manufacturing to ones based on services and the rise of consumerism;
- changes in family structures;
- proliferation of the mass media;
- suburbanization of cities;
- altered relations between men and women, parents and children;
- decline in deference to authority.

Further Reading

Loder, I. and Sparks, R. (2007). Contemporary Landscapes of Crime, Order and Control: Governance, Risk and Globalization, in Maguire et al. The Oxford Handbook of Criminology. Oxford University Press.

Criminal Cases Review Commission

The independent review body, established in 1997 as a result of the Criminal Appeal Act 1995 in the wake of the serious <u>miscarriages of justice</u> in 1980s, whose role is to

- consider suspected miscarriages of justice
- refer such cases to the Court of Appeal for reconsideration where there is a real possibility that a conviction would not be upheld
- make recommendations for <u>pardons</u>

It deals with more than 1000 applications per year (see Table 4).

Table 4 Case statistics: Figures to 2010

Total applications	12,613
Cases completed	11,924
Referrals	454
Heard by <u>Court of Appeal</u>	416 (295 quashed, 120 upheld, 1 reserved)

Source: www.ccrc.gov.uk/cases.

Further Reading
Criminal Appeal Act 1995 s13
www.ccrc.gov.uk

Criminal Conviction Certificate

A certificate provided to persons who request details about their criminal record from the Criminal Records Agency set up under the Police Act 1997.

Criminal Damage [Criminal Damage Act 1971]

A criminal offence which takes several forms:

* Simple Criminal Damage: intentionally/recklessly damaging property of another.
* Aggravated Criminal Damage: intentionally/recklessly damaging property with intent to endanger life.
* Arson: intentionally/recklessly damaging property by fire.

Criminal Defence Service (CDS)

The replacement service for the criminal legal aid scheme established in 2001 (Access to Justice Act 1999).

This service is not means-tested but the judge, at the end of the trial, may order the convicted person to pay some or all of his/her costs.

Criminal Defence Service Direct

A telephone advice service dealing with minor offences outside of the Duty Solicitor Scheme.

Criminal Injuries Compensation Authority (CICA)

The body, within the Ministry of Justice, responsible for administering the Criminal Injuries Compensation Scheme.

Further Reading
www.criminalinjurycompensation.org

Criminal Injuries Compensation Scheme

The government scheme which provides compensation to victims who have suffered physical or mental injury from violent crime reported to the police.

It is not essential that anyone has actually been convicted of the crime.

Until 1996 awards were set at the sum a successful civil action would have produced, but now they are fixed by statute and range from £1000 to £250,000.

Further Reading
www.cica.gov.uk

Criminalistics

The collection and examination of physical evidence of crime.

Criminality

Behaviour defined as criminal because it offends the law and collective morality and causes harm to individuals or society as a whole.

Concepts of criminality are dynamic and are influenced by public opinion, political, economic and moral considerations.

Definitions of crime, therefore, shift through time and behaviour; once considered criminal, it may be later decriminalized. Obvious examples include abortion, suicide and homosexuality.

Traditionally, two main theoretical approaches explained why conduct is defined as criminal:

* Consensus approach
  Conduct is criminalized because it is generally agreed to be unacceptable.
* Conflict approach
  Criminal law is constructed to protect the interests of powerful interest groups in society, seeking to impose their values over competing groups struggling for power.

Some would argue that criminality is, in effect, an artificial construct of the society which defines it.

Criminality Information Unit (CIU)

The agency set up to help improve the management of criminality information in the public sector, at home and abroad, with the overall aim of improving the protection of the public.

It extends beyond the criminal justice system to include health, education, care and immigration.

It is now called the Joint Public Protection Information Unit.

Criminalization

The concept or process of defining individuals and behaviours as criminal which is the opposite of decriminalization.

Criminal Justice

Criminal justice represents society's formal response to criminality, specifically breaches of the criminal law.

Traditional analysis has focused on the tension between different perspectives on criminal justice derived from various disciplines, including criminology, sociology, law and politics. These are called models of criminal justice and reflect different influences on policy and practice in criminal justice systems.

There are three distinct criminal justice systems in the UK; England and Wales, Scotland and Northern Ireland.

EU membership has led to increased integration between European criminal justice systems.

Further Reading

Davies, M. et al. (2005). Criminal Justice: An Introduction to the Criminal Justice System in England and Wales. Longman.

McConville, M. and Wilson, G. (2002). The Handbook of Criminal Justice Process. Oxford University Press.

www. cjsonline.govt/uk/publications/current.html

Criminal Justice Agencies

The departments and personnel which administer the criminal justice system.

Criminal Justice Consultative Council (CJCC)

A body established, along with its Area Committees, in 1992, to foster better communications between the main criminal justice agencies and to advise government on matters of practical application in the criminal justice system.

It acts as a forum for senior members of the agencies and legal system to address issues of crime at a national level. Its membership includes senior civil servants, judges, lawyers and police officers.

Criminal Justice System(s)

A system maybe described as a collection of parts working together to form a whole, implying co-operation, co-ordination and consultation.

A criminal justice system is an aggregate of centrally funded agencies that carry out criminal justice functions, namely, law enforcement, adjudication, punishment, crime prevention and deterrence.

Law enforcement is the responsibility of the police and prosecuting agencies, while the courts are adjudicatory bodies.

Punishment is primarily the concern of the prison and probation services, and crime prevention and deterrence could be said to involve all of these and other related agencies.

There has been criticism that multiple and competing aims are often pursued by different agencies. This is not easy to reconcile with the concept of a system, especially where there is competition for funding and responsibility.

The main agencies include the police, CPS, Courts, National Offender Management Service, Criminal Defence Services, Probation Trusts, Prison Service, Youth Justice Service and the Serious Organized Crime Agency.

Subsidiary agencies would include the Forensic Science Service, Criminal Injuries Compensation Authority, HM Inspectorates, Parole Board, Victim Support, Coroners and the Legal Profession.

Laypersons are also involved in criminal justice as jurors, witnesses, paralegals and reporters of crime. Ultimately, as the electorate they also influence policy.

Various government departments have responsibilities in relation to criminal justice. These include the Home Office, Ministry of Justice, Serious Fraud Office, HM Revenue and Customs and local government agencies.

Some view the criminal justice system as a series of stages through which a case proceeds, namely, investigation, arrest, charge, trial and sentence. Collectively these stages could also be seen as the criminal justice system.

Further Reading

Davies, M. et al. (2005). *Criminal Justice: An Introduction to the Criminal justice System in England and Wales.* Longman.
McConville, M. and Wilson, G. (2002). *The Handbook of Criminal Justice Process.* Oxford University Press.
www.cjsonline.org

Criminal Law

The body of (public law) which prescribes an act or omission as a crime and punishable by the state in criminal proceedings. It defines the elements of these crimes and the defences and sentences available for them.

The aims of the criminal law could be said to

1. forbid and prevent conduct which unjustifiably inflicts or threatens to inflict harm to public interests,
2. subject to public control persons whose conduct indicates that they are disposed to commit crimes,
3. safeguard conduct that is without fault from criminalization,
4. give fair warning of the nature of conduct that is criminal,
5. differentiate between serious and minor offences.

There is no single criminal code in the UK, so the law is found in both common law and statute.

Criminal law is classified as

- Offences against the person (fatal/non-fatal), for example, murder, manslaughter, assault and battery.
- Offences against property, for example, theft ,criminal damage and burglary.
- Offences against the state, for example, treason.

Further Reading

Allen, M. J. (2009). *Textbook on Criminal Law.* Oxford University Press.
Jefferson, M. (2008). *Criminal Law.* Pearson Education.

C

Criminal Libel

The common law offence of publishing a false, written statement which is defamatory of a person's character or reputation.

Criminal Lifestyle

The lifestyle adopted by criminals.

More specifically, it has been used to define persons convicted of criminal activity over a period of time (6 months or more) from which that person had derived benefit [The Proceeds of Crime Act 2002].

Criminal Liability

The legal responsibility for one's crimes which will result in conviction and punishment by the criminal courts.

Criminal Records Agency (CRA)

The body which provides information about criminal records in the form of a criminal record certificate.

Further Reading

www.criminalrecordsagency.co.uk

Criminal Records Bureau (CRB)

The executive agency of the Home Office, launched in 2002 to assist recruiting organizations in the public, private and voluntary sectors by identifying applicants who may be unsuitable for work with children or other vulnerable persons. It provides a wider access to criminal records than was available in the past.

Criminalization

The process of defining conduct as criminal by means of the criminal law.

It is estimated that the government has defined more than 3000 crimes since 1997 – almost one per day. This compares with about 494 offences created by the Conservatives 1988–96.

The new offences include criminalizing the sale of grey squirrels! [The Natural Environment and Rural Communities Act 2006]

The Sex Offences Act 2003 created 61 offences while the Crime and Disorder Act 1998 was responsible for 11 new offences, including nine racially aggravated crimes.

Other statutes relate to mobile phones, gambling, data protection and terrorism.

For perspective however, it should be borne in mind that some of these replaced existing offences.

Criminal Statistics

See Statistics.

Criminology

The study of the nature and causes of crime and the means of dealing with crime and criminals.

It is an interdisciplinary area of study, with strong roots in the humanities and natural sciences. Its prime focus is on improving understanding of criminal behaviour rather than on legal reform although, obviously, it is also very influential on the latter.

Its origins go back to the late 1700s and there are many major schools of Criminological Theory.

Criminological Theories

There is no single theory of criminology; different schools of thought and disciplines have attempted to explain the phenomenon of crime.

Some of the main theories are outlined below.

- Classical Theory
  This theory is often, although not invariably, said to represent the origins of criminology at the beginning of the nineteenth century and represented a challenge to the earlier dominance of the spiritual and religious Natural Law School.

  Classical criminologists (e.g., Beccaria, Bentham, Mill) focus on the criminal act which the state, under its social contract with citizens, has power to punish provided it does so proportionately.

  Crime is seen as a matter of individual choice; in that individuals are rational beings, free to choose criminal or non-criminal lifestyles, dictated by the pain/pleasure principle, that is, rational people will choose courses of action likely to produce pleasure rather than pain. It assumes that individuals will weigh up the costs and benefits of crime.

- Positivist Theory
  Classicalism is essentially a philosophical and subjective theory rather than one based on research evidence and was therefore challenged by positivists (e.g., Darwin, Lombroso) whose work is based on scientific research and objectivity.

  It focuses on the nature and characteristics of the offender rather than the criminal act itself and downgrades the significance of free will, arguing that an individual's behaviour may be influenced or determined by outside forces, over which he/she has no control and which might be biological or psychological.

  Behavioural problems are seen in terms of pathology or deficiency. Deviants are regarded as having personal difficulties related to biological/psychological factors which have to be identified and corrected by experts and so this approach tends towards treatment rather than punishment.

  Systematic study is emphasized and so methodologies from the natural sciences are adopted in order to find causal determinants of human behaviour. These, in turn, facilitate predictions and modifications of future behaviour.

Two strands of Positivism may be identified:

(i) Biological Criminology
    Epitomized by Lombroso, this strand involves a theory based on criminal anthropology whereby criminality resides in the nature of the offender who is viewed as biologically inferior to non-criminals. This inferiority is identifiable by reference to physical characteristics, namely, intelligence and genetic factors which predispose individuals to delinquency.

In 1940's, for example, three main body-types were identified (see Figure 2):

- Endomorphic (endomorphs): soft /round, medium height, likely to be relaxed, sociable and fond of food; tolerant, extrovert and inclined towards delinquency and occasional fraud.
- Ectomorphic (ectomorphs): thin/fragile, sensitive, tense, thoughtful, inhibited, likely to be brainy, articulate and inclined towards theft.
- Mesomorphic (mesomorphs): muscular/strong, lacking in empathy, aggressive, assertive; most likely to become criminal with inclination towards homicide, assault and battery.

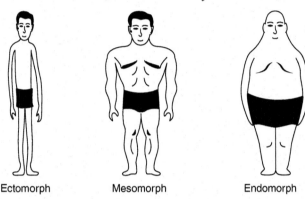

Ectomorph   Mesomorph   Endomorph

Figure 2   Body types

Further Reading

Sheldon, W. et al. (1970). Varieties of Delinquent Youth. Hafner Publishing Co. Ltd.

(ii)   Psychological Criminology

Epitomized by the British psychologist <u>Eysenck</u>, this strand theorizes that crime is a result of biological problems, externally caused (e.g., by war injury or childhood trauma) or internally caused (e.g., by mental illness or the subconscious).

Essentially, therefore, <u>deviancy</u> is linked to the offender's personality.

- Sociological Theory

This theory predicates that <u>criminality</u> is best understood by reference to social factors external to the individual. It views crime as a manifestation of social rather than individual <u>pathology</u>. There are a number of strands within this theory including

(i)   Consensus Theory (e.g., <u>Durkheim</u> 1895)

These theorists take for granted that criminality exists and do not attempt to explain it but rather focus on the role of law as an expression of social and moral consensus which is a means of defining and dealing with crime.

(ii)   Conflict Theory (e.g., Sellin 1938)

Linked with Marxism, this theory considers the role of the State and the powerful in defining crime; its focus is on <u>discrimination</u> and divisions in society.

(iii) Feminist Theory (e.g., Smart 1976)
There is no single feminist theory but this perspective draws from other theories to describe how women are affected by inequalities and structural oppression that exist in society and the criminal justice system, in particular.

From the 1970s feminist criminologists pointed out that criminological theories either ignored women or assumed that theories applicable to men were equally applicable to women – which is palpably untrue.

- Social Disorganization Theory (e.g., Shaw and McKay 1942)
This theory is linked with the Chicago School of 1920s which claimed that disorder, poor integration and lack of social stability encourage crime.

Criminality is seen as a normal response to abnormal environmental circumstances (such as industrialization, urbanization, poor accommodation, transient populations, decay, illiteracy and migration) resulting in social instability and lack of attachment to community.

- Differential Association Theory (e.g., Sutherland 1939)
Also linked with the Chicago School, this approach sees criminal behaviour as being learnt and transmitted via social interaction, often within intimate social groups or subcultures.

Criminality is thus learnt by association and imitation of criminals.

- Strain Theory (e.g., Merton 1938)
This theory maintains that where there is inequality (Strain) between goals in society (e.g., pursuit of wealth/status) and the means to achieve these goals (e.g., employment/education), such disparity will drive some individuals to resort to illegal means to achieve goals.

Strain, which is linked to Anomie, creates frustration and resentment which then becomes the motivation for crime.

- Status Frustration Theory (Cohen 1955)
Developed from Strain and Anomie this theory has it that frustration at being denied legitimate means for goal achievement weakens commitment to a law-abiding life.

Cohen argued that working-class males, coming into contact with middle-class values in school have a choice of whether to try to conform (and likely fail) or to reject those values and create their own instead. This improves their self-esteem but makes living up to this new subculture's standards/expectations much more important than societal (e.g., parents/teachers) expectations.

- Drift Theory (e.g., Sykes and Matza 1964)
These theorists believe that adolescents drift between conventional and criminal behaviour, not necessarily occupying one position but choosing when to be criminal or not. Their perception of being freed from conventional values encourages them to commit crime.

- Control Theory (e.g., Hirschi 1969)
This approach is different to most theories; in that it does not ask why people become criminals – but rather why they obey the law!

People comply because they are controlled and offend when this control breaks down.

Hirschi proposed that delinquency occurs when an individual's bond with society is weakened or broken; if he becomes alienated form others'

C

values and expectations, social activities or the law itself, he is more likely to act criminally.

- Labelling Theory (e.g., Becker 1963, Giddens 1993)
  This theory argues that the labels given to deviants by those in power (e.g., criminal justice agencies) can stigmatize and therefore create or reinforce criminality.
  Crime is seen as a social process and the impact of the criminal justice experience on individuals cannot be ignored; crime is not an objective phenomenon but an outcome of specific types of human interaction.

- Marxist Theory (e.g., Chambliss 1978)
  This theory continues the notion of inequality in society and sees crime as a product of class divisions, exploitation and alienation, reflecting the values and interests of the powerful.
  It characterizes criminal justice systems as operating in the interests of capitalism and the powerful who define and enforce their own form of social order.
  The causes of crime thus lie in the structure of unequal class relations in society.

- Realist Theory (e.g., Wilson 1975)
  This theory proposes a shift towards a more realistic approach to criminality which would provide ideas useful for policymakers and reminds that crime cannot be divorced from the wider political and economic environment.
  Two strands can be identified:
  (i) Right realism
      In 1980s conservative ideology was dominant in many countries, especially Britain and USA, and with this came less concern about the causes of crime and more concern with public protection, law and order, punishment and deterrence.
      Fundamentally crime is seen as a freely chosen option and the way to reduce it is to emphasize that crime does not pay by the use of hard-line policies and punishments (e.g., zero-tolerance strategies, increased police powers, extended sentences of imprisonment).
      Certain groups in society (e.g., homeless, state benefit dependant, single parents) are seen as responsible for the majority of crime and need to be made more responsible and accountable.
  (ii) Left realism
      A reaction to the punitive exclusionary policies of the Right, this theory advocates inclusionary, co-operative responses from criminal justice agencies, and community involvement.
      Crime prevention programmes, concern for victims, local safety projects characterize this approach with a view to long-term reform and equality.
  These theorists see the causes of crime as being a combination of bad economic conditions (especially in inner city working-class areas), unemployment, and hard-line criminal justice policies.

- Restorative Justice Theory (e.g., Braithwaite 1989)
  A relatively modern theory which emphasizes the need to find holistic and constructive ways to deal with offenders and victims.
  The impact of the particular crime on its victims is of crucial importance and to this end offender-victim meetings, family group conferences, reparation and reassurance are its focus.

- Cultural Theory (e.g., Katz 1988)
  An approach which attempts to understand the meanings and emotions associated with crime and crime control.
    This includes studying the hedonistic nature of offending (adrenaline and visual impact, for example).

It should be remembered that different theories lend themselves to different criminal justice policies and these will change through time; how popular any theory or policy is will often depend on the political climate of the time. At the beginning of the twentieth century the two main competitors were <u>Classical Theory</u> (free will) and <u>Biological Theory</u> (determinism). As the century advanced, the number and variety of theories proliferated and led to calls for integration (<u>Integrative Theory</u>) which may be achieved in the twenty-first century.

Further Reading

Newburn, T. (2007). Criminology. Willan Publishing.
Newburn, T. (ed.) (2009). Key Readings in Criminology. Willan Publishing.
Hopkins-Burke, R. (2005). An Introduction to Criminological Theory. Willan Publishing.
Tierney, J. (2006). Criminology: Theory and Context. Pearson Education.
Lanier, M. and Stuart, H. (2005). Essential Criminology. Westview Press.

Crisis of Imprisonment

A broad term associated with the problems and tensions in modern prisons.
    These have been documented in criminological literature as

  (i)   Visibility crisis: which refers to the limited public access to, and information about, prisons which, in turn, perpetuates maltreatment, violence, drug abuse and bad conditions.
 (ii)   Authority crisis: which is the complaint of prison personnel who complain that changes in prison rules and practices have undermined prison authority and made maintenance of order more difficult, thereby increasing staff stress.
(iii)   Conditions crisis: which refers to the poor conditions and state of repair in a number of prisons, especially those built in the Victorian era and made worse by lack of resources and overcrowding.
 (iv)   *Containment crisis*: which highlights how overcrowding and lack of recreational time and facilities affect staff-inmate relations, threaten security and increase the likelihood of disturbances and escape attempts.
  (v)   Legitimacy crisis: which encompasses the arguments that there is no real justification for imprisonment which in fact does not work (as evidenced by the high rates of recidivism) and which is a class-based system in which the working classes are disproportionately represented. Legitimacy is also undermined when rules and procedures are not followed or where staff do not act professionally.

Further Reading

Cavadino, M. and Dignan, J. (2007). The Penal System. Sage Publications Ltd.
www.prisonreformtrust.org.uk

Critical Criminology

A label used to bring together a range of different theories concerned with the various ways that the state subtly uses its power to maintain and support itself, recognizing that it has vested interests in the way that things are (status quo) rather than the way they might be.

These thinkers focus on how

- racism, sexism, class and discrimination are an intrinsic part of the way policies are developed and institutions operate;
- some state practices marginalize and criminalize some groups and not others;
- some people are more likely to be seen as victims than others;
- economic policies may force individuals to turn to crime as a survival mechanism;
- moral panics about crime being out of control are used to deflect attention from structural conflicts;
- crime control measures are incapable of dealing with the crimes of the powerful in the state;
- criminal laws are riddled with gender assumptions about what constitutes reasonable, normal behaviour;
- crime control has developed into a growth industry, dominated by multi-national interests;
- crime and other social problems cannot, and should not, be regulated by the criminal justice system;
- crime is the product not the object of criminal justice philosophies and institutions.

These criminologists advocate the dismantling of the criminal justice system, which has vested interests in ensuring that crime remains out of control. This, they argue, would eliminate many of the problems caused by the system itself.

Other agencies and forms of resolution should be adopted and funded to seek solutions which might include restorative justice, co-operation, community justice and inclusionary rather than exclusionary punitive measures.

Cross-examination

See Examination.

Crown

The legal entity in which the state is vested, namely the government, as opposed to the monarch (Queen) in her personal capacity.

Criminal prosecutions are brought by the Crown in the Queen's courts.

Crown Court

The criminal court which sits usually with a jury trying indictable crimes and appeals from Magistrates' Courts.

Crown Prosecution Service (CPS)

The body, headed by the DPP and independent of the police which is responsible for

- deciding if a prosecution should be brought,
- charging and presenting the prosecution case in court,
- advising the police,
- discontinuing criminal proceedings.

The criteria for determining if a prosecution should be mounted are laid down in the Code for Crown Prosecutors.
  The CPS is organized on a regional basis, each area having a chief prosecutor.

Further Reading
www.cps.gov.uk

Cuffing

The term for the police practice of deciding not to create a crime record ('non-criming') in respect of incidents reported by members of the public.
  This may occur where

- reports are regarded as mistaken or false
- evidence is unavailable or perceived as likely to be inadmissible
- complaint is not supported or withdrawn by the victim

Pragmatically, the police may wish to do this to avoid generating unsolvable crimes which will affect their clear-up rates.

Culpability

The state of having committed an offence for which responsibility must be taken.

Cult

A group, generally regarded as extremist, and often religious, whose followers live unconventionally and often under a charismatic leader.
  Some of these have been notoriously criminal such as

- Charles Manson Cult ('The Family') which carried out horrific murders in America in the late 1960s.
- Jim Jones Cult which, having killed an investigating US Congressman, committed mass suicide in Guyana in 1978.
- David Koresh Davidian Cult which, after its 1993 gun-battle with federal officers in Wako, Texas, led to a 51-day siege which ended in a blaze which left Koresh and 82 members dead.
- Aum Shrini Kyo Cult whose followers were responsible for the nerve gas attack in the Tokyo subway which killed 12 and injured thousands in 1995.

C

- Heaven's Gate whose members committed mass suicide in California in 1997.
- The Ugandan Movement for the Restoration of the Ten Commandments of God which committed mass murder and suicide in 2000.
- Baader-Meinhof Gang, founded in the 1970s which was one of post-war West Germany's most violent and prominent groups who advocated communist-inspired terrorism and engaged in armed resistance against what they deemed to be the fascist state. It operated from 1970 to 1998 and was held responsible for 34 deaths, including many secondary targets – such as chauffeurs and bodyguards – and many injuries in its almost 30 years of activity.

Further Reading

Melton, J. Gordon (1992). The Encyclopaedic Handbook of the Cults. New York: Garland Publishing.

Culture

A society, organization, institution or group with shared values, attitudes and goals at any particular time.

Cultural Criminology

The theory that places criminality and its control in the context of culture.

Cultural Deviance Theory

The theory that maintains that persons from different origins or ethnic groups have different cultural heritages. One group/culture may dominate and become regarded as mainstream while the values and behaviours of others may be criminalized, thus creating criminals of persons who are really only conforming to their own, albeit minority, values.

Cumulative Sentence

A criminal who has been convicted of two or more different crimes, instead of being sentenced for both crimes separately, can be sentenced for both of them jointly and be required to serve for the crime with the longer time of imprisonment.

Curfew Order

A bespoke court order aimed at reducing the opportunity for offending and so protect the public by, effectively, coercing an offender (16 years +) to stay indoors and out of public or specific places at particular times.

Typically, it might involve electronic monitoring of an offender's movements.

An order can last for 2–12 hours per day for 6 months (maximum).

Custody

Detention of a suspect or offender for questioning at a police station, remand pending trial or imprisonment following the imposition of a custodial sentence by a court.

The Criminal Justice Act 2003 provided for innovative changes to short-term sentences:

- Custody Plus: consisting of a short period of imprisonment (2–13 weeks) followed by a longer period of community supervision (26 weeks minimum).
- Custody Minus: consisting of giving the offender the opportunity to be punished in the community on conditions which, if they are not observed, will carry the threat of imprisonment.
- Intermittent Custody: consisting of a custodial sentence spread over a longer period which might include weekend imprisonment, thus allowing employment to continue uninterrupted.

These measures have not yet been implemented.

Custody Officer

A police officer in all police stations responsible for ensuring that the rights of suspects and detainees are observed.

Cybercrime

Criminal activity which occurs in virtual space using computer network technologies.

It can, therefore, transcend national boundaries.

It includes the illegal accessing, intercepting, damaging, deleting or alteration of computer data as well as misuse of devices, identity theft and electronic fraud. It has become a high-profile crime in recent years with the development of child pornography and grooming.

C

Dangerousness

The concept which determines whether an <u>indeterminate sentence</u> is imposed on a dangerous offender for the public protection [Criminal Justice Act 2003].

In assessing dangerousness the court must be satisfied that the offender poses an ongoing significant risk of serious harm to the public.

The court takes account of all information available to it about the nature and circumstances of the offender's crime and any other information, if any, about patterns of behaviour which might not have actually resulted in conviction but be relevant to risk assessment, such as hanging about near parks or playgrounds in the case of sex offenders.

Thus, for example, where an offender has been convicted of a serious violent offence and has a prior conviction for indecent assault, the court must assume the requisite risk unless it is unreasonable to do so.

This therefore, provides a safety net to ensure that offenders convicted of two relevant offences are assumed to be dangerous.

There is no such presumption in respect of under-18-year olds and the courts look at cases on an individual basis.

The concept of 'danger' should not be confused with 'risk'; danger refers to actual exposure to harm or the propensity of offenders to cause harm while risk relates to the probability that a harmful event/behaviour will occur.

The use of the word 'significant' is to ensure that remote risks are not taken into account.

Further Reading
Ward, R. and Davies, M. (2005). The Criminal Justice Act 2003: A Practitioner's Guide. Longmans.

Dangerous Offenders

See *Dangerousness*.

Dark Figure

The amount of 'invisible' crime which is not officially known about or recorded in official crime <u>statistics</u> and which undermines statistical measurement of actual crime in society.

Crime surveys have enabled this dark figure to be somewhat more accurately configured.

Further Reading
Coleman, C. and Moynihan, J. (2002). Understanding Crime Data: Haunted by the Dark Figure. Open University Press.

Darwin, Charles (1809–82)

The father of evolutionary theory whose ideas strongly influenced <u>criminological theories</u> (e.g., <u>biological positivists</u> such as <u>Beccaria and Lombroso</u>).

Further Reading

Robinson, D. and Groves, J. (1999). Introducing Philosophy. Icon books UK.

Date Rape

<u>Rape</u> perpetrated in the context of a date or other-would-be-romantic situation.

It is said to be common among young women and adolescents. Drugs and/or alcohol may be used to undermine judgement, inhibition, resistance and motor control as well as inhibiting the victim's memory of the event.

The most common substances reported in association with sexual assaults are alcohol, cocaine and marijuana but, more recently, other drugs have also been reported such as <u>rohypnol</u>, <u>ketamine</u> and ecstasy.

Death Penalty

See Capital Punishment.

Decarceration

Criminal justice policies and practices which aim at the reduction of imprisonment by providing alternative measures, usually in the community.

Given the huge rise in the prison population from the 1990s, this would not seem to be very evident or successful today.

Declaration of Incompatibility

See Human Rights Act.

Deconstruction

A method of analysis which aims to undo or undermine theories in a way that explains why they appear to be real or convincing at first sight.

Deconstructual approaches include <u>anarchism</u> and <u>absolutionism</u>.

D

Decriminalization

The process of making conduct legal which was previously illegal. Examples include adult, consensual homosexuality in private and <u>suicide</u> which were decriminalized by the Sex Offences Act 1967 and Suicide Act 1961 respectively.

De facto

The expression indicating an actual state of affairs, in fact/reality as opposed to <u>de jure</u> the term for a legal state of affairs.

Default

An offence of ommission, it is often used to refer to neglect of a legal duty or non-appearance in court in which case judgement may be given against the defaulting party.

Defence

An issue of law or fact which, if proved, will relieve a defendant of criminal liability, wholly or partly.

Insanity, for example, will wholly exempt the defendant whereas diminished responsibility or provocation will only reduce the charge from murder to manslaughter. Other defences include self-defence, necessity, duress and intoxication.

Defence, the

The defendant's case/argument as opposed to the prosecution's case in a criminal trial.

Defendant

A person charged with a criminal offence.

Deindividualization

The term used to describe loss of individual identity and lowered self-awareness, often temporary, resulting from being a member of a group. The loss of self-awareness may lead to the individual focusing rather on their group and their own role within it and striving to achieve group norms. This can have the effect of reducing inhibitions, making persons feel they are less responsible for their own actions and thus may make them more likely to commit crime. It has been used to explain cult behaviour and even the Holocaust.

Dejuvenization

The term used from 1990s referring to the erosion of the welfare principle of treating young offenders differently or separately from adults.

Extending adult sentences (e.g., electronic tagging) to young persons and allowing them to be publicly identified are illustrations of this process.

Delegated Legislation

Law made by subordinate bodies conferred with law-making powers by Parliament by a parent/enabling Act. This includes Orders-in-Council, regulations and byelaws made by the Privy Council, ministers and local authorities respectively.

De jure

See De facto.

Deferment (sentence)

A court may delay (6 months maximum) passing a sentence on a convicted offender, with his/her consent, pending observation of future behaviour or change of circumstances. This is said to be deferment of sentence.

Delinquency

The term often used to describe juvenile misbehaviour or criminality.

Demonization

The identification of individual(s) as 'Folk-devils', usually by exaggerated media coverage which may cause a moral panic.

Further Reading
Cohen, S. (1973). Folk Devils and Moral Panics. Routledge.

Denunciation

The disapproval of conduct, often by society or its representatives.

In the context of the philosophy of sentencing denunciation is expressed in the form and severity of the sentence imposed.

Department of Constitutional Affairs

The government department, established in 2003, responsible for running the court service but replaced by the Ministry of Justice in 2007.

Determinism

The counter-notion of self-determination suggesting that individuals may be inclined to criminality by factors over which they may have little or no control. It is linked to Positivist and Biological Criminology.

Deterrence

See Theories of Punishment

D

Deviance

Behaviour deviating from the normal, and thus socially disapproved of, but which may not always be proscribed by the criminal law, for example, adultery.

Deviance Amplification

The process by which attempts to control deviance by the state has the opposite effect and actually increases it.

Labelling Theory supports this concept.

Differential Association Theory

See Criminological Theories.

Dimantia

See Amentia.

Diminished Responsibility

A partial criminal <u>defence</u> under the Homicide Act 1957 available to a murder charge which, if successful, reduces the charge to <u>manslaughter</u> to which it is then treated as a <u>guilty plea</u>. Its advantage lies in the fact that the sentence for manslaughter is discretionary as opposed to the mandatory life-imprisonment sentence for murder.

In order to establish diminished responsibility the defendant must prove, on a <u>balance of probability</u>, that his/her mental responsibility at the time of the killing was substantially impaired by an abnormality of the mind which might include disease, injury, mental subnormality, clinical depression or irresistible impulse.

The defence was introduced in the era of the <u>death penalty</u> to enable disturbed killers who could not satisfy the strict requirements of the <u>insanity</u> defence to be convicted of manslaughter.

Directors of Offender Management

Regional Directors (10) responsible for prison and probation services in the ten government regions in England and Wales. They are part of the <u>National Offender Management Service (NOMS)</u>.

Director of Public Prosecutions (DPP)

The head of the Crown Prosecution Service (<u>CPS</u>), appointed by the Attorney-General (<u>A-G</u>) who is a lawyer and is responsible for the conduct of criminal prosecutions. He/she has powers to discontinue prosecutions and his/her consent is required for certain criminal proceedings, for example, <u>incest</u> and official secrecy prosecutions.

Discharge

The release of a convicted defendant without punishment, absolutely or conditionally.

Technically this is a <u>sentence</u> and is placed on the defendant's criminal <u>record</u>.

A <u>conditional discharge</u> releases the defendant subject to a condition of non-reoffending for a specified period; in the event of another conviction within the time he/she may be sentenced also for the original <u>offence</u>.

D

Disclosure

Formerly called 'discovery of documents', this refers to the rules requiring the disclosure of specific evidence by the <u>defence</u> and <u>prosecution</u> to each other in advance of criminal trial proceedings.

The Criminal Justice Act 2003 increased the disclosure obligations on both the prosecution and defence in criminal proceedings. A prosecutor will henceforth have to disclose material which might *reasonably* be considered capable of undermining the prosecution case. More controversially, the defence must supply names, addresses and date of birth of proposed defence <u>witnesses</u> as well as details of any defences which will be raised and ensure that such details are regularly updated.

Further Reading
The Criminal Justice Act 2003 Part V

Discounts (sentence)

The practice of offering discounts in the length of <u>sentences</u> in return for a <u>plea</u> of guilty to a criminal charge, incriminating a co-defendant(s) or otherwise assisting the prosecution.

Further Reading
www.sentencingcouncil.org.uk

Discrimination

The judgement or treatment of persons by reference to legally irrelevant factors, for example, colour, race, ethnicity, gender or age.

It may take several forms:

- Direct discrimination: deliberate considerations of inappropriate considerations.
- Indirect discrimination: structural and institutional processes and expectations which are not intentionally designed to treat persons differently but which, in fact, do so.
- Contextual discrimination: differential outcomes and treatments.
- Positive discrimination: policies which take differential factors into account so as to promote equal opportunities and advantages for the underprivileged.

Further Reading
Sex Discrimination Act 1975
Race Relations Act 1976
Race Relations (Amendment) Act 2000
Disability Discrimination Acts 1995, 2005
Equality Acts 2006, 2010

D

Disparity

The term used to describe divergent sentencing practices for the sentencing of similar cases which is facilitated by the discretionary nature of sentencing in the UK criminal justice system.

Dispersal Order (Anti-social Behaviour Act 2003)

An order which enables the police in a designated area ('dispersal zone') to disperse groups of two or more whose presence or behaviour has resulted, or is likely to result, in harassment, intimidation or distress to the public.

The order may last for up to 6 months (renewable) in England and Wales or 3 months in Scotland. Failure to comply is a criminal offence.

Dispersal Zone

See Dispersal Order.

Displacement

The theory that crime *has* to occur in society (because of problems such as social, psychological, economical or biological) and if it is prevented in some particular form at some particular time and place, it will merely transfer to another time or place or in some other form.

Discretion

The ability to make decisions or act (or not) according to one's own judgement. Discretion is one of the most contentious concepts in criminal justice because it is so important and yet so difficult to define and contain.

Discretionary powers are given and exercised by all the criminal justice agencies: police officers, prosecutors, lawyers, judges, prison and probation officers, among others.

Sentencing discretion is particularly evident in the UK penal system as illustrated by the following features:

- Judges have a choice from a wide range of sentences, custodial and non-custodial, with special consideration being given to juvenile offenders.
- There are no overall statutory aims of sentencing policy.
- There are relatively few prescribed maximum, minimum or mandatory sentences.
- While judges are generally required to give reasons for their judgements, they need not give reasons when imposing sentence.
- Sentencers may consider mitigating factors and consult other professionals (doctors, psychiatrist and social workers) before imposing sentence.

Many factors, formal and informal, may influence the exercise of discretionary powers, including

- the seriousness of the offence
- harm caused to the victim(s) and public
- dangerousness of the offender
- mitigating or aggravating factors
- professionals' reports
- character of the offender, his/her remorse and reform potential
- need for public protection

- prevailing theories of punishment
- government policy and sentencing guidelines
- research and statistical material regarding the efficacy of sentencing policies and practices
- resource availability
- need for consistency and avoidance of sentencing disparity and
- judicial awareness of the likely scrutiny of their sentences by the appeal courts, police, social workers, the media and the public, especially in sensational cases

Sentencing discretion is contentious and several mechanisms have developed to limit and constrain it. These include prescribed maximum, minimum and mandatory sentences for certain offences, sentencing power limitations (e.g., Magistrates' Courts), age restrictions for sentences, sentencing guidelines, A-G's referral powers regarding unduly lenient sentences, Sentencing Advisory Panel and Council and financial restraints.

Judges have, at times, resisted these constraints on the basis that a wider discretion gives them greater opportunity to do justice in individual cases. On the other hand, public and policy pressures have more usually been in favour of limiting judicial discretion so as to reduce the injustice of inconsistency. The correct balance is not always easy to achieve.

Further Reading

Easton, S. and Piper, C. (2005). Just Constraints? Sentencing Discretion and Retributivist Principles, in Sentencing and Punishment. Oxford University Press.

Discretionary Life Panels

Bodies set up in 1992 to determine whether and when a prisoner serving a discretionary life sentence should be released.

They consider more than 200 cases per annum and approximately 10–15 per cent are released. Panels decide on the basis of a dossier, compiled by the Prison Service, to which the Home Secretary and prisoner concerned also contribute documentation. The whole process is (surprisingly) short; the average hearing being about an hour and a half.

The prisoner is heard as well as relevant witnesses such as probation officers, prison staff, psychiatrists, family and friends.

The factors taken into consideration include

- Positive conduct and attitudes during the sentence, for example, acceptance of responsibility and punishment for the crime, insight into the offence and sensitivity to the victim(s), engagement with educational and offender-behaviour programmes and attitude to authority.
- Negative conduct and attitude during sentence, for example, disruptive behaviour, lack of respect for authority or rules and committal of further offences while inside.
- Initial offence.
- Security classification.
- Age.
- Family and friends' support.

Further Reading

Padfield, N. and Leibling, A. (2000). An Explanation of the Decision-making at Discretionary Life Panels. HO Research Study No 213.

Padfield, N. (2002). Beyond the Tariff. Willan Publishing.

Discretionary Life Sentence

A sentence of life imprisonment imposed at the discretion of a judge based on the perceived risk of the offender towards the public owing to his/her dangerousness. It is distinguished from the mandatory sentence of life imprisonment for murder. It is usually for a fixed period of incarceration (tariff) followed by a second period upon which release will only be granted when a Discretionary Life Panel determines that the prisoner poses no danger to the public.

This sentence may be given for, for example, attempted murder, manslaughter, infanticide, rape, sexual intercourse with a girl under 14 years, incest, kidnapping, burglary and having possession of Class A drugs for supply.

There are approximately 900 prisoners serving discretionary life sentences.

Disqualification Order

An order made by the Crown Court disqualifying an offender from working with children [Criminal Justice and Court Services Act 2000].

District Judge(s)

Full time judge(s) in the Magistrates' Courts, formerly known as stipendiary magistrate(s).

Diversion

The criminological approach which advocates keeping offenders out of the criminal justice system. It advocates diversion from the courts and custody wherever appropriate.

Examples include increased use of police cautioning, especially of juveniles, and court diversionary schemes which bring together medics, psychologists and the CPS to address the specific needs of alcohol and drug offenders. It is hoped that these measures may be more successful in helping to reduce stigmatization and recidivism by not exposing these groups of offenders to the more sophisticated criminal environment of custodial institutions.

Diversity

The range of diverse identities found within a population (local, national, global) such as male/female, young/old, rich/poor, powerful/minority, indigenous/immigrant, racial, religious, ethnic groups, heterosexuals and homosexuals.

Large complex social populations, obviously, have more diversity and some attempt to manage it by, for example, gated or secure housing schemes and immigration policies which are often controversial.

D

Divided Legal Profession

See Legal Profession.

Divisional Court(s)

The High Court exercising its appellate jurisdiction, hearing appeals in its Chancery, Family and Queen's Bench Divisions.

The principal criminal jurisdiction is hearing appeals by case-stated from Magistrates and Crown Courts.

Dizygotic Twins

Another term for non-identical twins where two eggs have been fertilized rather than one which then splits into two, resulting it identical (monozygotic) twins.

DNA

Material used as evidence that contains deoxyribonucleic acid in which genetic characteristics are encoded in a way that is unique to each individual found in, for example, nails, blood, hair, tissue and bodily fluids. The generic name for this material is forensic evidence.

English law, controversially, enables DNA evidence to be kept for prevention, detection or prosecution purposes for some persons arrested regardless of whether they are prosecuted, convicted or acquitted. Indeed it has been speculated that it is police practice to arrest suspects in order to obtain such samples. The English courts upheld the lawfulness of such retention but recently the European Court ruled that the indefinite retention of such samples was unlawful, disproportionate and a breach of the European Convention of Human Rights (Art 8). As a result the government is proposing to limit the retention period.

Further Reading

R (on the Application of S) v Chief Constable of South Yorkshire [2004] UKHL 39
S and Marper v UK [2009] 48 EHRR 50

D

Dock

The place in a criminal court where the defendant is positioned while on trial.

Doe (John)

An unidentified deceased who is a likely victim of a crime.

Doli Incapax

The Latin term meaning incapable of wrong.

The age of criminal responsibility in England, Wales and N. Ireland is 10 years (12 in Scotland since 2010) and so a child under that age is deemed incapable of committing a crime.

Traditionally there has been a presumption that young persons aged between ten and 14 years will only be tried if, in addition to committing a criminal act, they knew that what they were doing was "seriously wrong." It was up to the prosecution to prove this beyond reasonable doubt. The abolition of this presumption was recommended in 1960 and eventually it was implemented by the Crime and Disorder Act 1998.

Domestic Violence

Violence within the family which can take many forms, including physical and sexual assault, psychological and emotional abuse, financial pressure(eg dowry-related violence) and control over movements and social contacts.

It is only since the 1980s that it has been taken seriously, largely as a result of the feminist movement and the opening of women's refuges.

Reported incidences vary considerably depending on what is culturally seen as acceptable but generally it is rooted in the dynamics of power.

Causal factors have been identified as:

* patriarchy
* tacit cultural tolerance of such violence
* women's primary role as carers and consequent exclusion from the work place
* marital instability and conflict
* economic stress and poverty
* low educational attainment
* dysfunctional families
* Weak community sanctions

Dopomine

See Neurotransmitter.

Double Jeopardy

The (former) principle that once acquitted of a crime a person could not be retried (autrefois acquit). Controversially, this right was modified by the Criminal Justice Act 2003 (effective 2005) in respect of indictable trials; a new trial may be ordered if new and compelling evidence or techniques become available which throw doubt on the earlier acquittal.

Crimes to which it is applicable include murder, manslaughter, rape, kidnapping, armed robbery and serious drug offences. All cases must be approved by the Director of Public Prosecutions and the Court of Appeal must agree to quash the original acquittal.

The first person to be convicted under this new rule was William Dunlop in 2006 after he had been acquitted of murder in 1991 and admitted his guilt some years later. He was sentenced to life imprisonment with a recommendation that he serve no less than 17 years. This has also occurred in other sensational murder cases including the Stephen Lawrence and Rachel Nickell prosecutions.

The abolition of the centuries-old double jeopardy rule has been criticized as creating a novel concept – the conditional acquittal.

Dramaturgy

A research method which involves the researcher engaging in role-play (drama) with offenders in order to gather sensitive data through interactive, theatrical performance.

Drift Theory

See Criminological Theories.

Drive-by Shooting

The shooting of a victim(s) from a moving vehicle. This technique has been employed in political assassinations, organized crime and gang murders as well as terrorist killings; journalists have also been the targets of such shootings.

Drug Abstinence Order

An order which certain courts may make requiring an offender to abstain from abusing specified Class A drugs for a period (3 years maximum) and to give samples for testing during that period.[Criminal Justice and Courts Services Act 2000].

Drug-mule(s)

Drug couriers who often swallow packets of drugs in order to smuggle them in or out of a country.

Drug Rehabilitation

Formerly known as a Drug Treatment and Testing Order, Drug Rehabilitation is commonly included as a requirement of community sentences.

It usually requires attendance at an accredited drug programme and aims to deal with reoffenders who seem to commit crime in order to fund their drug habit. It has been subject to a number of criticisms; in that

- it effectively makes treatment compulsory
- it fails to provide appropriate post-treatment support
- it over-simplifies the link between crime and drugs and
- it is overly used for petty offenders

D

Drug Testing and Treatment Order

A court order, introduced in 1998, which could be imposed where an offender (16 years +) was convicted if the court was satisfied that the offender was drug-dependant, susceptible to treatment and consented to comply with its conditions.

It has been renamed Drug Rehabilitation.

Drug Trafficking

Trading, distributing, manufacturing, storing, importing or smuggling illegal drugs.

The Crown Court is required to impose a confiscation order where a person who has benefited from drug trafficking is sentenced for a related offence. The order covers the proceeds of the offender's trafficking or, if less, the amount realized from the sale of his/her assets [Drug Trafficking Act 1994].

Due Process

Principles guaranteeing fair trials and protections for defendants in court.

These are also seen as the features of the due process model of criminal justice and include the following:

- presumption of innocence
- onus and standard of proof
- choice of plea (guilty/not guilty)
- right to silence
- exclusionary rules of evidence
- principle of integrity
- disclosure rules
- rules of natural justice
- ECHR (Articles 5, 6)

While these protections are identifiable in the trial process in England and Wales, there are many limitations which can also be identified:

- The onus and standard of proof may be partially reversed where a defendant raises a criminal defence and has to satisfy the evidential burden of proof on a balance of probability.
- There are incentives for defendants to enter a guilty plea and the right to silence has been undermined by the introduction of the adverse inference rule. Likewise the double jeopardy rule has been eroded.
- The rules of natural justice and ECHR guarantees all have permissible limitations on them and the police have increased stop and search powers and extended permissible periods of detention of suspects, particularly suspected terrorists.
- The serious miscarriages of justice cases which were eventually overturned by the appeal courts were largely the result of serious disregard for the due process rights of the defendants.
- Ultimately the Executive's domination of Parliament and the legislative programme means that due process rights are susceptible to erosion as can be seen in the limitations described above.

Due Process Model

See Models of Criminal Justice.

Dunblane Massacre

The massacre which occurred at Dunblane Primary School in the Scottish town of Dunblane in March 1996. Sixteen children and one adult were killed by the attacker, Thomas Watt Hamilton, before he committed suicide. It remains the deadliest single targeted mass murder of children in UK history. Hamilton's motives remain unclear, though they may have been paedophilic as there were complaints to police regarding his suspicious behaviour towards young boys who attended the youth clubs he directed as a Scout leader.

Duress

Unlawful coercion or pressure, actual or threatened, on a person in order to persuade them to act or not to act. It constitutes a defence to some crimes (e.g., driving offences) excluding murder or attempted murder. If successful, it results in acquittal.

During Her Majesty's Pleasure

The phrase used to describe a period of detention imposed on a defendant found not guilty by reason of insanity. He/she is admitted to a hospital and remains there until released by the authorities.

Young persons convicted of murder may be thus detained.

Durkheim, Emile (1858–1917)

Regarded as the founder of sociology, he was also a key contributor to sociological criminology, specifically consensus theory.

He claimed that while crime is problematic for society, it is also functional; in that it allows members of society to express disapproval of unacceptable behaviour. In producing such a social reaction, which then translates into sanctions and punishment, it strengthens society as a whole.

Deviance is also valuable in challenging established norms and values, perhaps leading to reform.

He argued that crime is normal in society because there is no actual dividing line between criminal activity and acceptable activities. The dividing line is, in fact, the continuous process of demarcation and labelling of which criminalization is just a strong form. As members of society see the effects of punishment and feel outraged by offenders, they come to associate with right and wrong; thus crime could be seen as an integral, beneficial part of social organization. The issue, therefore, is one of balance: a society without any crime would be overregulated and oppressive whereas one with too high a crime rate is one in which individuality and regulation are not in balance.

D

Hence the concept of <u>anomie –</u> a state in which individuals feel estranged from the prevailing value system and are willing to engage in anti-social activity.

Further Reading

http.Durkheim.itgo.com/anomie

Duty Solicitor(s)

<u>Solicitor</u>(s) who provide free legal assistance to persons who do not have access to their own solicitor.

Two schemes operate in England and Wales:

- The Police Duty Solicitor Scheme which enables a person arrested or charged to consult a solicitor (in person, by telephone or both) while in police custody and
- The Court Duty Solicitor Scheme which allows persons charged with offences to consult and be represented in the <u>Magistrates' Courts</u>.

The schemes are managed by the <u>Legal Services Commission</u>.

D

Ecological Psychology

The study of how environmental factors prevail on an individual's mind so as to affect behaviour. This school developed as a reaction against medical models such as psychotherapy and advocates making resources available for education and enabling people to fit into society.
Community policing is based on this approach.

Ectomorphs

See Biological Criminology.

Ego

See Freud.

Egotism

In layman's language this is a term used to describe an exaggerated sense of self-importance.

In psycho-analysis, according to Freud, it refers to the part of the psyche which keeps us in touch with reality and mediates between the pleasure-seeking *id* and the moralistic *super-ego*.

Electroencephalography (EEG)

The process which measures brain wave patterns in the central nervous system, responsible for conscious thought and voluntary movement – and therefore behaviour. It does so by measuring the electro-chemicals in the brain.

There is some evidence that 5–20 per cent non-criminals have abnormally slow wave patterns whereas in criminals this abnormality rate rises to 25–50 per cent and is even more marked in violent recidivists. Thus there seems to be some link between criminality and EEG ratings but the exact relationship is not yet fully understood.

It is also possible that, since EEG measurements are usually taken after crime has been committed, slow rates are a consequence of the criminal activity or of the experience of the criminal justice system itself.

Further Reading

Reyes, A. C., Amador, A. A. (2009). Qualitative and Quantitative EEG Abnormalities in Violent Offenders with Anti-Social Personality Disorder. Jo. Forensic Leg Med., Feb, 16(2): 59–63.

Electronic Facial Identification Technique (E-fit)

A facial identification technique producing a composite of a suspect from a detailed description from a witness.

Electronic Monitoring/Tagging

A community-based punishment which enables a convicted offender to be kept under surveillance. Its aim is to reduce custodial sentences while still protecting the public and deterring recidivism.

Originating in USA, it was introduced into Britain in the late 1970s as a complement to curfews. It was virtually abandoned in 1993 but reinstated by the New Labour after 1997 and extended to failed asylum-seekers in 2006.

Tracking devices (tags) have ranged from indelible ink and magic bracelets to sophisticated satellite trackers and voice recognition techniques. More controversially the use of microchips has been introduced to monitor paedophiles.

Empanelment

The process of swearing in a jury for a criminal trial.

Empirical Research

Research based on the analysis of data rather than concepts.

Endomorphs

See Biological Criminology.

Enlightenment

The era when the significance of the church and religious explanations declined and were replaced by the secular, liberal philosophy that truth, reason, planning and science can ensure social progress.

Entrapment

The encouragement and setting up of bogus opportunities for criminal activity, usually by the police in order to secure a conviction.

They are sometimes referred to as 'sting', 'decoy' or 'manna from heaven operations' and typically have been employed in the context of drugs and sex crime, burglary, theft and organized crime.

These proactive methods of policing are controversial and have raised concerns about privacy, arbitrary state interference and human rights infringement. Thus both the UK and European Courts have sometimes held that trials of such offences may not proceed. However not all proactive methods have been ruled out and the House of Lords has held that the police may target individuals if they:

- have reasonable grounds to suspect the individual of involvement in an offence

- are authorized to act by relevant codes of practice
- do no more than provide the individual with an unexceptional opportunity to offend rather than an extra temptation (Looseley 2001)

Environmental Criminology

Criminological theory which focuses on the relationship between crime, space and the environment.

Epistemology

Literally meaning 'theories of knowledge', the term refers to researchers' views about the nature of subject-matter under research (e.g., criminality) and how such knowledge should be obtained:

> should research be objective and value-free (positivist) or subjective and interpretive (interpretivism)?

Positivist epistemology underpins quantitative research methodology while interpretivism is employed in qualitative methodology.

Error of Law/Fact

A mistake of law or fact in a court judgement which may constitute grounds for an appeal.

Essentialism

The belief that people and/or phenomenon have a fundamental and unchanging 'essence'. Specifically the term is used in a number of senses:

- The view that for any specific kind of entity there are a set of characteristics possessed by all entities of that kind.
- The assumption that there are natural and unchangeable differences between men and women.
  This view has influenced radical feminism; the assumption that all men have the same power over their own and women's lives and that they all share in the same relationship with their masculinity in its expression through sexual violence.
- The use of biological, physiological and genetic causes as explanations for human behaviour rather than psychological or cultural explanations.
  For example, the argument that men are more aggressive than women which is inevitably due to hormonal differences (biological).
- Generalized assertions that certain properties possessed by a certain group are universal and which therefore which ignore cross-cultural differences or historical factors, for example, statements that men are more visual than women or women are more empathic than men in all cultures at all times. Context is ignored.
- Claims that some things are wrong in an absolute sense, for example, murder breaks a universal, objective moral law.

E

Essentialism is a rather problematic concept and has its critics, particularly as it ignores or denies difference and may close off the possibility that human behaviour is changeable.

It is contrasted with non-essentialism which has it that, for a given entity, there are no specific characteristics or properties which entities of that kind must possess.

Further Reading

Fuchs, S. (2005). Against Essentialism. Harvard University Press.

Fuss, D. (1990). Essentially Speaking: Feminism, Nature and Difference. Routledge.

Ethics

The consideration of what is moral or acceptable in the pursuit of personal or scientific goals or enquiry.

Codes and guidelines exist to ensure that criminological research is conducted ethically; especially that it is in the best interests of the participants and with their informed consent. Ethics committees scrutinize projects to ensure that this is the case which is crucially important given that much criminological research requires the collection of sensitive data.

The British Society of Criminology Code of Ethics provides that

- researchers should make every effort to respect the rights, interests, sensitivities, privacy and confidentiality of research participants;
- strategies should be devised to achieve this;
- informed <u>consent</u> should be obtained at the beginning and throughout all projects;
- participants should be allowed to withdraw, fully or partially, without adverse consequences;
- confidentiality issues should not be disclosed.

Further Reading

King, R. and Wincup, E. (eds) (2007). Doing Research on Crime and Justice. Oxford University Press.

www.britsoccrim.org

Ethnicity

A term often used interchangeably with race, and referring to social groups based on a shared identity, rooted in geography, culture and history.

Common elements for an ethnic group have been identified as including

- language, religion, race, homeland and <u>culture</u>
- perception by members that this is the case and
- shared activities built around these factors

Ethnic Minority

A term used to denote people who are the minority within a defined population on grounds of race, colour, culture, language, religion or nationality.

Further Reading

Rex, J. and Mason, D. (eds) (1986). Theories of Race and Ethnic Relations. Cambridge University Press.

www.nacro.org.uk/publications/racecriminal

Ethos

The prevailing attitude or disposition in a community or institution.

This can have considerable impact on decision-making and styles of management in organizations such as police forces.

Ethnography

Research based on anthropology and the study of people in their natural environment.

These researchers engage first-hand with crime in everyday contexts (interviews, case studies and fieldwork) and then write about it so as to reflect how it is viewed by the subjects of the research.

Eugenics

The practice of selective breeding aimed at improving the human gene pool and thus the human species. It was quite popular in the early twentieth century but became seriously discredited after its association with the Holocaust and the Nazi racial policies of Jewish extermination in the name of racial purity.

European Community (EC)

The economic and political association of European states created in the post-war years by the Treaties of Paris 1951 and Rome 1957 and developed in subsequent treaties. Its objectives include the promotion of economic development and elimination of internal customs duties, free movement of goods, persons, services and capital, European citizenship, unity and co-operation between member states.

The UK joined the EC on 1 January 1973 [European Communities Act 1972].

EC Law

The primary (e.g., treaties) and secondary (e.g., regulation, directives) laws of the EC made by its institutions. Some of it has direct effect in member states without any implementation by national parliaments.

European Convention of Human Rights and Fundamental Freedoms

The European treaty defining the human rights and freedoms which the signatory member states guarantee to their citizens and which came into

E

force in 1953. These rights are contained in the Articles of the Convention and include

- Right to Life (Art. 2)
- Freedom from Torture or Inhuman or Degrading Treatment or Punishment (Art. 3)
- Freedom from Slavery, Forced or Compulsory Labour (Art. 4)
- Right to Liberty and Security of the Person (Art. 5)
- Right to Due Process and Fair Trial (Art. 6)
- Non-retrospectivity of Criminal Trials or Sentences (Art. 7)
- Right to Privacy, Family Life and Correspondence (Art. 8)
- Freedom of Thought, Conscience and Religion (Art. 9)
- Freedom of Expression (Art. 10)
- Freedom of Association and Assembly (Art. 11)
- Right to Marriage and Family (Art. 12)
- Enjoyment of Convention Rights without Discrimination (Art. 14)

The rights are supplemented periodically by mini-treaties called Protocols.

The Human Rights Act 1998 effectively incorporated these Convention Rights into UK law which means that UK citizens may now enforce them in UK courts rather than being obliged to go to the European Court of Human Rights, as was the case in the past.

European Court of Human Rights (ECHR)

The court, sitting in Strasbourg, which hears allegation of breaches of the European Convention of Human Rights and whose decisions the UK courts take into account so far as is possible in human rights cases concerning the Convention.

Further Reading
www.echr.coe.int

European Court of Justice (ECJ)

The court of the EU, sitting in Luxembourgh, responsible for interpreting, developing and enforcing EC law and determining the validity of acts of Community institutions or member states. Its decisions are to be respected by member states although there are no formal enforcement mechanisms.

European Courts

The European Court of Human Rights and the European Court of Justice.

European Union (EU)

The entity created by the Maastricht Treaty 1993 representing the extended co-operation agreement between member states of the EC into areas including common monetary, foreign and security policy, police and judicial co-operation in criminal matters and political integration.

Although a political rather than a legal entity like the EC, the two terms are often used synonymously in everyday language.

Europol

A Europe-wide body, established in 1996, for the exchange and analysis of criminal intelligence in areas such as terrorism, drug/person-trafficking and other serious organized crime.

Euthanasia

The term applied to so-called mercy killing; the act or practice of intentionally killing someone painlessly because they have a terminal or incurable illness. It derives from Greek, literally meaning 'a good death'.

It is not legal in the UK. In fact the Netherlands is the only country where it is openly practised (although not authorized by statute) if doctors follow prescribed guidelines.

These require that there is an express, direct, voluntary and considered request by the patient, made repeatedly. Moreover the patient's condition must be intolerable, with no prospect of improvement.

A distinction is made between

- Voluntary euthanasia which is where a mentally competent person with a terminal illness requests that their life be ended by a doctor or carer. It is sometimes called assisted suicide.
- Involuntary euthanasia which is where a person's life is ended without their consent although they are competent to make decisions about treatment. This constitutes murder.
- Non-voluntary euthanasia which is where a person's life is ended when they are not competent to make decisions about treatment because, for example, they are unconscious. This is also known as mercy killing.

A further distinction is also made between active and passive euthanasia: actively causing a person's death, for example, by giving them an overdose of drugs or passively allowing them to die by withholding treatment.

Pain relief which might have the effect of shortening life is not considered as euthanasia and is acceptable in all countries.

Evidence

Material which tends to prove the existence or non-existence of fact(s).

It may be written (e.g., records, deeds, affidavits) or oral (e.g., witness, testimony) and may also be classed as primary, best or secondary evidence.

The law of evidence governs the admissibility and presentation of evidence in court. Admissibility concerns what material is allowed to be considered in legal proceedings and is determined by relevancy. Irrelevant material is inadmissible but even relevant material may be inadmissible if it falls within the exclusionary rules of evidence.

Competence refers to the legal ability to be a witness.

The following terms may be useful to know:

- Testimonial: evidence given by a witness.
- Documentary: written evidence, for example, affidavit.
- Direct: evidence given in the form of a witness statement in court as proof of any fact(s) stated by the witness.
- Extrinsic: evidence of matters not referred to in a document offered in evidence to explain, vary or contradict the document's meaning.
- Primary: evidence which is the best available, for example, original of a document.
- Secondary: evidence which is available but which may not be the best, for example, copy of a document.
- Conclusive: evidence which cannot be disputed, for example, certificate of incorporation of a company.
- Circumstantial: indirect evidence from which a court might infer facts but which does not itself prove the facts, for example, finger prints, DNA samples.
- Parol: oral evidence (governed by the parol evidence rule).
- Corroboration: evidence which confirms the accuracy of other evidence. Generally this is no longer required in English law but a judge has discretion to warn a jury of the dangers of relying on particular uncorroborated evidence, for example, confessions, accomplice or sex offence complainants' evidence.

Evidential Burden of Proof

The legal burden of proving the fact of guilt which normally lies on the prosecution in criminal proceedings. Exceptionally, however, where a defendant is raising a defence (e.g., insanity, diminished responsibility, self-defence), he/she is required to show sufficient evidence to raise it as an issue on a balance of probability, that is, it was more likely than not that he/she was acting in self-defence. This is called the evidential burden which the prosecution has then to refute.

Examination

The questioning of a witness on oath or affirmation in court. This may involve 'examination in chief' of a witness by the party calling him/her in order to elicit facts favourable to that party. This may be followed by 'cross examination' by the opposing party and 're-examination' by the original party.

Exclusion Requirement

A requirement which can be part of a community order prohibiting an offender from entering a place specified in the order for a period of time.

Exclusionary Rules of Evidence

Rules excluding particular types of evidence or methods of proof.

All irrelevant evidence is deemed to be excluded as is <u>hearsay evidence</u> or evidence which might be unfairly prejudicial to a defendant or otherwise have an adverse effect on legal proceedings.

Executive, the

The government.

Exemplary Sentence

A sentence which is more severe than would usually be given for a particular offence so as to operate as a deterrent from further offending.

Exhibit

A piece of <u>evidence</u> produced in court for inspection by the judge, jury, party or witnesses during a trial.

Exhumation

The digging up of buried human remains which requires legal authorization.

Expert Evidence

Opinions of a specialist <u>witness</u> (e.g., medic) as opposed to evidence of facts in general.

This is a way in which scientific evidence can be provided to inform a court's decision. This type of <u>evidence</u> has been discredited in some criminal prosecutions of sexual abuse and cot death syndrome.

It has been said that the objectivity of experts may be compromised because of their background and discipline which may affect their evaluation of evidence.

Extended Sentences

See Public Protection Sentences.

E

Extradition

The surrender of a person by one state to another for an <u>extradition crime</u> under an extradition treaty.

Where extradition is available between the UK and a foreign state, a person may be arrested and returned to that state provided that

- they are accused of an extradition crime in that state or they are unlawfully at large after conviction for an extradition crime in that state;
- the <u>offence</u> is not of a political nature or only of a military offence;
- the requested return is not made for the purpose of prosecuting or punishing the person on racial, religious, nationality or political affiliation grounds.

Extradition Crime

Conduct in a foreign state or Commonwealth country/Colony which, if committed in the UK, would constitute an offence punishable by imprisonment for 12 months + and which is also punishable under the law of that state or country.

Ex Turpi Causa

The defence based upon the principle that courts may refuse to hear a claim arising out of the claimant's own illegal or immoral act(s).

A fellow criminal, injured during a joint criminal enterprise, may thus be unable to sue for injuries sustained during their joint criminal activity, for example, car chase.

Eysenck, Hans (1916–97)

A key thinker in psychological criminology who believed that criminality is located within an individual's personality; some people are more inclined towards anti-social behaviour because of their personality.

He suggested that the central nervous system of criminals differs from that of non-criminals and that the former are more sensitive to stimuli and therefore more excitable and less self-controlled.

He identified various personality traits, some of which were predisposed to criminality:

- Extroversion: Extrovert individuals are inclined to seek out stimulation constantly which can result in impulsive and aggressive behaviour.
- Neuroticism: Persons who are low in neuroticism tend to be calm and stable in contrast with neurotics who are likely to be moody, anxious and irritable.
- Psychoticism: Psychotic individuals are likely to be hormonal, solitary, cold, cruel and lacking in fear.

He concluded that the most hard-core criminals were likely to score highly on these three scales of personality because they find it difficult to learn from, or condition themselves to, the social environment.

E

Fair Trial

See Due Process.

False Confession

A false admission of guilt by a suspect or defendant.

How often these occur is unknown and criminal justice agencies tend to be reluctant to accept that they do occur. It is difficult to establish whether a confession is false which has led some researchers to classify confessions as proven false, disputed false, unsafe and probably false.

Certain interview techniques have been identified as likely to lead to false confessions, particularly those that involve threats, inducements, trickery or psychological tactics.

Five distinct types have been distinguished:

1. Voluntary false confessions: given without any external pressure or inducement. These may be given for a number of reasons, for example, desire for celebrity status, enhancement of self-esteem, need to impress, attempt to relieve guilt, inability to distinguish fact from fantasy, desire to protect the real offender, failure in a lie-detector test, despair at proving innocence, pre-emption of further investigation or to hide other, non-crimia, facts (e.g., adultery).
2. Coerced-compliant false confessions: given usually after a pressurized police interview or to avoid interview at all.
3. Stress-compliant false confessions: given as a result of the interview situation itself (unfamiliar setting, isolation, fear, emotional intensity, lack of control) which produces such distress that the suspect confesses to escape the situation.
4. Coerced-internalized false confessions: given where, in the course of the interview, the suspect comes to believe that it is more likely than not that they have committed the crime.
   Internalization refers to the private acceptance of beliefs espoused by others, often where the confessor has no memory of having committed the crime and thus has little confidence about their own innocence.
5. Coerced-reactive false confessions: given as a result of coercion from an outside source, other than the police.

Suspects are likely to withdraw coerced false confessions as soon as the pressures are removed but voluntary false confessions are much less likely to be withdrawn.

Several measures have been introduced to try to prevent false confessions, such as recording of police interviews, the presence of legal advisors or appropriate adults to safeguard the interests of interviewees and the requirement for corroborative evidence in support of confessions.

Further Reading

Gudjonsson, G. H. (1990). One Hundred Alleged False Confessions. British Journal of Clinical Psychology, 29, 249–50.

Gudjonsson, G. H. (1999). The Making of a Serial False Confessor. Journal of Forensic Psychology, 10, 416–26.

False Imprisonment

Unlawful restriction of a person's freedom of movement which includes false arrest and detention, not necessarily in a prison or police station. A writ of habeas corpus may be issued by a court to secure the detainee's liberty.

False Memories (Memory Distortion)

Incorrect beliefs about past events or experiences which become incorporated as genuine memories for an individual who perceives them as true and accurate. Childhood sex abuse cases in the 1990s raised controversy and heated debate about the authenticity of some of the victims' memories. The debate focused on the conditions under which memories were recovered, the power of suggestion in the creation of false recollections and the role of experts who advise the courts in these matters.

Studies suggest that suggestive interview techniques, memory implantation and imagination distortion can all affect or alter victims' memories and beliefs; the more plausible the distorted or suggested event, the more likely it will be acceptable to the subject (Nezdek et al. 1997).

There has also been concern about the use of hypnosis in memory recovery.

Falsify

To alter a document or account with intent to deceive.

F

Family Intervention Programme (FIP)

A programme which targets and supports households demonstrating extreme anti-social behaviour. Assistance with parenting, financial and budgeting skills may be provided in order to assist these families.

Fear of Crime

Concern, worry or anxiety about the level or incidence of crime and the likelihood of victimization among members of the public.

Alarmed by such fears, individuals may adopt extreme methods of guarding against it such as CCTV cameras, spiked fencing and guard dogs – what some writers refer to as 'angry lawns syndrome' (Davies 1992).

Further Reading
See Moral Panic(s).

Feminist Criminology

See Criminological Theories.

Fine

A financial penalty which an offender is ordered to pay on <u>conviction</u>. Most <u>summary</u> <u>offences</u> are punishable by fine; the seriousness of the offence and the ability of the offender to pay are relevant considerations for the court imposing the fine.

Fingerprints

A record of skin patterns and other physical characteristics of fingers or palms of hands which is used as a means of identification.

Controversially, fingerprints and samples taken during a criminal investigation may under present legislation be retained for the purposes of the prevention, detection or prosecution of a criminal offence. The courts have held that this is generally unlawful in the context of <u>DNA</u>.

Firearm

A potentially lethal or prohibited weapon that can fire a shot, bullet or other missile [Firearms Act 1968].

There are a number of criminal offences involving firearms, including, for example, purchase or possession without a licence, carrying in a public place without reasonable excuse and possession with intent to endanger life, commit <u>rape,</u> <u>burglary</u> or <u>robbery</u>.

In the wake of the <u>Dumblane Massacre</u> 1996, all privately owned handguns were banned, subject to certain exceptions.

'Fishing Expeditions'

Police searches (persons/property) in order to find <u>evidence</u> justifying a formal search when, in fact, there should first be reasonable grounds for suspicion in advance of any search.

F

Fixed Penalty Notices

Originally introduced in 1950, these were notices affixed to a stationary vehicle offering the opportunity to avoid conviction for a criminal offence (usually minor parking offences) by the payment of a sum specified in the notice.

Their use has now been vastly extended to deal with a wide range of offences including <u>anti-social behaviour</u>, disorder, environmental crime, truancy, <u>criminal damage</u> and residential night noise (11pm–7am).

The number of fixed penalty notices for crimes of disorder, such as thuggery and petty violence, for example, rocketed from 63,000 when they were introduced in 2004 to 362,889 in 2007. This is a matter of concern for the Metropolitan Police Commissioner especially as more than half of the offences tend to be dealt with outside of the courts; 624,000 of the 1.374 million offences were dealt with by a caution, fixed penalty or official warning.

Further Reading
Antisocial Behaviour Act 2003 [s23 (truancy)]
Noise Act 1996 [s2 (night noise)]
Clean Neighbourhoods and Environment Act 2005

'Foils'

See Identity Parade.

Folk-devils

A class or group which becomes identified, usually by the media, as the personification of evil within a society. Once identified as such, they become a primary focus of 'moral panic'.

> 'Once a category has been identified in the media as consisting of trouble-makers – from then on all mention of representatives of the new category revolves around their exclusive negative features'.
>
> (Good and Ben Yehuda 1994)

Social and legal forces can then be mobilized against them which might include scapegoating, legislation, police targeting, arrest, prosecution and exemplary sentences.

Further Reading
Cohen, S. (1973). Folk Devils and Moral Panics. Routledge.

Foreign Travel Orders

A measure to deal with sex tourism allowing the police to prevent a person subject to such an order from travelling abroad provided that it is established that such person has convictions for offences against children, that there are indications of reoffending and that there are no realistic alternatives to such an order.

Further Reading
The Sex Offences Act 2003 s 97–103, 114–122.

Forensic Evidence

The generic name for material discovered from a crime scene or recovered from a suspect or his/her home/belongings which may be put forward as evidence for a crime (forensic means with reference to the legal system).

F

Forensics/Forensic Science

Scientific techniques of evidence-collection relying on personal samples such as body fluids, fingerprints, hair and skin or items of clothing or tools left at crime scenes. These materials may then be matched with police records of past offences, offenders, suspects or information on databases.

Forensic Science Service (FSS)

A government-owned company providing analysis and interpretation of forensic science evidence for criminal justice agencies in England and Wales.

It was also responsible for pioneering the development of DNA profiling technologies.

Forensic Toxicology

The science of the detection, identification and measurement of poisons in human biological materials. It is to be differentiated from clinical toxicology which recognizes poisons from symptoms and is concerned with the care and treatment of the poisoned patient.

Foresight/Forseeability

The test applied in determining legal liability requiring that, at the time of the act/omission of the defendant, certain consequences are perceived as likely or possible by the defendant.

In homicide, for example, a defendant will not be liable if the required consequence (death) was not a reasonably foreseeable consequence of his/her act or omission.

Forgery [Counterfeiting Act 1981]

Intentionally making a false instrument (e.g., document) in order that it be accepted as genuine, thereby causing loss to others.

Foreman (Jury)

A member of a jury elected by jurors as spokesperson for the jury in the delivery of its verdict.

Foucault, Michael (1926–84)

An innovative and controversial thinker whose theories focused on how power operates in the criminal justice world.

Further Reading

Foucault, M. (1975). The Discipline of Punishment. Vintage Books.

F

Fraud

The criminal offence created by the Fraud Act 2006 which may be committed in three ways:

- Fraud by false representation: dishonestly making a false representation intending to make a gain for oneself/another or a loss/risk of loss to another.
- Fraud by failing to disclose information: dishonestly failing to disclose information where there is a legal obligation to disclose intending to make a gain for oneself/another or a loss/risk of loss to another.
- Fraud by abuse of position: dishonestly abusing a position (in which one is expected to safeguard the financial interests of another) intending to make a gain for oneself/another or a loss/risk of loss to another.

A representation is false if it is untrue or misleading and the person making it either knows that it is or might be.

Further Reading

Fraud Act 2006 s2–4

Freud, Sigmund (1856–1939)

The founder of psychoanalysis, a theory based upon personality structure and its influence on behaviour, including criminal behaviour.

The human mind, he argued, comprises three key elements, namely,

- Id: present at birth, driven by basic instincts operating on pleasure-seeking/pain-avoidance principles.
- Super-Ego: acquired by socialization, the moral part of personality (conscience) operating on pride and satisfaction/shame and guilt principles.
- Ego: the part of the mind striving to control basic instincts and drives.

He believed that the demands of the Id and the Super-Ego are, inevitably and constantly, in competition, requiring the Ego to resolve this conflict between the wishes of the individual and the demands of society.

F

Freezing Order

An order made by the Treasury prohibiting persons providing funds to a

'person(s) specified in the order provided that there are reasonable grounds to believe that such persons are acting or likely to act in a way that is threatening to the UK economy or the life or property of UK residents'.

[Anti-terrorism, Crime and Security Act 2001]

Fugitive

A person accused or convicted of an extradition offence in a foreign state and who is in HM's Dominions or suspected of being there. Such a person is liable to be surrendered under extradition procedures.

Functionalism

A social theory that posits that society consists of institutions and rules that work together to maintain social stability.

Its essence is that there is a consensus of core values within a society which reflects the needs of its members, and the task of its institutions (e.g., family, schools) is to socialize individuals to conform to such values.

F

Gang

A group of people who share a common identity.

It originally referred to a group of workmen but its modern usage tends to be rather negative, connoting criminal associations in opposition to mainstream norms and values.

There are many types of gangs, including

- Street gangs which are often involved in <u>street crime</u>, for example, <u>mugging, drug trafficking</u>, extortion and <u>murder</u>.
- Prison gangs which are formed for mutual support and advancement in prison institutions.
- Organized crime gangs which are often involved in drug and people trafficking, kidnapping and contract-killing, the most notable being the <u>Mafia</u>.
- Biker gangs which may or may not be criminal such as the Hells Angels.
- Military-style gangs which use military skills, knowledge and weapons to facilitate criminal activities such as theft and sale of military weapons, ammunition and equipment.

Further Reading
www.knowgangs.com

Gangbanger

The (slang) term for a member of a gang (often a youth gang).

Further Reading
www.merriam-webster.com/dictionary/gangbangers

Gender

The term used for categorizing persons as male or female.

It is often used interchangeably with sex but in fact there is a difference: sex is based on biological criteria. For example, genital, hormonal and reproductive roles while most gender differences are ascribed by social processes and relate to role expectations.

There is a strong body of literature on gender and crime.

Further Reading
Evans, K. and Jamieson, J. (eds) (2008). Gender and Crime; A Reader. Open University Press.
Hale, C. et al. (2009) Criminology, Chapter 7. Oxford University Press.
www.fawcettsociety.org.uk

Gene(s)

A part of the chromosome of an organism that carries biological information in the form of DNA and which determines heredity characteristics.

Their discovery by Gregor Mendol in 1865 led to them to being seen as an explanation for criminality; crime being the outcome of some genetically conveyed heritable factor(s), for example, impulsivity, low arousal to pain or brain dysfunction.

Humans are thought to have between 30,000 and 40,000 genes.

Further Reading

Williams, K. S. (2001). The Influence of Physical Factors and Genetics on Criminality, in Criminology: A Textbook. Oxford University Press.

Genetics

The study of genes and hereditary characteristics.

Genocide

The systematic, planned killing of a cultural, national, ethnic or religious group.

It is regarded as a war crime and can now be prosecuted in the International Criminal Court. The court has convicted at least 24 genocide suspects and a number are on appeal.

Notorious genocides include the Holocaust (1939–45) and the killings in Armenia (1915–22), Cambodia (1975–9), Rwanda (1994) Bosnia (1992) and Darfur (2004).

Further Reading

Schabas, W. (2000). Genocide in International Law. Cambridge University Press.
Heidenrich, J. G. (2001). Governments, Citizens and Genocide: A Comparative and Interdisciplinary Approach. Oxford University Press.

George, Barry

The victim of a miscarriage of justice who was convicted of the murder of Jill Dando in 2001.

He was cleared after a retrial was ordered following his second appeal in 2008.

Further Reading

Henderson, R. (2001). Barry George and the Celebrity Effect; a Miscarriage of Justice in the Making. Libertarian Alliance.

Graffiti

The illegal writing or painting on public premises (e.g., subways, railways, billboards, walls) by individuals or groups. Technically it constitutes the crime of criminal damage.

Derived from the Italian word meaning 'scratch', it has a long history, having been found in Roman ruins and medieval churches. During the twentieth century it came to be associated in the US and UK with urban gangs and subcultures where writers used graffiti as a way of communicating with each other by tags, murals or other symbols. Messages or meanings could be conveyed concerning, for example, drug-dealing territories and deals and interpersonal street or gang violence.

Green Paper

A discussion and consultation document issued by government concerning proposed legislation and which precedes a White Paper.

Grievous Bodily Harm (GBH)

The term used in criminal law meaning really serious bodily injury caused by crimes such as murder, wounding and burglary.

Grey Area

See Dark Figure.

Grooming

The practice of befriending young persons with a view to sexual exploitation.

This has been facilitated by the internet and chat rooms where adults can, anonymously, pretend to be of similar age as their intended victims.

An attempt to deal with this growing problem was made by the Risk of Sexual Harm Order (RSHO) introduced 2003. The police can apply for this order if they observe a pattern of behaviour developing with a sexual component to it. Fines and imprisonment can be imposed for breach of such an order.

Further Reading
The Criminal Justice Act 2003, ss123–9

Group 4 Securicor

Group 4 Securicor is the largest security systems and services company in the world. It provides a range of security services such as transportation, training and prison management to both the public and private sector.

Guildford 4

The three men and one woman who were falsely convicted of the Guilford pub bombings of 1974 in which four soldiers and a civilian were killed and 65 injured. The pub was targeted by the Provisional IRA because of its popularity with British army personnel.

Their convictions were eventually quashed on appeal in 1989 but only after they had spent 15 years in prison.

This classic miscarriage of justice was a result of unreliable confession evidence, obtained under pressure, as well as fabrication and concealment of relevant evidence by the police. Neither the bombings nor the wrongful imprisonment resulted in further convictions although a public apology was issued by the then prime minister, Tony Blair, in 2005.

Further Reading

Woffinden, B. (1987). *Miscarriages of Justice*. Coronet Books.
Conlon, J. (1990). *Proved Innocent*. Penguin Books Ltd.
In the Name of the Father. 1993 (film)
www.innocent.org.uk/cases/guildford4

Guilty Plea/Finding

An <u>admission</u> of guilt to a criminal <u>charge</u> which will usually result in a criminal <u>conviction</u> by a court.

The majority of defendants plead guilty or, failing to appear, are found guilty in their absence (60 per cent <u>Crown Court</u>, 92 per cent <u>Magistrates' Courts</u> (Sanders and Young 2006)).

Guantanamo Bay

The highly controversial containment facility in Cuba that provided for indefinite detention for non-US citizens suspected of international <u>terrorism</u>.

This was made possible as a result of the Cuban-US Treaty 1903 which gave a perpetual lease of the territory to America where it established a Naval base which became the detainment camp in 2002.

There were many charges of torture and cruelty towards detainees and President Obama signed an executive order for its closure in January 2009.

Further Reading

Worthington, A. (2007). *The Guantanamo Files: The Stories of the 774 Detainees in America's Illegal Prison*. Pluto Press.
www.globalsecurity.org/military//guantanamo-bay

Gun Crime

Gun-related violent crime.

G

Habeas Corpus

One of the oldest remedies in English law used to secure freedom from unlawful detention.

Deriving from the royal prerogative, it was originally granted by the Sovereign but is now issued by the High Court. Its modern use is often as a means of challenging immigration detentions.

Hacking [Computer Misuse Act 1990]

Unlawful access to a computer system.

Handling [Theft Act 1968]

The criminal offence of handling stolen goods which is committed by a person who, knowing or believing them to be stolen, dishonestly receives the goods, or dishonestly undertakes or assists in their retention, removal, disposal or realization by, or for the benefit of, another person, or arranges to do so.

Hanging

The method of carrying out a sentence of death on a convicted offender in the UK until capital punishment was abolished in 1965.

Harassment [Public Order Act 1994]

The offence of causing harassment, alarm or distress to a victim.

Harm (Principle)

A crucial element in defining crime, for example, death, physical and psychological injury, property damage and financial loss.

Hate Crime

Racial or other prejudicially motivated criminal behaviour.

The crime has developed along with increased awareness of how minority groups experience crime.

In the UK there was no special legal status delineating it from other forms of crime so that the actual behaviour may be the same as any other crime but a special focus is on the victim. This is in contrast to the US where it is a specific crime category defined as behaviour motivated by personal prejudice because of diversity (race, sex, religion, ethnicity or disability). However UK legislation has now created a number of what could be regarded as hate crimes:

* The Crime and Disorder Act 1998 created a number of new racially and religiously aggravated offences.
* The Criminal Justice Act 2003 introduced tougher sentences for offences motivated by hatred of the victim's sexual orientation (this must now be taken into account by the sentencing court as an aggravating factor, in addition to race or religious hate motivation).
* The Racial and Religious Hatred Act 2007 which makes it a criminal offence to use threatening words or behaviour with the intention of stirring up hatred against any group of people because of their religious beliefs or their lack of them.

Further Reading

Bleich, E. (2007). Hate Crime Policy in Western Europe. American Behavioural Scientist, vol. 51(2), 149–65.

Hearing

The trial of a case in a court.

Hearsay Evidence

Second-hand evidence, essentially, where a witness gives evidence of statements made by another person to prove the truth of what that other person said.

Generally it is not admissible in criminal trials because it is not given on oath and not subject to cross-examination. There are, however exceptions to this rule for statements of deceased persons, dying declarations and voluntary confessions.

Hegel, George (1770–1831)

The German philosopher who supported retributivism as justification for punishment.

Specifically he argued that

* The criminal is a rational individual who, by voluntarily committing crime, consents to being punished; in fact it is his/her right to be punished!
* Punishment is recognition of the criminal as a rational being.
* Crime is annulled by punishment and this retribution amounts to just deserts provided it is proportionate.

Further Reading

Robinson, D. and Groves, J. (1999). Introducing Philosophy. Icon Books UK.

Hegemony

A term meaning leadership or dominance.

H

Criminologists introduced the concept of hegemonic <u>masculinity</u> whereby many crimes are said to be best understood as a means of asserting masculinity ('doing masculinity'). Thus, it is said, an understanding of masculinity is central to understanding crime.

Further Reading

Newburn, T. and Stanko, E. (eds) (1995). *Just Boys Doing Business: Men, Masculinities and Crime.* Taylor and Francis Ltd.

Winlow, S. (2004). Criminal Justice Matters 55, 18–19.

Heteronomy

See Autonomy.

High Court of Justice

The court hearing criminal <u>appeals by case-stated</u> in the <u>Queen's Bench Divisional Court</u>.

High jacking

Seizure of an aircraft or ship in transit by the use/threat of force.

It is an offence under both national and international law.

The term derives from the greeting 'hi jack' used when illegal alcohol was seized from bootleggers during the US Prohibition era.

Hindley, Myra

See Moors Murderers.

Hired Guns

A colloquial term for an <u>expert witness</u>.

HM's Court Service

The executive agency responsible for providing support for <u>courts</u> and tribunals in England and Wales.

HM's Inspectorate of Constabulary

The body responsible for the efficiency of <u>police</u> forces.

Her Majesty's Inspectors are appointed by the <u>Crown</u> on the recommendation of <u>the Home Secretary</u> and report to Her Majesty's Chief Inspector of Constabulary (HMCIC), who is the Home Secretary's principal professional policing adviser. The HMCIC is independent both of the Home Office and of the Police Service.

H

HM's Inspectorate of Prisons

The independent inspectorate, sponsored by the Ministry of Justice, which reports on the conditions and treatment of persons in prisons, young offender institutions and immigration centres.

Further Reading

www.homeoffice.gov.uk/justice/prisons/insp.prisons/index.htm

HM's Pleasure (Detention)

The mandatory, indeterminate sentence for murder committed by young persons (10–18 years).

Further Reading

Mowbray, A. (1996). Detention During HM's Pleasure. Journal of Forensic Psychiatry and Psychology, vol. 7(3), 600–6.

Home Office

The government department responsible for immigration and passport control, criminal justice policy and administration including the police, security and counter-terrorism.

Further Reading

www.homeoffice.gov.uk

Home Secretary

The government minister in charge of the Home Office.

Homicide

Literally meaning 'killing of a man', this is the generic term for killing.
  There are three categories:

- Justifiable homicide: which includes capital punishment (where legal), use of reasonable force in the prevention of crime or in effecting a lawful arrest.
- Excusable homicide: which includes killing by misadventure or accident or in defence of self, others or property.
- Criminal homicide: which covers murder, manslaughter and infanticide.

Homophobia

Derived from the Latin (man) and Greek (fear) it is the term used to describe fearful, irrational, and discriminatory attitudes towards homosexuality.
  It appeared in the literature of the 1970s and was then adopted by psychologists and gay activists.

H

There is now an offence of inciting homophobic hatred (incitement to hatred on grounds of sexual orientation) to which there is a so-called free speech defence which provides protection for persons telling jokes or criticizing sexual conduct or practices. There have been numerous attempts to abolish this defence but so far all have been defeated. This law, in force in 2010, brings protection for gay persons into line with laws against racial and religious hatred.

Further Reading
The Criminal Justice and Immigration Act 2008
www.stonewall.org.uk/info

Honey-pot

See Entrapment.

Honour killing

Homicide deriving from the distinctive cultures of certain minority groups. It is usually, but not exclusively, associated with the killing of Asian women who are perceived as having brought dishonour to their family.

Hormones

Secretions of the endocrine gland and some nerve cells in the brain which are transferred by the blood and serve as chemical messengers or receptors affecting physiological and behavioural functions.

The male hormone, for example, can cause an increase in aggressive behaviour.

Hostage

A person taken as security in order to compel a state, government, organization or individual to take or not take action.

One who threatens to kill, injure or continue to detain a hostage commits a criminal offence.

Further Reading
The Hostages Act 1982.

Hostile Witness

A witness who refuses to testify on behalf of the party which calls him/her and who may, then, with permission of the judge, be cross-examined by that party.

House of Commons

The elected (lower) House of Parliament comprising Members of Parliament (MPs).

The majority party after a general election becomes the government and its leader the Prime Minister.

House of Lords

In its *legislative* capacity it is the (presently) unelected (upper) House of Parliament, comprising hereditary and life peers. In its *judicial* capacity it is the highest appellate court in the land hearing appeals on points of law of general public importance only. Its judges are called Lords of Appeal in Ordinary (commonly known as 'Law Lords') and the court usually sits with five members although there may be up to nine in exceptional cases.

It is now renamed the Supreme Court.

Howard League

The oldest independent organization and registered charity, set up in 1866, which campaigns for the reform of the penal system. It is funded by voluntary donations.

Further Reading

www.howardleague.org

'Hue and Cry'

The old common law process of facilitating the apprehension of criminals; citizens who witnessed a crime were exhorted to make a loud noise and fuss until the offender was caught!

Human Rights

The rights and freedoms regarded as adhering to every human being and protected by international, national and European (e.g., ECHR) law.

Human Rights Act 1998

The statute whereby the UK effectively incorporated the European Convention of Human Rights into national law in October 2000 by creating the concept of Convention Rights [Articles 2–12, 14, 16, 18 ECHR].

The provisions of the Act are outlined below:

- ECHR Jurisprudence (s2)
  Courts are required to take account of decisions of the European Court so far as they are relevant to the national proceedings in question.
- Interpretive Obligation (s3)
  Courts should read and give effect to primary and secondary legislation (past and future) in a way which is compatible with Convention Rights wherever possible. If this is not possible national law should be applied.
- Declarations of Incompatibility (s4)
  Courts (High Court and above) may make a declaration that national law is incompatible with Convention Rights but this does not invalidate the offending legislation.

H

- Remedial Orders (s10)
  Following a declaration of incompatibility a government minister may make a fast-track order amending the incompatible legislation if there are compelling reasons to do so.
- Public Authorities (s6)
  Public authorities (including the courts and <u>criminal justice agencies</u>) must act compatibly with Convention Rights unless prevented from doing so by <u>statute</u>.
- Victims' Enforcement (s7)
  Victims of a breach of Convention Rights may bring an action against the public authority in national courts.
- Remedies (s8)
  Courts may grant such remedies as appear just and appropriate provided they are within their existing powers.
- Statements of Compatibility (s19)
  A statement of compatibility with Convention Rights must be made when a public <u>Bill</u> is introduced into parliament unless the minister is prepared to make a statement that the government knows that it is incompatible but intends to proceed nonetheless.

This Act is of great significance as, for the first time, individuals are given a charter of positive rights, enforcible against the state in national courts rather than having to go to the European Court in Strasbourg.

An example of a controversial use of s(4) occurred in relation to the Anti-Terrorism Crime and Security Act 2001 when the <u>House of Lords</u> declared the power of indefinite executive detention of foreign terrorist suspects (s23) to be incompatible with the right to personal liberty (Article 5 ECHR) in 2004. The government accepted this and the offending provisions of the Act were repealed.

Further Reading
A v Secretary for the Home Department [2004] QB 335.

Hung Jury

A <u>jury</u> unable to reach a <u>verdict</u> in a criminal case.

Hypermasculinity

The exaggeration of male stereotypical behaviour, often by the media, which emphasises strength and aggression and may reinforce the perceived link between power and masculinity and support the theory of hegemony.

Hypothesis

A theoretical assertion about the relationship between two or more variables which can be tested.

Hypnosis

An artificially induced sleep-like condition which represents an altered level of consciousness.

This technique has been used in the <u>criminal justice system</u> to assist the memory recovery of witnesses and victims, especially in sex abuse cases but has proved controversial.

It is referred to as forensic or investigative hypnosis.

Further Reading

Neihaus, J. (1999). Investigative Forensic Hypnosis. CRC Press LCC.

Howitt, D. (2009). Introduction to Forensic and Criminal Psychology. Pearson Education.

McCorkery, K. and Sheehan, P. (1995). Hypnosis, Memory and Behaviour in Criminal Investigation. Guildford Press.

www.eHow.co.uk

H

Id

See Freud.

Identity (ID) Cards

Documents identifying individuals and linked to their owners by unique biometric identifiers (e.g., finger prints).

They are a result of the Labour government's controversial decision to introduce the National Identity Scheme in 2006.

Biometric residence permits were introduced for foreign nationals in 2008 and it was anticipated that ID cards might be issued to British citizens, but this remains controversial and is most unlikely after the change of government in 2010.

Further Reading
Identity Cards Act 2006

Identity Fraud

The criminal obtaining and use of a person's personal information to, for example, bank accounts, credit cards, state benefits, driving licences, birth certificates or passports.

Further Reading
Fraud Act 2006

Identity Parade (Line-up)

A police line-up of a suspect alongside innocent individuals ('foils') often in front of a two-way screen. Witnesses then view the line-up covertly to see if they can identify the suspect. Members of the parade are usually all presented together (simultaneously) but may sometimes be presented one at a time, followed by a decision on each one individually (sequentially).

Video and photo identity parades are also used.

One of the criticisms of this type of evidence is that there is scope for bias which may take the form of

- Presentation bias: where the suspect is distinctive and stands out from the other participants.
- Expectation bias: where witnesses believe that the offender is in the line-up and are thus influenced to make an identification which may not be accurate.

- Investigator bias: where the police may unintentionally pass on information to a witness or undermine their confidence.

It has been found that false identification is more common in simultaneous presentations than in sequential ones. This may be because the witness knows the size of the parade and is looking for the person most resembling the culprit; in sequential parades the size is unknown and there may be less pressure to make an identification at any point in time (Lindsey and Wells (1985)).

Ideology

A system of values, ideas and beliefs that supports a society or group.

Ignorance of the Law

It is no <u>defence</u> to legal proceedings to plead ignorance of a relevant law ('ignorantia legis neminem excusat').
Ignorance or mistake of fact(s) may, however, be an excuse.
This was well explained in an old case:

'The rule is not that a man is always presumed to know the law but that no man shall be excused from an unlawful act'.

(R v Bailey 1800)

Immunity

The state of having protection from criminal liability.
In criminal law this is granted to certain persons for different reasons such as:

- Judicial immunity: judges acting in their official capacity have immunity from prosecution while serving in the courts.
- Sovereign immunity: the Queen and foreign sovereigns cannot be prosecuted for crime committed in the UK.
- Diplomatic immunity: ambassadors and other foreign representatives are usually granted immunity and will be deported rather than prosecuted for any crimes committed in UK territory.
- Witness immunity: criminals may be offered immunity from <u>prosecution</u> in return for giving evidence against other alleged offenders in criminal trials.

There are exceptions to these rules and some crimes are not covered by immunity and there are often other avenues available to deal with immune persons who commit crimes, for example, deportation.
Some critics are opposed to immunities in principle, believing that perpetrators should always be subject to prosecution for their crimes. However, immunities do allow governments to protect foreign relations and expedite serious criminal trials.

Implication

An inference of something arising from a set of facts or circumstances.

Imputation

The attributing of fault or responsibility (e.g., for a crime) to an individual.

Since 2003 where a defendant makes imputations against another's character, he may then, with leave of the court, be cross-examined as to his own previous convictions or bad character [Criminal Justice Act 2002].

In Camera

The holding of a trial in private (usually in the judge's room in the court) rather than as a public hearing which is normal in adult courts.

Exceptionally, this might occur if a public hearing might be unfair to the parties or not be in the public interest.

Incapacitation

Punishment which is based on a risk assessment of future offending and the need for public protection.

Incapacitation assumes that certain offenders will commit crimes over a given time if they are not deprived of the opportunity to do so. Indeterminate sentences of imprisonment and castration of sex offenders would fall under this heading.

Further Reading

Zimring, F. E. and Hawkins, G. (1995). Incapcitation: Penal Confinement and the Restraint of Crime. Oxford University Press.

Incarceration

Imprisonment or some other form of detention.

Incest [Sex Offences Acts 1956 and 2003]

Sexual intercourse between relatives of prohibited degree.

These include mother, father, son, daughter, brother, sister, half brother, half sister and grandparents. This is a crime, irrespective of consent, provided that the parties are aware of the relationship.

The consent of the DPP is required for a prosecution.

Incitement

The act of urging or persuading criminal action by another; even if that person does not commit the crime, the offence of incitement has been committed.

Inclusion Institute

The institute set up in the International School for Communities, Rights and Inclusion (ISCRI) at the University of Central Lancashire in 2009. ISCRI itself was established in 2008, comprising two centres and three institutes dedicated to multicultural, cross-disciplinary study of the relationship between individuals and society, challenging injustice and ensuring equality and human rights.

The Inclusion Institute carries forward the work of the National Social Inclusion Programme (NSIP) which was established in 2004 as a 4-year programme to implement the government's action plan from the Social Exclusion Unit (SEU). The Institute acts as an academic centre for studies related to social inclusion. It aims to develop and support work and practices on social inclusion by building a practical evidence base on inclusion linked to support for development and practices in the community.

Further Reading
www.socialinclusion.org.uk

Inchoate Crimes(s)

Incomplete crimes which must be connected to a substantive crime in order to get a conviction.

The defendant must have the intention to commit the full crime; effectively he/she was preparing to commit the crime. Conspiracy, attempt and incitement are inchoate crimes. A person may be found guilty where the full crime did not occur owing, perhaps, to arrest, impossibility or an accident.

Incrimination

The suggestion of involvement in a criminal offence.

A witness in court cannot be required to answer a question if, in the judge's opinion, it might be self-incriminatory.

Indecent Exposure

The crime of wilfully exposing one's body in public in a way which outrages public decency.

Indecent Assault

The sex offence which has been replaced by that of sexual assault [Sex Offences Act 2003].

Independent Monitoring Boards

The bodies which replaced prison disciplinary Boards of Visitors in 2003 whose main role is to monitor prison regimes, to hear complaints, ensure proper standards of care, fair treatment of prisoners and to report to prison management and the Secretary of State, if necessary.

They are intended to be independent watchdogs but, as they are appointed by the <u>Home Office</u>, it is sometimes said that they do not inspire total confidence among prisoners themselves.

Independent Police Complaints Commission (IPCC)

A public body, fully independent of the <u>police</u>, which oversees the police complaints system in England and Wales since 2004.

It may manage or supervise police investigations into a complaint or independently investigate the more serious allegations (e.g., <u>serious organized crime</u>, allegations against senior police officers, racism or perverting the course of justice).

Indeterminate (Sentence)

A criminal <u>sentence</u> which is open-ended, that is, not for a fixed period.

Its aim is usually <u>rehabilitation</u> of the offender or protection of the public.

Indeterminate Sentence of Imprisonment for the Public Protection (IPP)

A sentence which may be imposed on a person, aged 18 years or over, convicted of a serious (sexual or violent) offence which enables the offender to be detained either for life or for an indeterminate time for the public's protection.

The court must be satisfied that there is a significant risk to members of the public of serious harm caused by the commission of further specified offence(s) by the offender.

Further Reading
Criminal Justice Act 2003 s224–9, Schedule 18

Indictment

A formal written document containing a criminal <u>charge</u>(s) against a defendant in the <u>Crown Court</u>. It is read out formally at the trial and states the particulars of the alleged offence.

Indictable Offence

A serious criminal offence triable only on <u>indictment</u> in the <u>Crown Court</u>.

<u>Murder</u>, <u>manslaughter</u> and <u>rape</u> are all indictable offences.

Individualism

The philosophy which stresses the primary importance of the individual, self-reliance, independence and self-interest over that of society.

It is often contrasted with collectivism which is more society or group focused.

Individualism is associated with the belief that individuals know best and that there must be compelling reasons for public authorities to interfere with personal freedom of choice, especially of lifestyle; the state should protect individual freedoms as long as they do not interfere unduly with the rights of others.

Further Reading

Brown, S. (1993). The Politics of Individualism: Liberalism, Liberal Feminism and Anarchism. Black Rose Press.

Whatt, I. (1996). Myths of Modern Individualism. Cambridge University Press.

Infanticide [Infanticide Act 1938]

The killing of a child under 12 months by its mother, when at the time her mind was unbalanced because of childbirth or lactation.

The charge will be reduced from one of <u>murder</u> to <u>manslaughter</u> and, although life imprisonment is a possible sentence, <u>probation</u> or a <u>discharge</u> are more common.

Informant

A person who gives information to the police about crime(s) committed by others. This may be the <u>defendant</u> himself who offers information in anticipation of a reduced charge or sentence.

In a broader sense the police are sometimes characterized as information brokers who collaborate with other organizations to identify crime risks and, perhaps target deviant groups.

Information

A statement, usually in writing, by which a <u>magistrate</u> is informed of the offence for which a <u>summons</u> or <u>warrant</u> is required so as to secure the appearance of an offender in court.

It is the usual way of instituting criminal proceedings.

Inns of Court

Professional legal 'clubs' for the <u>Bar</u> where <u>barristers</u> meet, dine, train and network with each other.

There are four Inns, namely Grays Inn, Lincolns Inn, Inner Temple and Middle Temple which were all established in the fourteenth century.

They are governed by officers named <u>Benchers</u>.

Innocent agent

A person who unknowingly, unintentionally or under <u>intimidation</u> commits a crime on behalf of another.

Further Reading

Glanville Williams Innocent Agency and Causation. 1992 Criminal Law Forum vol. 3 no. 2, 289. Participating in Crime Act 2006

Inquest

An inquiry into a sudden or suspicious death, conducted by a coroner, assisted by a jury (7–11 persons).

Inquests are not criminal proceedings and may be adjourned if a criminal prosecution is likely. They are held to determine when and how a death occurred rather than criminal responsibility for the death.

Further Reading

The Coroners and Justice Act 2009

Inquisitorial System

The court procedure adopted in Continental legal systems whereby the judge conducts an enquiry into the facts of the case in order to discover the truth.

The judge takes a lead role in the investigation and examines evidence and witnesses unlike the adversarial system which operates in the English legal system.

Insanity (Defence)

A defence to a criminal charge if a defendant can prove that, at the time of the alleged offence, he was insane within the M'Naghten Rules.

The onus of proving this defence is on the defendant as everyone is presumed sane unless they can prove otherwise. A successful plea of insanity results in a special verdict of 'not guilty by reason of insanity' with the defendant usually being subject to discretionary detention in a special hospital (e.g., Broadmoor).

A person who claims to be insane at the time of trial, in the sense that he/she is unable to understand the charge and cannot properly instruct a defence lawyer, may be found unfit to plead and a range of discretionary measures are then available to the court.

Insider-dealing [Criminal Justice Act 1993]

A criminal offence whereby an insider in an institution (e.g., director, employee) takes advantage of confidential financial information and deals with it so as to make a profit or avoid a loss. Improperly disclosing or encouraging disclosure of such information is also an offence.

International Centre for the Prevention of Crime (ICPC)

See Crime Prevention.

Integrative Theory

A criminological approach, developed post 1979, which, instead of developing new theories to compete with existing ones, attempts to combine the best elements of existing theories.

'The combination of two or more pre-existing theories, selected on the basis of their perceived commonalities, into a single, reformulated theoretical model with greater comprehensiveness and explanatory value than any one of its component theories'.

(Farnworth 1989)

This approach is opposed by some critics on the grounds that theory competition is preferable to integration.

Further Reading

Barak, G. (2002). Integrating Criminologies, in Encyclopaedia of Crime and Punishment. Sage Publications Ltd.

Intention

The mental element (mens rea) which needs to be proved for many crimes.

There are two forms:

- Direct Intention: which denotes the defendant's primary purpose which he/she is aiming to achieve and
- Oblique Intention: which is not the defendant's main purpose but rather is a virtually certain consequence of his/her action.

Crimes are sometimes referred to as *basic intent crimes* (requiring proof of intention or recklessness as to the unlawful act and its consequences, e.g., manslaughter, rape, assault and battery) or as *specific intent crimes* (requiring proof of additional intent, e.g., wounding with intent, murder, theft, robbery).

The difference between basic and specific intent crimes is of particular significance with regard to intoxication which maybe a defence to a specific intent but not to a basic intent crime.

Interception of Communications

The modification or interference with a communications system or its operation or monitoring of its transmissions.

It is a criminal offence to intercept, intentionally and without authority, in any place in the UK, any communication in the course of its transmission by means of a public or private telecommunications system.

Permitted exceptions (provided duly authorized) include interceptions to

- prevent or detect crime
- investigate or detect unauthorized use
- ensure effective operations
- ascertain compliance with regulatory practices

Recently an attempt to allow interception evidence to be admissible in criminal trials failed.

Further Reading
Regulation of Investigatory Powers Act 2000.

International Criminal Court (ICC)

The first permanent criminal court established by the Rome Statute in 2002 to try the gravest international crimes.

These include <u>genocide</u>, <u>war crimes</u> and <u>crimes against humanity</u>.

It usually sits at the Hague in the Netherlands but may sit elsewhere if appropriate. It is an independent entity, not part of the United Nations (UN), based upon a treaty signed by over one hundred states (excluding China, Russia, Israel and the US which is particularly hostile to it and has pressurized many states not to recognize it). It takes referrals from member states, international organizations, individuals and the UN Security Council but will only try cases which are not investigated by a national judicial system unless national proceedings are not genuine.

To date four states (Uganda, Democratic Republic of Congo and Central African Republic) have referred situations and the Security Council has referred the situation in Dafur, Sudan.

The ICC's first trial, of Congolese militia leader <u>Thomas Lubanga</u>, began in January 2009 followed by the second trial, in November 2009, against Congolese militia leaders <u>Germain Katanga</u> and <u>Mathieu Ngudjolo Chui</u>. It is presently preparing to try the main perpetrator of the Rwandan genocide (1990s) who was surrendered in October 2009.

Further Reading
The Official Journal of the ICC
www.icc-cpi.int

'Internet Eyes'

An Internet scheme designed to give citizen crimewatchers the chance of winning cash by monitoring closed-circuit television cameras over the Internet.

Financed by the security cameras' owners, it was set up as a pilot in 2009 but has been criticized as a 'snooper's paradise' by civil liberties groups.

Further Reading
www.interneteyecj.coium

Intervention Order

See Controlled Drugs.

Interpol

The largest international police organization, created in 1923, with over 180 member countries. It formulates cross-border police co-operation and supports all organizations whose aim is to combat international crime.

Further Reading
www.interpol.int

Interrogation

See Interview.

Interview

A critical stage of criminal investigation aimed at obtaining further information about crime and to link a suspect to a crime.

Sometimes a distinction is made between interviews and interrogation. Interviews are said to be non-accusatory, the purpose being to determine whether the suspect is likely to be guilty while interrogation is accusatory, aiming to obtain a confession from the suspect.

A popular technique employed is the Nine Steps Approach.

Institutional Racism

Collective discrimination within an institution or organization.

It can be evidenced in attitudes, behaviours and processes which, although not necessarily intentional or conscious, amount to discrimination on the basis of prejudice, stereotyping, thoughtlessness and insensitivity-particularly towards ethnic minorities. There has long been tension between the police and immigrant groups who have claimed that lack of scrutiny of the police has encouraged disproportionate, oppressive and arbitrary practices against them. The stereotyping of black people as offenders was reinforced when young blacks were involved in the civil disturbances in deprived areas of Britain (Toxteth, Brixton) in the 1980s.

Although major changes were implemented within the police after the introduction of PACE in 1984, mistrust persisted.

The Macpherson Inquiry into the racist murder of Stephen Lawrence in 1993 focused on this and found that the failure of the murder investigation was due to institutional racism in the police, and the criminal justice system overall.

Instruction

The process by which a solicitor engages a barrister to act on behalf of a client.

Intimidation

The use of violence or threats to frighten or compel a person to do or abstain from doing something.

A person who commits a crime under intimidation will have a defence.

Intoxication

The state of being under the influence of alcohol or drugs.

It may constitute a <u>defence</u> to some, but not all criminal offences: it may be a defence to a <u>specific intent</u> but not to a <u>basic intent</u> crime unless it is involuntary intoxication (e.g., spiked drink). Intoxication may, however, be a <u>mitigating</u> factor as far as sentence goes, that is, it may operate to reduce the severity of sentence imposed on an offender.

Irrebuttable Presumption

See Presumption.

Joint Public Protection Information Unit

Previously called the Criminality Information Unit, this is the unit, established in 2008, to help improve the way public protection information is managed and used across public sector agencies (Public Protection Network) at home and abroad. It is hoped that this will be achieved through closer collaboration on risk management, technology and resources.

Further Reading

Joint.public.protection.unit@homeoffice.qsi.gov.uk

Joyriding

The colloquial term, usually applied to young offenders, for the criminal offence of taking a conveyance (e.g., car).

Judicial Activism

The approach adopted by some judges in their decision-making whereby they take a rather creative attitude and liberal view of the separation of powers doctrine which requires the courts to be subservient to Parliament when interpreting statutes and applying the law.

Judges of this persuasion will be inclined to broadly interpret statutes and to create case law where they perceive reform to be required.

Judge

An official who presides, alone or with others, in a court to adjudicate a trial or an appeal in a criminal offence.

Judicial officers include

- Lord Chief Justice who is head of the judiciary in England and Wales, Head of Criminal Justice and Head of the Court of Appeal (Criminal Division).
- Master of the Rolls who is the second most senior judge and Head of the Court of Appeal (Civil Division).
- President of the Family Division of the High Court who is the Head of Family Justice.
- Justices of the Supreme Court (called Law Lords in the House of Lords) and who now sit in the highest court in the UK.
- Lord Justices of Appeal who sit in the Courts of Appeal of England and Wales.
- High Court Judges who sit in the Divisions of the High Court.

- Circuit Judges who sit in the Crown Court, County Courts and specialist divisions of the High Court.
- Recorders who sit as part-time Circuit Judges in the Crown Court.
- Masters who sit in the High Court below the level of High Court Judges.
- District Judges some of whom sit as full-time magistrates in the Magistrates' Courts while others sit in the County Courts.
- Justices of the Peace who are laypersons who sit as judges in the Magistrates' Courts.

Judge-alone Trial

A trial on indictment without a jury in the Crown Court.

The prosecution has been given the right to apply for such a trial before a judge alone where

- the subject matter is very complex and the trial is likely to be lengthy
- there is a real and present danger of substantial jury interference or intimidation
- the parties are allowed to make representations
- approval is given by the Lord Chief Justice

If the application is granted the judge decides the issues of both law and fact but, unlike a jury, must give reasons for conviction.

A right of appeal lies to the Court of Appeal against such a decision to allow judge alone trial. The aim is to prevent trials collapsing because of jury tampering and also to spare jurors the anxiety or inconvenience of lengthy trials but it is seen by many as yet another attempt by the government to cut down on the availability of trial by jury.

The first such no jury trial started in early 2010 when three men faced trial for a raid on Heathrow airport. The Court of Appeal granted it as there were fears of jury tampering.

Further Reading
The Criminal Justice Act 2003 s 43, 44

Judgement

A decision of a court.

Judicial Appointments Commission

The public body created by the Constitutional Reform Act 2005, responsible for the independent selection of judges in England and Wales.

It is composed of 15 members: 5 judges, 2 lawyers, 1 lay magistrate, 1 tribunal member and 6 laypersons (including the chair).

Further Reading
www.judicialappointments.gov.uk

Judiciary

The collective term for the courts and judges.

Judicial Review

Administrative Court proceedings challenging the legality or fairness of public bodies' decisions or delegated legislation.

Specifically the grounds of challenge are *illegality* (e.g., excess or abuse of powers), *irrationality* (e.g., unreasonableness) and *procedural impropriety* (e.g., bias or breach of natural justice). A successful challenge may result in the decision or delegated legislation being set aside.

Judiciary

The collective term for the judges and courts.

Jump Bail

Failure to observe bail conditions.

Jurisdiction

The power of a court to hear specific cases.

Magistrates' Courts and the Crown Court have *first instance jurisdiction* over summary and indictable offences respectively while the High Court, Court of Appeal (Criminal Division) and the Supreme Court have *appellate jurisdiction*.

Jurisprudence

Traditionally the term denotes the philosophy or science of law involving the study of the principles and theories on which a legal system is based as distinct from the study of the system itself. It also looks at the historical, moral and cultural foundations of legal concepts such as the nature of law, the evolution of criminal and civil responsibility, justice and morality, to name but a few.

A number of schools of jurisprudence can be identified including

- Formalism which maintains that law is a science based on logic and deductive reasoning (e.g., Coke, Dworkin),
- Realism which holds that law is a synonym for politics – in that judicial decisions are the product of political affiliations and value judgements based on the experience of particular judges (Llewellyn, Bentham),
- Positivism which suggests that law should be confined to written ('black letter') rules enacted or recognized by state entities such as the legislature or the courts. (Austin, Hobbes),
- Naturalism which requires that law should also reflect the universal principles of justice and morality (Locke, Jefferson),
- Historical Jurisprudence which considers that history, tradition and culture determine the law and legal decisions (Holmes, Cardozo).

The lines between these schools are not watertight and often become blurred leading some academics to consider that it is more appropriate to regard jurisprudence as a spectrum of legal thought.

J

It should be noted that jurisprudence is also taken to mean case law in the European context, that is, decisions of the European courts.

Further Reading

Kavanagh, A. and Oberdiek, J. (2008). *Arguing About Law*. Routledge.
Veitch, S. et al. (2007). *Jurisprudence: Themes and Concepts*. Routledge-Cavendish.
Dworkin, R. (1977). *Taking Rights Seriously*. Harvard University Press.
Holmes, O.W. (1963). *The Common Law*. Boston Little Brown.
Llewellyn, K. (2000). *Jurisprudence: Realism in Theory and Practice*. Union, N. J. Lawbook Exchange.

Juror

A member of a 12-person jury, selected at random from the electoral register, who swears on oath 'to faithfully try the issues and give a true verdict according to the evidence'.

The selection of a juror for a particular case may be challenged on certain grounds, for example, physical infirmity, potential bias, illiteracy or language inadequacy. During a trial the judge may discharge a juror who becomes ill or commits an impropriety provided such discharge does not reduce the number of jurors to below nine. The entire jury may also be discharged and a retrial with a fresh jury may be ordered if inadmissible evidence is disclosed or if it cannot reach a verdict.

Jury

Criminal cases in the Crown Court are tried before a judge and jury, usually of 12 persons. Its role is to determine the facts of the case and to deliver a guilty or not guilty verdict. It is directed on points of law by the judge who also sums up the evidence before leaving the jury to consider its verdict.

Verdicts should, if possible, be unanimous but since 1967 majority verdicts are permissible. It is delivered by the jury foreman whose first delivery is not final as the judge may ask the jury to reconsider. Ultimately, however the jury can bring in a verdict contrary to the judge's wishes.

It is a criminal offence (contempt of court) to attempt to influence or disclose a jury's deliberations.

Juries also feature in coroners' inquests.

Jury Foreman

The chair of a jury elected by its members before considering its verdict.

Jury Nobbling

The attempted bribery or intimidation of jurors so as to ensure a favourable outcome in a case.

Jury Service

The performance of jury duty by jurors.

Jury Vetting

A practice whereby the DPP or police may check the names of potential jurors in order to ascertain whether they have criminal associations, connections, sympathies or antagonisms towards a defendant or in relation to a particular case.

It is most common in cases involving terrorism or official secrecy.

Although legal, it is controversial as many believe it interferes with random jury selection and also because it is available only to the prosecution and not to the defence in criminal proceedings.

Just Deserts

See Theories of Sentencing.

Justice of the Peace (JP)

A lay magistrate.

Justice

The concept or principle which could be seen as the moral ideal behind social policy, law and the legal system. It is a relative concept in the sense that what is regarded as just may depend on prevailing values in each society or on individual perceptions of a particular situation; legal injustice may be perceived by individuals who view a decision as failing to represent their values. Thus a well-meaning citizen who intervenes in a lawful arrest, believing an innocent person is being arrested, would be unlikely to consider his subsequent conviction for obstruction of the police as just!

The two forms of justice which are sometimes referred to are (a) *corrective justice* which aims at achieving justice as between parties in dispute and (b) *distributive justice* which is concerned with the just distribution of resources (wealth, jobs, education, healthcare, etc.) in society.

Justice is not, therefore always synonymous with law.

Obstacles to justice may be identified as

- Human error: a solicitor who fails to notify parties of a date for a court hearing or who mislays documents can have a detrimental effect on a case.
- Bias: criminal justice agencies may be biased in favour of, or against, certain groups or individuals.
- Access: excessive delay, lack of financial assistance or inadequate disclosure of evidence may hinder parties in legal proceedings.
- Legal formality: technicality of procedures and legal language may intimidate and confuse litigants and defendants.
- Malpractice, corruption or intimidation may effect decisions to initiate or pursue legal cases.

Devices for securing justice and limiting these obstacles may also be identified, for example, due process protections, human rights guarantees, the rule of law, immunities and defences, rules of evidence and judicial review and appeals processes and sentencing guidelines.

Further Reading

Rawls, J. (1971). A Theory of Justice. Belknap Press.
Rawls, J. (2001). Justice as Fairness; A Restatement. Belknap Press.

Judicial Studies Board

The body responsible for the training and continuing education of judges.

Further Reading

www.jsboard.co.uk

Juvenile

A young person between the ages of 10–17 years who is charged with, or convicted of, a criminal offence in a Youth Court.

J

Kant, Immanuel (1724–1804)

The German philosopher who supported retributivism as the justification for punishment.
Specifically he argued that

- all individuals (including offenders) are rational, autonomous beings whose choices should be respected, including the decision to offend;
- the moral foundation of punishment is the need to make individuals take responsibility for their choices and rests solely on the fact of the offending;
- law cannot use individuals as a means to an end, even if it is a noble end (e.g., common good);
- the consequences of punishment are irrelevant; the sole issue is the guilt of the offender;
- the form and degree of punishment must be proportionate to the crime;
- if crimes go unpunished by society, this amounts to collaboration by society in the violation of justice.

Further Reading
Kant, I. (1996). The Metaphysics of Morals. Cambridge University Press.
Robinson, D. and Grove, J. (1999). Introducing Philosophy. Icon Books UK.

Keeping the Peace

Behaving in a way so as not to threaten or cause a breach of the peace or public disorder.
Magistrates' Courts have power to bind persons over to keeping the peace or require them to enter into recognizances if they fail to do so.

Keeping Terms

Dining the required number of times by a student at his/her Inn of Court in order to be called to the Bar.

Kerb-crawling

Solicitation of a prostitute in a street by a driver in a vehicle.

Ketamine

A general anaesthetic used in medicine.

Its illicit use to facilitate <u>date rape</u> has been widely reported which is of particular concern as there is currently no readily available detection test for the drug.

Kiszko, Stefan

The man wrongly convicted of the murder of a young girl in 1976 and who spent 16 years in prison before the trial was declared a <u>miscarriage of justice</u> in 1992 because of non-disclosure of police and forensic science evidence and a confession obtained under duress in the absence of a solicitor.

Stefan died shortly after his release.

The real killer was convicted on the basis of <u>DNA</u> evidence obtained in an unrelated sexual assault in 2005.

Further Reading

Rose, J. (1997). Innocents: How Justice Failed Stefan Kitzko and Lesley Molseed. Fourth Estate.

A Life for a Life–The True Story of Stefan Kiszko (1998) [DVD]

Kleptomania

An irresistible impulse to steal.

Klinefelter's Syndrome

See XYY Syndrome.

K

Labelling Theory

A criminological theory which focuses on the ways in which actions and actors are defined as deviant.

Some criminologists (e.g., Howard Becker) argue that there is no such thing as deviance per se but that it is a product of the criminal justice system which criminalizes individuals by applying the label 'criminal' to them. They then identify with the label and act deviantly. This can then trump other forms of self-identity or occupation and lead to increased criminality and social exclusion.

Further Reading

Becker, H. (1963). Outsiders: Studies in the Sociology of Deviance. Free Press of New York.

Laissez-faire

The ideology, popular in the nineteenth century, which advocated minimal state intervention in citizens' lives.

This translated into the criminal justice attitude that criminals were individuals freely deciding to adopt criminality as a way of life ('rational choice theory') and crime being seen as a product of individual pathology and not as having a social aetiology.

Law Commission

A permanent, statutory, independent body of lawyers established in 1965 to conduct research and consultations in order to systematically recommend reform of the law.

Its Chair (3 years) is an Appeal or High Court judge and its five Commissioners are appointed (5 years extendable) by the Lord Chancellor and Secretary of State for Justice.

Law Lords (Lords of Appeal in Ordinary)

The judges, formerly in the House of Lords (renamed the Supreme Court) comprising 12 legally qualified life peers sitting as the highest appellate court for criminal cases in England, Wales and N. Ireland.

Law Officers of the Crown

The Attorney-General and his deputy, the Solicitor-General, who act as the chief legal advisers to the Crown in England and Wales (Lord Advocate in Scotland).

They are members of government.

Lawrence, Stephen

The black student who was fatally stabbed at a London bus stop by a gang of white youths in 1993.

Although five suspects were arrested, the police prosecution of two of them collapsed and three were acquitted in the private <u>prosecution</u> brought by the Lawrence family.

This murder led to the <u>Macpherson Report</u> which found that the bungled police investigation was affected by institutional racism in the Metropolitan Police. This set the agenda for wide-ranging reforms within the <u>criminal justice system</u>, including the modification of the <u>double jeopardy</u> principle.

Further Reading

Macpherson, Sir W. (1999). The Stephen Lawrence Inquiry. HMSO.

Law Reports

Detailed reports of cases tried in the courts and their judgements. They are published periodically and include the *All England Reports (All ER)*, *Weekly Law Reports (WLR)* and the *Criminal Appeal Reports (Cr. App. R)*. They are an important source of the <u>common law</u> which is made up of judicial decisions which form a body of <u>precedents</u> found in the law reports.

Law Society

The governing body of the <u>solicitors'</u> branch of the <u>legal profession</u>.

It is responsible for training, examining and admission of entrants to the profession as well as internal discipline of its members.

Left Realism

See Criminological Theory.

Legal Aid

See Criminal Defence Service.

L

Legal Profession

See Divided Legal Profession.

Legal Representation

Representation in court by a lawyer who puts forward the client's arguments in the legal proceedings.

Legal Services Commission

The body responsible for the legal aid scheme in England and Wales which in the criminal law context is the <u>Criminal Defence Service</u>.

Legislation

See Act of Parliament.

Legislature

The body which makes legislation, namely Parliament.

Level of Service Inventory Revised

A tool for risk assessment based upon a range of eight risk variables, namely,

- Anti-social attitudes
- Anti-social thoughts
- Anti-social personality
- Anti-social history
- Employment
- Family
- Leisure activities
- Substance abuse
- Anti-social/criminal associations or peers

Lie Detector (Test)

See Polygraph Test.

Life Licence

The release of a person, sentenced to life imprisonment, after the minimum tariff has been served and the prisoner is considered eligible for parole.

This can be revoked by the Home Secretary if its conditions are breached or if there is concern about his/her behaviour; the prisoner must then serve the remainder of the sentence in prison.

Life Sentence

A sentence of imprisonment for life imposed on persons over 21 years who are convicted of murder or other serious offences. There are several types:

- A mandatory life sentence is one automatically imposed for murder.
- A discretionary life sentence is one which may be imposed for a serious offence where the court thinks that the offender's risk of committing another serious offence will continue for an indefinite time provided that
  - o the offence carries a life imprisonment (maximum) sentence
  - o the offender represents a significant public risk
  - o the seriousness of the offence itself justifies a life sentence.
- An automatic life sentence existed from 1997–2005 which could be imposed on an offender convicted of a second violent or sexual offence. This has been replaced by an indeterminate sentence of imprisonment for public

protection which is applicable on offenders (over 18 years of age) convicted of a serious specified violent or sexual offence carrying a penalty of 10 years or more and who are considered dangerous by the court.

Line-up

See Identity Parade.

Lord Advocate

See Law Officers of the Crown.

Lombroso 1836–1909

A medical practitioner and the founder of the Italian Positivist school who put forward the concept of the "born criminal" who was a throwback to primitive times and socially inferior.

He termed this atavism and concluded that this trait was discernible in the bodies of offenders that he had researched.

Lord Chancellor

A senior member of government and cabinet who is appointed by the Queen on the advice of the Prime Minister.

His previous legislative and judicial roles were removed by the Constitutional Reform Act 2005. At present he is head of the Ministry of Justice, responsible for the administration of the courts, constitutional reform and has a (reduced) role in relation to judicial appointments, acting on the advice of the Judicial Appointments Commission. He also performs various ecclesiastical duties (e.g., appointment of some clergy and ecclesiastical court judges) and acts as a Visitor for many universities, colleges, hospitals and charities.

Lord Chief Justice (LCJ)

The head of the judiciary.

Lord Justice of Appeal

A judge in the Court of Appeal.

Lord of Appeal in Ordinary

See Law Lords.

L

Macpherson Inquiry

The official public inquiry into the <u>Stephen Lawrence</u> murder which had raised widespread concerns about racism within the Metropolitan Police. It resulted in the <u>Macpherson Report</u> in 1999 which found that these concerns were justified; institutional racism, although unintentional and unconscious, nevertheless affected the processes, attitudes and behaviour of the force and amounted to discrimination and stereotyping which disadvantaged ethnic minorities.

It made far-ranging recommendations for reforms both within and beyond the <u>criminal justice system</u> and is regarded by some as a defining event for race relations in Britain.

Further Reading
Macpherson, Sir W. (1999). The Stephen Lawrence Inquiry. HMSO.

Macpherson Report

See Macpherson Inquiry.

Mafia

The notorious Sicilian <u>organized crime</u> group, known as the 'Cosa Nostra' operating in criminal fields such as protection, drugs, arms and people trafficking.

Magistrate

A judge in a <u>Magistrates' Courts</u> or <u>Youth Court</u>.

These are either unpaid lay <u>Justices of the Peace</u> (JPs) or full-time paid lawyers which are now called <u>District Judges</u> (formerly stipendiary magistrates.) and total more than 29,000 today.

Further Reading
www.magistrates-association.org.uk

Magistrates' Courts

Courts, usually comprising <u>Justices of the Peace</u> (JPs) and a <u>District Judge</u>, which try <u>summary or triable-either-way offences</u> and conduct <u>committal proceedings</u>. They may also commit convicted offenders to the <u>Crown Court</u> for sentencing if a sentence beyond the magistrates' powers is considered appropriate.

Magistrates National Training Incentive (Minty)

A mentor system under which experienced magistrates assist new magistrates in their role.

Maguire 7

The six members of a family and one friend who were wrongly convicted of possession of explosives in 1976 and served long prison sentences.

In 1991 the Court of Appeal quashed their convictions on the ground of unreliable evidence but did not rule them as miscarriages of justice. However they received a public apology from prime minister Blair in 2005.

Malice Aforethought

The mental element (mens rea) which must be proven for the crime of murder, namely, an intention to kill (express malice) or to cause grievous bodily harm (implied malice).

This can be misleading to laypersons as neither ill-will nor premeditation need to be established.

Managerialism

A criminal justice model which is focused on finding the most efficient and economic way of crime management as opposed to welfare or justice approaches.

M'Naghten Rules

The principles governing the criminal defence of insanity established in M'Naghten's Case 1843.

Daniel M'Naghten killed the Prime Minister's secretary, mistaking him for the Prime Minister and acting under the delusion that the government was persecuting him. He was acquitted of murder on grounds of insanity.

The Rules require the defendant to show that at the time of the offence he/she was suffering from a defect of reason caused by disease of the mind (not limited to recognized mental illness but including any internal factor which impair mental function, e.g., epilepsy, diabetes, arteriosclerosis, sleepwalking, schizophrenia and paranoia but excluding, e.g., neurosis, abnormality) with the result that

M

- either he did not know the nature and quality of his act (referring not to its legal or moral status but rather to its physical nature, e.g., slitting a person's throat believing he was slicing a loaf of bread rather than killing them)
- or he did not know it was wrong in law. This maybe if he knew he was killing someone but did not know that this was wrong, for example, killing in 'self-defence' while under the delusion that his victim was a would-be assassin.

Mandatory Sentence

A sentence prescribed for an offence which, on conviction, the defendant must be given; the sentencer has no discretion.

These are usually prescribed by statute.

Murder carries a mandatory sentence of life imprisonment [Murder (Abolition of the Death Penalty) Act 1965].

If the offender is under 18 years, the equivalent is detention during Her Majesty's Pleasure [Children and Young Persons Act 1933].

In addition to the mandatory life sentence for murder, there are also certain presumptive sentences which sentencers have to give unless the facts of the case fall within defined exceptions, for example, mandatory disqualification for drunken driving unless 'special reasons' prevail and mandatory activation of a suspended sentence on reoffending.

Minimum sentences are also prescribed for some firearms offences [The Firearms Act 1968].

More draconian is the 'Three Strikes legislation' [Crime (Sentences) Act 1997] which operates where there is repeat offending in certain categories of offences which include

- Trafficking in Class A drugs: a minimum 7 years imprisonment for a third conviction.
- Domestic Burglary: a minimum 3 years imprisonment for a third conviction.
- Certain listed sexual or violent offences: automatic life imprisonment for a second conviction.

These operate as mechanisms to curtail judges' sentencing discretion, along with sentencing guidelines and are also meant as reassurances to the electorate that politicians are being 'tough on crime'.

The use of mandatory measures has been criticized as unduly restrictive on sentencers, ineffective in terms of deterrence or protection, and tending to result in more 'guilty pleas' and consequent increase in the workloads of the courts and additional expense to the criminal justice system. In practice, therefore, they are sometimes circumvented by judges and lawyers in the interests of justice. There may be 'escape clauses' in the legislation, for example, allowing the courts not to impose the mandatory sentence if 'it is unjust in all the circumstances'. This is open to wide interpretation. Another example is plea bargaining whereby lawyers negotiate a lower charge in return for a guilty plea to avoid a charge that would carry a mandatory sentence on conviction.

Manslaughter

Homicide which does not amount to murder and which may take two forms:

- Voluntary manslaughter: where the defendant has the mens rea for murder but establishes a defence such as provocation, diminished responsibility, or killing in pursuit of a suicide pact which reduces the charge to manslaughter or

- Involuntary manslaughter: where the <u>defendant</u> does not have the <u>mens rea</u> for <u>murder</u> and kills by an unlawful, dangerous act (constructive manslaughter) or through gross negligence or recklessness.

<u>Corporate manslaughter</u> now is included in the latter form.

Marital Rape

Non-consensual sexual intercourse by a husband with his wife. Until 1991 there was no such offence on the reasoning that

'the husband cannot be guilty of a rape committed by himself upon his lawful wife, for by their mutual matrimonial consent and contract the wife hath given herself up in this kind unto her husband which she cannot retract'.

(Hale 1736)

However the <u>House of Lords</u>, recognizing that marriage is now a partnership, abolished this marital exemption in 1991 and <u>legislation</u> was amended in 1994.

Further Reading
R v R [1992] I AC 599 HL

Mass Murderer

A person who kills a number of persons, typically in a single location, which thus distinguishes him/her from a <u>serial or spree-killer</u>.

Master Status

The dominant social identity adopted by an individual, for example, 'deviant', 'criminal'.

Mediated Crime

A concept in <u>cultural criminology</u> which focuses on the complex interconnections between the mass media, crime and <u>criminal justice systems</u>.

Much of the work around this concept derives from <u>Cohen</u>'s 1972 classic model of '<u>folk-devils</u>' and '<u>moral panics</u>'. It examines the cultural dynamics by which certain activities come to be constructed as crime and therefore threatening.

Further Reading
Newburn, T. (ed.)(2009). Key Readings in Criminology, Chapter 4. Willan Publishing.
Jewkes, Y. (2004). Media and Crime. Sage Publications Ltd.
Glover, D. (1984). The Sociology of the Mass Media. Causeway Press.

Megan's Law

The US law requiring states to give open access to sex registers and on which <u>Sarah's Law</u> in the UK is based.

M

Mens Rea (guilty mind)

The mental state or element which the <u>prosecution</u> must prove a <u>defendant</u> had at the time of committing a crime in order to secure a <u>conviction</u>.

For most crimes it is not sufficient to prove that the defendant committed the wrongful act (<u>actus reus</u>) but the requisite criminal state of mind must also be proven. The precise mens rea will vary with the crime but it will generally include intention (<u>murder</u>), recklessness or gross negligence (<u>manslaughter</u>) or knowledge (receiving stolen goods).

Mercy Killing

See Euthanasia.

Mesomorphs

See Biological Criminology.

Metropolitan Police Service [MPS]

The police force responsible for policing within Greater London, excluding the City of London. It is also referred to as <u>Scotland Yard</u> (because of its original location around Great Scotland Yard in Whitehall).

It is the largest police force in the UK and the second largest in the world, after NYPD. It is headed by the <u>Commissioner of Police of the Metropolis</u>.

MI5 and MI6

See Security Services.

Ministry of Justice

The government department set up in 2007 and headed by the <u>Secretary of State for Justice</u>, which is responsible for the justice system, modernization of the constitution and protection of <u>human rights</u>.

Specifically, in the context of criminal justice, it manages the <u>courts</u>, <u>prisons</u>, <u>national offender management service</u> and acts in partnership with other agencies to reform the law and support victims.

Further Reading
www.justice.gov.uk

M

Miscarriages of Justice

Failures in the <u>criminal justice system</u> resulting in questionable or wrongful treatment, convictions or acquittals.

They can occur as direct or indirect miscarriages; a decision affecting an individual which lacks factual justification could be seen as direct while an indirect miscarriage affects the community as a whole as when there is a lack of moral integrity within criminal justice agencies (McConville and Wilson).

High-profile examples of miscarriages include the convictions of Judith Ward, Birmingham 6, Maguire 7, Guildford 4, Bridgewater 3, Stefan Kiszko, Barry George and Sally Clark, all of whose convictions were quashed because of evidential flaws or fabrication or non-disclosure of relevant evidence.

Derek Bentley's hanging in 1953 is regarded as one of the most notorious and tragic miscarriage cases. More recent examples include Stephen Lawrence and Winston Silcott which highlighted the institutionalized racism in the police.

Further Reading

Walker, C. and Starmer, K. (eds) (1999). Miscarriages of Justice: A Review of Justice in Error. Oxford University Press.

Lean, S. (2007). No Smoke: The Shocking Truth about British Justice. Diggory Press.

Mischievous Discretion

The legal ability to know right from wrong.

The common law presumption (doli incapax) that a child between the ages of 10 and 14 years cannot be guilty of a crime can be rebutted by the prosecution proving that, in addition to the actus reus and mens rea, the child knew what they were doing was seriously wrong (not merely naughty).

This additional mental element is known as mischievous discretion. The presumption was abolished in 1998.

Mitigation/Mitigating Factors

After conviction but before sentence is passed, the defence may enter a plea in mitigation giving reasons supporting the imposition of a less severe sentence. These might include personal, family or financial circumstances, previous good character of the offender or provocation.

Models of Criminal Justice

The different perspectives on, or ways of looking at criminal justice systems, derived from different disciples and values which may influence the nature of any particular system.

The models include

M

- Due Process Model (Packer)
  This model derives from the concept of the Rule of Law; emphasis is placed on the need for rules protecting defendants and ensuring a fair trial, equality between parties in criminal proceedings and restraint on arbitrary state powers.

- Crime Control Model (Packer)
  The underlying values of this model are the repression and punishment of crime and maintenance of public order – even if this may be at the expense of individual offenders' rights.

  High levels of apprehension and conviction are seen as crucial and the emphasis in on speed, informality and finality with restrictions on appeal opportunities. Due Process protections are often seen as obstacles to be overcome.

Essentially the difference of emphasis is on the *reliability* of convictions (due process) and the *efficiency* of processing as many cases as possible (crime control).

Crime control is more tolerant of error (e.g., doubtful convictions) than due process which requires the elimination of error as much as possible.

Packer's analogy is to a factory in which lax quality controls are acceptable if it increases quantitative output (crime control) whereas due process prioritizes quality controls even if this reduces output (convictions).

- Liberal Bureaucratic Model (Bottoms & Maclean)
  This model takes a pragmatic approach which recognizes that defendants' rights need to be respected but that they must have limits so as to enable criminal justice resources to be used effectively, and so defendants must be deterred from asserting their rights too vigorously.

- Rehabilitation Model (King)
  This model takes the view that criminality is wholly or partly affected by individual, social and environmental factors. At every stage of the criminal justice process the main focus should be on the individual offender and how best to treat him/her.

  It advocates wide discretionary powers for criminal justice agencies to facilitate individualized treatment opportunities.

- Bureaucratic Efficiency Model (King)
  In this model the emphasis is on the management of crime and criminals so as to take into account the pressures on the system to operate within limited resources and efficient management.

- Denunciation Model (King)
  The emphasis of this model is on the value of public trials and punishment as a means of stigmatizing offenders and reassuring law-abiding citizens.

  Criminal justice systems are seen as serving the important function of reinforcing social values.

- Power Model (King)
  Influenced by Marxist notions that criminal justice systems reinforce the role of the powerful in society, in this model the state is seen as acting in the interests of dominant classes and elite groups.

  Advocates would point to the over-representation of persons from the poorer and disadvantaged sectors of society in penal processes and institutions and the alienation of this group from the criminal justice system.

- Social Exclusion/Inclusion Models (Falkner)
  These models focus on the attitudes towards, and treatment of offenders by, the system.

  Criminals may be seen as 'the enemy' to be defeated and humiliated and crime must be prevented by efficient detection, predictability of conviction and severity of punishment (*Social Exclusion*).

  Alternatively, the aim of law should be to preserve and maintain freedom, and solutions to crime should lie in the community if the criminal justice system is to be respected (*Social Inclusion*).

M

- Just Deserts Model
  The importance of proportionality of punishments is stressed in this model; offenders should be punished in the light of the seriousness of their offences and their blame-worthiness rather than in terms of revenge – punishments should fit the crime.

These models illustrate the range of value choices that can underlie criminal justice policies and practices but, in reality, no criminal justice system will apply a pure form of any particular model but will rather be a mixture of many of their values.

Further Reading
Davies et al. (2009). Criminal Justice, Chapter 1. Longman.

Mode of Trial

The decision as to whether a triable-either-way offence should be tried in the Magistrates' Court or the Crown Court.

Money Laundering

The process by which criminals try to conceal the true sources and ownership of the proceeds of their criminal activities so as make them appear legitimate. They do this by disguising sources, changing the form and moving finances from country to country.

In the past the term was applied specifically to organized crime but today it is equally applicable to terrorist activity, tax evasion, bribery and corruption, and trafficking (drugs/people).

Further Reading
Terrorism Act 2000 s18
Anti-terrorist, Crime and Security Act 2001
Proceeds of Crime Act 2002 s340
Serious Organized Crime and Police Act 2005 Chapter 6
Money Laundering Regulations 2009

M

Monozygotic Twins

See Dizygotic Twins.

Moors Murderers

The infamous couple, Ian Brady and Myra Hindley, who murdered children in Manchester between 1963 and 1965 and buried them on Saddleworth Moor in Yorkshire.

The pair were convicted of the murder of three children and sentenced to life imprisonment in 1966. Another grave and body was discovered in 1987 nearly 20 years after their trial and the body of another victim is also suspected to be buried there but as of 2011 has not been found.

Brady was declared criminally insane in 1985 and has been held in a high security hospital ever since. Hindley made three unsuccessful appeals against her life sentence and died, aged 60 years in 2002.

Further Reading

Goodman, J. (1986). The Moors Murderers: The Trial of Myra Hindley and Ian Brady. David and Charles Publications.

Moral entrepreneur

A powerful person or group seeking to impose a moral (or legal) agenda by canvassing for a new category of crime or criminal justice policy.

Moral Panic

A term used to describe disproportionate social reaction to a perceived threat to social values from a group, characterized as 'folk devils' by the media, in particular.

Current panics surround parent-child relations, paedophilia and other forms of child abuse.

Further Reading

Greer, C. (2008). Crime and Media: A Reader. Routledge.

Mugging

The term, introduced by the press in the 1970s, referring to street robbery.

Murder

Homicide accompanied by malice aforethought; involving the unlawful killing of a human being, born alive (not a foetus) and having an existence independent of the mother.

A conjoined twin falls within this definition, despite not having independent organs.

Murder carries a mandatory sentence of life imprisonment since capital punishment was abolished in 1965.

Further Reading

R v A (Conjoined Twins) 2001 Fam 147

M

National Community Safety Plan

See Community Safety.

National Crime Recording Standards [NCRS]

A protocol, introduced in 2002, to standardize crime recording practices among police forces.

It requires the police to record a crime if the circumstances, as reported, amount to a crime as defined by law and there is no credible evidence to the contrary.

National Crime Squad (NCS)

A specialist national policing unit, established in 1997, with its own police authority to target international drug-trading, money laundering, terrorism and illegal immigration. It normally operates in conjunction with local police forces but may also act entirely separately.

National Criminal Intelligence Service (NCIS)

A specialist national intelligence policy unit, established in 1997, to assist law enforcement and other agencies (national and international) by gathering, storing and disseminating criminal intelligence, giving guidance and analysing major criminal activity.

National Criminal Justice Board (NCJB)

A body set up in 2003 with a view to improving communication, making the criminal justice agencies more co-ordinated and transparent in order to reduce crime and improve public confidence in the system.

It makes recommendations on overall aims and targets and monitors the performance of the criminal justice system as a whole.

Further Reading
www.icjb.cjonline.gov/ncjb

National Identity Scheme

See Identity Cards.

National Offender Management Model

See National Offender Management Service.

National Offender Management Service (NOMS)

The statutory body responsible for the management and efficiency of the Probation and Prison Services along with the Home Office.

It aims to enable offender management to be delivered more easily and to strengthen its effectiveness. It is responsible for the commissioning and delivery of adult offender management services for England and Wales within the framework set by Government and it is expected to increasingly devolve responsibilities to the regional and local levels.

It has an important role in influencing government departments to address the needs of offenders, and in providing sentencers with information on the costs and benefits of sentence options.

Every offender who is sentenced to imprisonment or community order is subject to a reoffending risk assessment based on four tiers of risk:

- Tier 1: offender is punished.
- Tier 2: offender is punished and helped.
- Tier 3: offender is punished, helped and changed.
- Tier 4: offender is punished, helped, changed and controlled.

Compliance and enforcement are the essential criteria and an offender may be returned to court for non-compliance (breach) of an order.

There is a National Offender Management Model which gives guidance on tiering arrangements to be used in offender management to ensure compliance with national standards. There is also an important new development in the form of the Offender Assessment System (OASys-pronounced 'oasis') which is a standardized process for the assessment of offenders, developed jointly by the National Probation Service and the Prison Service. It supports the courts by providing up to date reports on offenders prior to sentencing. It aims to improve the quality of assessment by introducing a structured, empirical-based approach to the assessment of the likelihood of reconviction and the risk of harm the offender presents.

The Young Offender Assessment Profile (ASSET) provides a similar structured assessment tool for young offenders. It looks at the young person's offence(s) and seeks to identify a number of factors or circumstances – ranging from lack of educational attainment to mental health problems – which may have contributed to such behaviour. The information gathered from ASSET can then be used to inform court reports so that appropriate measures can be taken. Particular needs or difficulties which the young person has are also highlighted so that these may also be addressed.

Further Reading

www.noms.justice.gov.uk
www.justice.gov.uk/offender-assessment-system

National Policing Improvement Agency (NPIA)

A non-departmental government body, funded by the Home Office, which acts as a central resource for the police. It contributes to this through the development of police national databases, neighbourhood policing initiatives, leadership programmes and workforce strategies.

N

National Probation Service

See Probation.

Natural Justice

Rules of procedural fairness (due process) developed by the courts to ensure fair trials which also provide grounds for judicial review of public bodies' decisions. These include

- the rule against bias which requires that a decision-maker be impartial so that he/she must not have any interest (e.g., personal/financial/political) in the subject-matter of the decision and
- the audi alterem partem rule which requires that a party should know the details of the case against him in advance so as to be able to defend himself.

These are complemented by the European Convention of Human Rights [Arts 5, 6]

Natural Law

A school of legal thought, deriving from the ancient Greek philosophers and closely associated with morality, which considers God-given (divine) law to be supreme over man-made law to which the latter must conform or be regarded as invalid.

This school is contrasted with legal positivism.

Nature/Nurture Debate

The controversy revolving around the origin of human personality and behaviour: is it innate, caused by biological factors (nature) or learnt from social factors (nurture)?

Current thinking in criminology generally is that it is likely to be a combination of factors: biological, hereditary, cultural, physiological and environmental.

Further Reading

Bartol, C. R. and Bartol, A. M. (1998). Criminal Behaviour: A Psychological Approach. Prentice Hall.

Neighbourhood Policing

See Community Policing.

Netwidening

The term used to describe the trend for drawing increasing numbers of offenders, particularly juveniles, into the criminal justice net (e.g., by increased use of formal cautions) rather than diverting them from the system.

Neuroses

A general term used to describe a wide range of anxiety disorders.

Neutralization

The idea that, although persons may learn to behave conventionally, they also learn, under some circumstances, that immoral or even criminal behaviour is sometimes justifiable or acceptable – on the basis that 'everyone does it' or 'no harm is done'. Commitment to conventional values is thus neutralized by such justifications.

Neurotransmitter

Chemicals (e.g., serotonin, dopamine) released by electrical signals given off by the nerves which transmit information to the brain which, in turn, then instructs the body to respond.

Low levels of serotonin have been linked to impulsive aggression (Rubin 1987).

Some persons with low levels of dopamine have been found to have lower emotional arousal rates and a need for increased stimuli, often by high risk-taking activities. Such 'sensation seekers' may also have stronger propensities towards criminality (Ellis 1988).

New Start

A scheme introduced for disaffected young persons and drop-outs whose aim is to motivate and support such persons by developing their skills and providing opportunities for work experience or apprenticeships. It represents a multiagency approach involving schools, Further Education (FE) institutions, local authorities, training and enterprise councils, the youth service and voluntary organization.

Nolle Prosequi ('unwillingness to prosecute')

The power of the Attorney-General to discontinue a criminal prosecution where, for example, the defendant cannot be produced in court or stand trial owing to mental/physical incapacity or if it is deemed to be not in the public interest to continue the trial.

Unlike most acquittals, it does not bar a future prosecution.

Nine-steps Approach

An interrogation technique consisting of the following nine steps:

- Positive Confrontation: suspect is faced with real or fictional evidence of his/her involvement in the alleged crime.
- Theme Development: rapport and sympathy is given to the suspect in order to foster a (false) sense of security, or bluffing and intimidatory approaches

are used to exaggerate the seriousness of the offence, suggest <u>accomplice</u> co-operation or elicit admissions of guilt.

- Handling Denials and Overcoming Objections: suspect is discouraged repeating or elaborating defences or explanations or made to feel that such are futile.
- Retention of Attention: interrogator moves physically closer and may lean towards the suspect, maintaining strong eye-contact.
- Mood Handling: suspects may be urged to tell the truth by focus being placed on possible understandable reasons for the commission of the offence or the consequences for the victim which may elicit remorse from the suspect.
- Admission Opportunity: suspect is given the opportunity to provide an explanation or excuse which then may make admission easier to achieve.
- Oral Confession: the initial admission is developed into a detailed confession, using brief, gentle questions.
- Formal Confession: the oral confession is converted into a written confession.

Despite its popularity, especially in US, this technique has attracted numerous criticisms, namely, because of its potential for

- unethical practices by interrogators;
- a 'boomerang effect' whereby suspects who might otherwise be inclined to confess will not do so because they feel they have been treated unfairly;
- resentment and cynicism towards the police;
- post-traumatic stress of suspects, especially vulnerable interviewees.

Further Reading

Inbau, F. et al. (1986, 2001). Criminal Interrogation and Confessions. Aspen Publishers.

Walkley, J. (1987). Police Interrogations: A Handbook for Investigators. Police Review Publishing Company.

Nonce

Literally meaning 'not of normal criminal ethos', this is a slang term referring to a sex offender or child abuser.

Norm(s)

A synonym for rule(s) which prescribe behaviour and includes legal rules but also customs, conventions, etiquette, habit and morality.

Notification Order

A measure to deal with <u>sex tourism</u> which enables persons (UK and foreign nationals in the UK) to be added to the <u>sex offender register</u> if they offended and were convicted while abroad.

Further Reading
The Sex offences Act 2003 s 97–103

Not Guilty Plea

A defendant's denial of a criminal <u>charge</u> which, effectively, entitles him to be tried in <u>court</u>.

Novus Actus Interveniens

See Causation.

N

Oath

Swearing to the truth of facts, usually on a Bible.

Oaths are legally required for various purposes, for example, affidavits, jury service and testimonial evidence in court.

'I swear by Almighty God that the evidence which I shall give be the truth, the whole truth and nothing but the truth' is a typical witness oath in court.

An oath of allegiance to the Crown is also taken by Members of Parliament at the opening of Parliament.

Persons who object to swearing an oath, often on religious grounds, may make an affirmation of the truth.

Obiter Dictum

An aside by a judge in the course of a judgement which, although not forming part of the ratio decidendi, may constitute a persuasive precedent in later cases.

Objective Test

The so-called reasonable man test of legal liability whereby a defendant's guilt or liability is judged on the basis of what a reasonable person would or would not have done or foreseen.

This is contrasted with a subjective test whereby these matters are determined by reference to the particular defendant in the circumstances.

Objectivity

The idea that decisions are made through impartial consideration of relevant issues and principles.

Oedipus Complex

The psychoanalytical term given by Freud to the condition arising from the relationship (and often) conflict between a child and its parent.

Typically it is associated with incestuous feelings that a young boy may develop towards his mother, coupled with rivalry with his father.

Offence

Another word for crime which may be classified as

- Offences against the person, for example, <u>murder, rape, assault</u> and <u>battery</u>;
- Offences against property, for example, <u>criminal damage, theft, robbery</u>;
- Offences against the state, for example, <u>treason</u>.

Offences are also classified as <u>indictable</u> (serious), summary (less serious) and <u>triable-either-way</u> (medium serious).

Offender

A person who has committed a criminal <u>offence</u>.

Offender Assessment System [OASys]

See National Offender Management Service.

Offender Management

The term used to describe the process of working with offenders at different stages of the <u>criminal justice system</u> with the aim of reducing reoffending.
    There is now a <u>National Offender Management Service</u>.

Offender Manager

A member of the <u>National Probation Service</u> attached to offenders serving <u>community sentences</u>.
    The manager encourages offenders to consider ways in which they can improve themselves and reduce the chances of reoffending. An individualized action plan is then agreed which might include skills training, financial management advice, substance abuse programmes and help with homelessness, accommodation or employment difficulties. The offender is then expected to co-operate completely with the plan and will be regularly monitored by his/her manager.
    An offender in custody may have an <u>Offender Supervisor</u> who may help to arrange parts of an action plan.

Offender Supervisor

See Offender Manager.

O

Office for Criminal Justice Reform

The cross-departmental team supporting all criminal justice agencies in working together to improve services to the public. Its goal is to achieve the Criminal Justice Strategic Plan 2008–11 for how the agencies will work together to create a <u>criminal justice system</u> that

- is effective in bringing criminals to justice, especially for serious offences;
- engages the public and inspires confidence;
- puts the needs of victims at its centre;
- has simple and efficient processes.

Further Reading
www.cjsonline.gov.uk

Old Bailey

The <u>Crown Court</u> for central London.

Onus of Proof

See Burden of Proof.

Organized Crime

A generic term for serious, collective <u>criminality</u> which poses a particular threat to society. The term emanated from the US Prohibition era in the 1920s with the 'bootleggers' who ran illegal liquor sales.

Today it refers to criminal <u>gangs</u> such as the <u>Mafia</u>, drugs/people-trafficking, <u>money laundering</u>, individual and private sector fraud and terrorism.

The sophistication of modern communications and transport systems has allowed these criminal organizations to develop global networks and thus become more transnational in character.

Further Reading
Wright, A. (2006). Organized Crime. Willan Publishing.
www.organized-crime.de
www.soca.gov.uk

'Otherness'

A feminist criminological perspective which celebrates difference; it posits the notion of woman being the 'other' and positively represents this 'otherness' as diversity, plurality and openness.

Over-rule

The decision, usually of a higher court, to set aside an earlier decision of a <u>court</u>.

O

PACE

The Police and Criminal Evidence Act 1984 which provides the statutory basis for police powers and the limits on these powers which are expanded in Codes of Practice.

Paedophilia

Sexual attraction to children which frequently leads to predatory sex abuse and offending.

This group of offenders caused widespread public concern in the 2000s, with high-profile child murders such as Sarah Payne and the Soham murders.

There are real fears that Internet chat rooms and consequent grooming of young persons has increased the dangers from this group of deviants.

Further Reading

Silverman, T. and Wilson, D. (2002). Innocence Betrayed: Paedophilia, the Media and Society. Polity Press.

Panopticon Principle

A prison surveillance regime, associated with Jeremy Bentham, which consisted of a central tower surrounded by prison cells which could be observed by a single guard in the tower without the prisoners being aware that they were being watched at any given time.

Bentham believed that prisoners would be more likely to self-regulate, given this uncertainty, which would improve the efficiency of prison authorities.

Paradigm

A pattern or model which may serve as a set of values or practices for, for example, a (criminal justice) system.

Pardon

The exoneration of a convicted offender by the Crown under the royal prerogative of mercy.

There are three forms of pardons:

- absolute/free pardon which sets aside the sentence but not the conviction;

- conditional pardon which substitutes one form of sentence for another, for example, life imprisonment for capital punishment;
- remission which reduces the sentence without altering its character.

The Bentley family's quest for a pardon for Derek Bentely who was hanged in 1953 was the longest ever campaign and was only awarded posthumously in 1998. This is recognized as one of the most serious miscarriages of justice in of the system.

Further Reading

www.derekbentley.com
Let Him Have it. Film (1991).

Parenting Order

A court order (12 months maximum) requiring a parent/guardian of a child under 16 years to comply with such requirements as the court considers necessary for preventing offences being committed by the child.

The idea of a Parenting Order is to encourage the child's parents to make sure that he or she abides by the conditions laid down; failure to do so may result in a fine (£1000 minimum) or compulsory attendance at parenting classes.

Parliament

The legislature of the UK comprising the Queen and the Houses of Lords and Commons.

The maximum duration of a Parliament is 5 years, after which a general election must be held. The primary functions of Parliament are the passage of legislation, scrutiny of government and the sanctioning of taxation and public expenditure.

Parliamentary Executive

The overlapping composition of the Executive (government) and Parliament which is often said to threaten the separation of powers in the UK constitution as it undermines the accountability of the Executive which can dominate Parliament – leading to what a leading judge referred to as an 'elective dictatorship' (Lord Hailsham).

Further Reading

Lord Hailsham (1976). Elective Dictatorship. The Listener, 21 October 1976.

Parliamentary Supremacy (Sovereignty)

The legal theory whereby Parliament exercises supreme power in the UK; it may make or repeal any law which may not be challenged in the courts.

In practice this sovereignty is limited today in a number of ways including international treaties, EU membership and the principles of democracy.

Parole

Early, conditional release of a prisoner from prison.

Offenders sentenced to less than 4 years imprisonment will normally be released on licence after serving ½ of the sentence while those sentenced to 4 years or more may be paroled after serving ½ and must be released at the ⅔ point of the sentence.

The parolee may be recalled at any time by the Home Secretary, and if he/she reoffends while on parole, they may have to serve any of the original sentence which is outstanding.

Parole Board

The body responsible for considering reports and evidence relating to an application for parole and for deciding if the prisoner is to be released and, if so, the conditions of the licence.

The Board includes a judge/ex-judge, a psychiatrist and a person experienced in probation and offender treatment.

Further Reading

www.paroleboard.gov.uk

Parol Evidence

Oral evidence as distinguished from documentary evidence.

Parol Evidence Rule

The rule that oral evidence cannot be given to contradict or alter any written document unless there is suspicion of mistake or fraud.

Party/Parties

Person(s) involved in civil or criminal proceedings.

In criminal prosecutions the parties are the State (prosecution) and the defendant.

Pathology

The study of the nature, causes, processes and effects of disease.

Patriarchy

A term, often used by feminists, to describe social structures and practices in which men dominate.

Peace-making Criminology

Based on humanistic concerns, this school of criminology seeks to replace making war on crime with making peace on crime (Pepinsky and Quinney 1991, Dekeserody and Schwartz 1996).

P

Instead of escalating violence in society by responding to crime with state-sanctioned violence (penal sanctions), <u>criminal justice agencies'</u> response should be through reconciliation, mediation, conciliation, <u>social inclusion</u> and de-centralized structures.

The major criticism of this 'being nice' approach is that it is unrealistic and will not reduce offending.

Peers

Members of the <u>House of Lords</u> who either inherit the title (hereditary peers) or are appointed for life (life peers).

Penology

The study of methods of punishment and their impact on crime management and prevention.

Further Reading

Cavadino, M. and Dignan, J. (2002). The Penal System: An Introduction. Sage Publications Ltd.
Walker, N. (1991). Why Punish? Oxford University Press.

Perjury [Perjury Act 1911]

The criminal offence of knowingly/recklessly making a false statement to a court while under <u>oath</u> or <u>affirmation</u>.

Phenomenology

Study based on issues, as perceived by the individual being researched.

This <u>subjective</u> approach has it that the function of scientific research is to provide an explanation based on subjective interpretation of individuals' behaviour. Mind and action are thus internally and not externally determined.

Physiognomy

The study of a person's outward features, especially the face, in order to discover their temperament or character.

Phrenology

The study of the structure of the skull in order to determine a person's character and mental capacity (see Figure 3).

Plea

A formal statement in court by or on behalf of a <u>defendant</u> in response to a criminal <u>charge</u>, for example, guilty/not guilty.

A <u>not guilty plea</u> will be followed by a <u>criminal trial.</u>

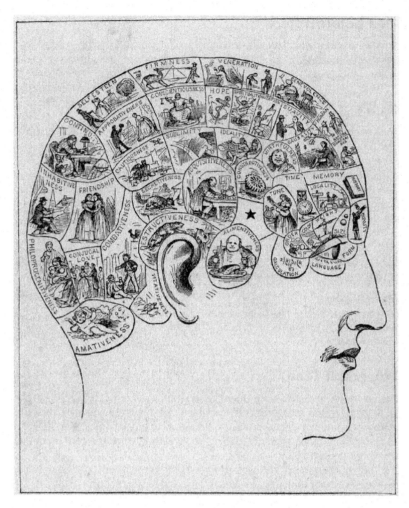

Figure 3 Phrenological chart of the faculties

If the defendant pleads guilty, there will be no trial; instead, the prosecution gives a statement of facts in <u>court</u> and the <u>judge</u> or <u>magistrates</u> will proceed to <u>sentence</u>.

Plea-bargain

An agreement (formal/informal) between <u>prosecution</u> and <u>defence</u> lawyers under which, in return for a <u>guilty plea</u>, the defendant will be charged with a less serious offence; the incentive being potentially a lesser sentence.

Plea-bargaining, although now quite common, can be controversial and often covert.

Plea before Venue

An arrangement which allows defendants, charged with a triable-either-way offence to indicate at an early stage whether or not they intend to plead guilty.

Police

The government agency responsible for the regulation and control of the community, particularly the maintenance of order, law enforcement, detection and prevention of crime.

Police powers are laid down primarily in PACE and its Codes of Practice.

In England and Wales there are 43 police forces employing over 233,000 personnel which includes police officers, police staff, police community support officers and special constables (volunteers).

The police also provide policy and programme support for a wide range of other agencies which assist them. These include the Serious Organized Crime Agency, Independent Police Complaints Commission, Criminal Records Bureau, Forensic Science Service and the National Policing Improvement Agency.

Further Reading

Newburn, T. (ed.) (2003). The Handbook of Policing. Willan Publishing.
Wright, A. (2002). Policing: An Introduction. Willan Publishing.
www.police.uk

Polygraph Test

Derived from the Greek 'poly' (many) and 'grapho' (to write), this refers to the lie detector test; a measuring device which can display, using ink pens onto charts or computer displays, a representation of physiological activity such as respiration, blood pressure, pulse and sweating which indicate deceptive answers to questions.

Although these tests are used as investigation and interrogation devices, they are not commonly regarded as reliable evidence in court.

Popularist Punitiveness

The term used to describe a perceived public attitude to punishment and the influence of public opinion on sentencing policy and decisions which are often justified on grounds of public demands for severe repressive sentencing measures.

Further Reading

Bottoms, A. (1995). The Philosophy and Politics of Punishment and Sentencing, in C. Clarkson and R. Morgan (eds) (1995). The Politics of Sentencing. Clarendon Press.

Positivism

The secular approach to legal theory, contrasted with natural law, which regards law as not necessarily synonymous with morality.

It denotes a scientific approach to the study of crime.

Postmortem

See Autopsy.

Power Model

See Models of Criminal Justice.

Precedent

A decision of a court, recorded in a law report, which is used as an authority to decide a subsequent similar case.

The English common law adopts a binding doctrine of precedent (stare decisis) whereby decisions of higher courts must bind lower courts, and some courts bind themselves. Thus, for example, decisions by the House of Lords (Supreme Court) must be followed by all courts but do not bind the House of Lords (Supreme Court) itself. The Court of Appeal binds lower courts and, generally, binds itself although there are exceptions.

Decisions of inferior courts (Magistrates and County Courts) do not create binding precedents. The binding part of a court judgement is called the ratio decidendi.

Prerogative of Mercy

See Pardon.

Prerogative Orders

The remedies available in judicial review proceedings, namely, quashing, mandatory and prohibitory orders.

Prerogative Powers

The old common law powers of the Monarchy which have now largely been subsumed by the Executive.

They include the powers to protect national security, declare and wage war, annex territory, administer the armed forces and civil service, make treaties and issue pardons.

Pre-sentence Report(s)

Reports commissioned by the courts from criminal justice agencies to assist in fixing appropriate criminal sentences.

They will often contain an account of the offence based on an interview with the convicted offender and include a risk assessment of likely future offending.

Further Reading

See Probation.

Presumption(s)

An inference made by the law of evidence which may be rebuttable or irrebuttable.

A *rebuttable* presumption may be contradicted by contrary evidence (e.g., presumption of innocence) while an *irrebuttable* one may not.

The most important presumption in the criminal justice system is the presumption of innocence whereby a person is presumed innocent unless the prosecution proves otherwise beyond reasonable doubt.

Rebuttable presumptions of statutory interpretation also act as guidelines for judges when interpreting statutes. These include presumptions that statutes

- do not bind the Crown
- are intended to comply with international obligations
- are not retrospective
- do not interfere with human rights

A presumption of death is also made where a person has been missing for 7 years.

Presumption of Innocence

See Presumptions.

Pre-trial

Preparatory stages in the criminal process before the trial and prosecution of a defendant.

These may include police and CPE investigations, committal and mode of venue, proceedings and jury empanelling.

Prima Facie (case)

The Latin phrase meaning 'on the face of it'.

A prima facie case is said to have been established where there appears to be sufficient evidence to support the initiation of criminal proceedings.

Principle of Integrity

The principle requiring that criminal justice agencies, particularly the police, observe the due process rights of persons they are dealing with in the system.

Breach of the PACE safeguards for suspects and defendants, for example, would threaten the prospects for a safe conviction.

Prison(s)

The criminal justice agency providing custodial confinement for convicted offenders.

There are different types of prisons including dispersal prisons (usually top security), remand prisons (containing persons awaiting trial) and young offender institutions (15–21 years).

The UK has one of the largest prison populations in western Europe. This continues to rise annually (25,000 increase in the last decade).

The average capacity of prisons has increased from about 400 to 800 with some holding 1300 or more inmates. This expansion has been expensive, estimated at £2.4 billion per annum which is approximately 16 per cent of the total law and order budget. This translates to taxpayers as about £508 a week per prisoner.

Prisons and prison conditions are regulated at national level [Prison Act 1952, Prison Rules] and European level [ECHR Art. 3].

The European Committee on the Prevention of Torture and Degrading Treatment has been established to inspect prisons and police stations in all member states and has made critical reports on British prisons.

According to the Howard League for Prison Reform, at least 60 per cent of prisons are over-crowded in England and Wales and this has been linked to riots, disturbances and increased suicide rates.

Undoubtedly, however, prison management and conditions have improved as evidenced by the abolition of past practices including dietary punishments (e.g., bread and water) and 'slopping-out' toilet facilities.

Literacy, occupational and therapy programmes are much more common now and visiting rights and conditions' inspections have also improved.

On the other hand, contemporary prisoners serve longer sentences and are subject to security measures unknown in the past (CCTV, wire-meshing, electronic locking systems and intensive surveillance). Strip-searching, random drugs testing, segregation and limited exercise facilities also characterize many modern prison regimes.

HM's Prison Service is now part of the National Offender Management Service (NOMS) within the Ministry of Justice and is responsible for prisons.

Privately managed prisons also exist since the controversial 'contracting-out' scheme was introduced in the 1990s.

Every prison in England and Wales is also served by an Independent Monitoring Board.

Further Reading

www.hmprisonservice.gov.uk

P

Prisoner(s)

Persons serving a custodial sentence in a prison or remanded in custody awaiting trial.

The Prison Service allocates prisoners according to their security risk. There are four main categories:

- highly dangerous prisoners,
- prisoners not requiring the highest security conditions but whose escape must be made very difficult,

- prisoners who cannot be trusted in open conditions but who have a low probability of attempting escape,
- prisoners who can be trusted in open prison conditions.

Prison Ombudsman

The official charged with investigating maladministration and reviewing decisions of prison personnel, including disciplinary findings and punishments. He/she reports to the Home Secretary.

Private Law

See Civil Law.

Private Prosecution

A criminal prosecution brought by a private individual rather than the State.
    In practice these are rare and are seldom successful.
    Examples include the Hillsborough Stadium football litigation and the Stephen Lawrence murder trial.
    The DPP has the power to take over or discontinue such prosecutions.

Probation

The colloquial term for the community order under which convicted offenders are supervised in the community.
    NOMS is the executive body in the Ministry of Justice which brings together HM Prisons and the Probation Service.
    The NPS operates 42 separate probation areas divided into ten regions throughout England and Wales. The NPS is responsible for the supervision of offenders in the community who are subject to a court order (70%) and also those who are released on licence from prison (30%). Offenders serving community sentences will have an offender manager from the Probation service.
    Probation staff are based in prisons to assist with sentencing planning and liaise with the NPS in the area where the prisoner will be released.
    Prisoners sentenced to a year or more imprisonment are supervised by the NPS on licensed release subject to conditions, breach of which could result in a breach action and lead to a re-sentence by the court or recall to prison (if on licence).
    A court may also ask the NPS to prepare a pre-sentence report (PSR) on a convicted offender to assist in the imposition of an appropriate sentence. These reports describe the facts and circumstances of the offence and the offender's potential risk to the public and may also include a recommended sentence which the sentencer may or may not adopt.
    Probation Trusts were set up by the Offender Management Act 2007.

Further Reading

Offender Management Act 2007
Gelsthorpe, L. and Morgan, R. (2007). Handbook of Probation. Willan Publishing.

www.probation.homeoffice.gov.uk
www.noms.homeoffice.gov.uk

Probation Trusts

The bodies which replaced Probation Boards under the Offender Management Act 2007 are responsible for commissioning and scrutinizing probation services from public and private providers both in terms of financial performance and outcomes effectiveness.

The first Trusts came into operation in 2008 and it is envisaged that eventually there will be one to represent each police force area.

Procedural Impropriety

A ground for a judicial review challenge to an act or decision of a public body on the grounds of procedural unfairness such as breach of the rule of natural justice or failure to comply with statutory procedural provisions, for example, consultation or publicity requirements.

Profiling

A behavioural investigative tool used to identify perpetrators of crime based on analysis of the nature and method of the offence and the psyche of an offender.

This information is then combined with physical evidence and compared to characteristics of known personality types (normal/abnormal) in order to develop a profile of the offender. Ideally this would include gender, age, race, IQ, educational level, status, lifestyle, personal relations and vehicle make.

Although profiling is often seen as a modern tool widely used in large-scale investigations, its origins can be traceable to the Middle Ages when inquisitions tried to identify heretics.

Originally profiling was intended to assist law-enforcement agencies to identify criminals by narrowing down a list of suspects or providing fresh avenues for investigation. It has since been extended to advising the police on interrogation and cross-examination techniques, planting information in the media to draw out offenders and prediction of dangerousness for sentencing purposes.

Notable criminals who were profiled include Jack the Ripper, Adolf Hitler, Ted Bundy and John Duffy.

TV programmes (e.g., *Cracker*) and movies (e.g., *Silence of the Lambs*) have popularized this practice and captured the public's attention.

Further Reading
Turvey, B. (2008). Criminal Profiling. Academic Press (Elsevier).

Proof

Evidence by which the existence of a fact(s) is established, including documentary and testimonial evidence of witnesses.

P

Prosecution

Legal proceedings (<u>trial</u>) brought against a defendant charged with a criminal offence.

The term also refers to the <u>party</u> bringing criminal proceedings, for example, <u>CPS</u>.

Provocation [Homicide Act 1957]

A partial <u>defence</u> to <u>murder</u> (only) where the <u>defendant</u> can prove that he/she lost self-control as a result of things said or done which were such that a reasonable person would similarly have lost control. A reasonable person, for these purposes, would be a person with similar characteristics or circumstances to the defendant, including age, gender, intelligence, disability but excluding intoxication.

A successful <u>plea</u> will reduce the charge to one of <u>manslaughter</u>.

Psychopath(y)

Literally a 'psychologically damaged person' representative of a small group (approximately10%) within the general population, genetically predisposed to serious <u>anti-social behaviour</u>.

A psychopathic personality checklist might include

- lack of remorse or guilt
- impulsiveness
- egocentricity and grandiose sense of self
- manipulation
- inability to learn from negative experience
- lack of sympathy
- superficial charm
- compulsive lying
- constant stimulation seeking

It has been estimated that about 25 per cent of patients in maximum-security hospitals in England have such tendencies.

Arguably one of the most problematic psychiatric concepts, it was statutorily defined as 'moral imbecility' in Britain in 1913. This was replaced by 'psychopathic personality disorder' often used interchangeably with sociopath.

The Mental Health Act 2007 made significant changes to the definitions of mental disorder providing a single definition ('any disorder or disability of the mind') and abolishes references to the various categories of disorder, including psychopathic disorder.

The possible causes of this type of disorder have been identified as brain-damage, genetic impairment, early childhood deprivation and poor socialization, truancy and <u>Oedipus</u> issues.

Psychological Criminology

See Criminological Theories.

Public Law

The branch of law which governs relations between the state and individuals, most typically, criminal law.

Public Protection Sentences

See Imprisonment for Public Protection.

Further Reading

Nash, M. (2006). Public Protection and the Criminal Justice Process, Chapter 10. Oxford University Press.

Punishment

A penalty inflicted for a criminal offence.

Further Reading

Walker, N. (1991). Why Punish? Oxford University Press.
Valier, C. (2002). Theories of Crime and Punishment. Longman.

P

Quash

The decision of an appeal court to overturn a criminal conviction or to set aside a decision after a successful judicial review.

Queen's Bench Divisional Court (QBD)

The Division of the High Court which hears appeals by case-stated from the Crown and Magistrates' Courts.

Queen's Counsel (QC)

A senior advocate appointed by the Queen who represents clients in the most serious and lucrative cases.

As they wear silk gowns in court, they are referred to as 'silks'.

Racialism

See Racism.

Racism

Ideology or beliefs, usually negative, based on perceived differences of race, which leads to prejudice and discrimination based on these beliefs.

Race is taken to account for differences in human character or capacity and that a particular race is inherently superior to another(s).Groups which have, historically, taken this view include South African whites and Nazi Germans.

In the context of white supremacy racism has been defined as

'Culturally sanctioned beliefs which, regardless of intentions involved, defend the advantages whites have because of the subordinated position of racial minorities'.

(Wellman)

There is a growing but controversial opinion that racism is a system of oppression involving attitudes, practices and institutions that combine to discriminate against certain racial groups.

A number of international treaties have sought to end racism such as the International Convention on the Elimination of All Forms of Racial Discrimination 1965 and most countries have race discrimination laws today.

Racism ought to be distinguished from racialism which refers to a belief in the existence and significance of racial characteristics and differences but which does not support the notion of racial supremacy.

Further Reading

Wellman, D. (1993). Portraits of White Racism. Cambridge University Press.
Niessen, J. and Chopin, I. (2004).The Development of Legal Instruments to Combat Racism in a Diverse Europe. Martinus Nijhoff Publishers.
Webster, C. (2008). Understanding Race and Crime. Open University Press.
www.nacro.org.uk/publications/racecriminal

Racist Violence

Violence – physical, mental or emotional – which is perceived to be racially motivated by the victim(s) or others.

Radical Criminology

See Criminological Theory.

Rampage killer

See Spree-killer.

Rape and Related Offences [Sex Offences Act 2003]

Penile penetration by a man of the vagina, anus or mouth of a victim (male/female) without consent and where the defendant does not reasonably believe that the victim consents.

Whether a belief is reasonable is determined by reference to all the circumstances, including any step(s) he has taken to ascertain whether there is consent.

There are now also three offences akin to rape:

- Assault by Penetration: which need not be penile but could be by an implement such as a bottle, for example.
- Sexual Assault: which involves intentionally touching another sexually (by the body or with something else) without consent and without reasonable belief in consent.
- Intentionally Causing a Person to Engage in Sexual Activity: which is without consent and without reasonable belief in consent.

A woman who forces a man to have intercourse could commit this offence.

Ratio Decidendi

See Precedent.

Rational Choice Theory

The theory based on the idea that patterns of behaviour reflect the personal choices made by individuals as they aim to maximize their benefits and minimize their costs.

In criminology the theory adopts the utilitarian belief that man is a rational person who weighs costs and benefits and makes a rational choice.

The central points of this theory therefore are

- A human being is a rational person.
- Rationality involves a cost/benefit analysis.
- People choose all behaviour (non-deviant and deviant) based upon their rational calculations of cost versus benefits.
- Choice, all things being equal, will be directed towards maximizing pleasure.
- Choice may be controlled by increasing awareness of potential pain or punishment that may follow anti-social conduct.

Thus the state's ability to maintain law and order is based on an understanding of this process of rational choice.

It is well explained in the context of crime in the following quote:

> 'According to this view, law-violating behavior should be viewed as an event that occurs when an offender decides to risk violating the law after considering his or her own personal situation (need for money, personal values, learning experiences) and situational factors (how well a target is protected, how affluent the neighborhood is, how efficient the local police happen to be). Before choosing to commit a crime, the reasoning criminal evaluates the risk of apprehension, the seriousness of the expected punishment, the value of the criminal enterprise, and his or her immediate need for criminal gain'.

(Siegel 1992)

As applied to crime prevention, this means that the focus shifts to the act of committing criminal behaviour; the issue becomes 'what can be done to make the criminal activity less attractive to the potential offender?'

> 'Crime prevention, or at least crime reduction, may be achieved through policies that convince criminals to desist from criminal activities, delay their actions or avoid a particular target'.

(Siegel 1992)

Rational Choice Theory is related to <u>Drift Theory</u> (Matza 1964) and <u>Routine Activity Theory</u> (Cohen and Felson 1979).

Further Reading
Siegel, L. (1992). Criminology. West Publishing.

Reasonable Man

See Objective Test.

Reasonableness

The objective standard for determining whether a person has acted or failed to act as a reasonable person would do in the circumstances.

    This will sometimes determine a person's criminal culpability or not, as the case maybe.

R

Reasonable Suspicion

The pre-requisite for the exercise of many police and other public bodies' discretionary powers under, for example, <u>PACE</u>.

Recidivist (ism)

A repeat or persistent offender.

Rates of youth reoffending are much higher than those of adults; official statistics suggest that 75 per cent young males and 63 per cent young females reoffend within 2 years of release.

Recklessness

The mental state of foreseeing a risk but consciously taking it.

It is the mens rea for some crimes.

However, not every case of foresight amounts to recklessness; the risk which the person chooses to run must be an unreasonable one, judged by an objective standard.

The factors which the law takes into account in determining this include the probability of the risk occurring and the nature and gravity of the potential harm. The main difference between this and intention is that, while in both cases the defendant must foresee the risk, in recklessness he/she need not be motivated to bring it about.

Further Reading

Simester, A. P. and Sullivan, G. R. (2007). Criminal Law: Theory and Doctrine, Chapter 5. Hart Publishing.

Recognizance

An undertaking to pay a specified sum of money if a specified event does, or does not, happen in a specified time.

An offender, for example, bound over to keeping the peace by a court maybe required to enter into a recognizance for £200 which will be forfeited if he fails to do so. Recognizances may also be required to ensure that a defendant appears in court on a specified date.

Record (Criminal)

A formal document listing a person's criminal conviction(s) or cautions.

If cautioned or convicted of a crime, offenders will retain their record even if given an absolute discharge. It will only be erased after 5 years (caution), 10 years (minor offence) or 20 years (serious offence). The purpose is to provide an offender's comprehensive criminal history and this may be used for numerous purposes including employment, immigration, background vetting, criminal investigation and sentencing.

Disclosure of criminal record information is made available to appropriate organizations by the Criminal Records Bureau (CRB)

Further Reading

www.crb.homeoffice.gov.uk

Recorder

A part-time judge in the Crown Court.

Recreational Drugs Use

Regular, but not usually excessive, use of drugs (e.g., cannabis, ecstasy) in a recreational context.

Reductivists

Theorists who believe that the aim of punishment is to reduce crime by reforming or deterring reoffending (Cavadino and Dignan (2002).

They are contrasted with retributivists whose focus is on blaming offenders and exacting retribution from them.

Further Reading

Cavadino, M. and Dignan, J. (2002). The Penal System: An Introduction. Sage Publications Ltd.

Regulatory Offence(s)

See Strict Liability.

Rehabilitation

See Theories of Sentencing.

Re-examination

The questioning of a witness by the party who originally called him/her to testify in court following cross-examination by the opposing party.

Re-examination is usually confined to matters arising out of cross-examination which may need clarification unless, exceptionally, the judge allows a new matter to be raised.

R (Regina)

The abbreviation used in the citation of a criminal case brought by the State in the name of the Queen.

Regulatory Offence(s)

Criminal offences which do not require proof of fault (mens rea) for conviction.

They are said to be strict liability offences and include selling contaminated food or alcohol to minors and discharging pollution into controlled waters.

Further Reading

Water Resources Act 1991 s 85

R

Re-hearing

A second hearing of a case already adjudicated upon.

There may be a complete rehearing of both parties' arguments or on a transcript of the trial evidence only.

Relativism

The theory that has it that concepts such as knowledge, truth or values are not absolute but relative to the person(s) or group(s) holding them.

In the context of criminology, relativism shifts attention away from the so-called facts of crime towards the social processes that define certain acts as criminal; crime is seen as a product of definition.

> 'Deviance is not a quality of an act the person commits, but rather a consequence of the application by others of rules and sanctions to an offender—deviant behaviour is behaviour that people so label'.
>
> (Becker 1963)

This view of crime is, of course, incompatible with biological criminology and the notion of 'born criminals'; if there is no crime but only acts labelled as such, how can it be said that some individuals are born good while others are born bad?

Further Reading

Beirne, P. (1983). Cultural Relativism and Comparative Criminology, Contemporary Crises, 7, 371–91.

Becker, H. (1963). Outsiders. The Free Press of Glencoe.

Relevance (Relevancy).

The concept in the law of evidence which describes the relationship between a piece of evidence and the facts at issue in a case. Relevant evidence is evidence which makes the matter requiring proof more or less probable.

Although most relevant facts are admissible in evidence, relevance is not the same as admissibility as relevant evidence may be non-admissible if it falls within the exclusionary rules (e.g., hearsay).

Remand

The custodial detention of an alleged offender or convicted offender pending trial or appeal respectively.

Remission

The release of a prisoner on licence, which is effectively a reduction of the term of imprisonment served.

All prisoners given a fixed term of imprisonment are eligible for remission at a certain point of their sentence, depending on the length of the original sentence. If the offender has spent time on remand in custody, this time will be taken as time served.

Most offenders will be supervised in the community on release.

Prisoners given an indeterminate sentence (e.g., life) may also receive remission from the Home Secretary on the recommendation of the Parole Board, Lord Chief Justice and the trial judge.

Reparation Order

See Sentencing.

Repeal

The revocation of an Act of Parliament by a subsequent Act.

Representation

Advocacy by a barrister or solicitor acting on behalf of a party in legal proceedings.

Respondent

The party opposing an appeal in court proceedings.

Responsibilization

A thesis (Garland 2001) which has developed out of the multiagency approach to crime prevention introduced by the Crime and Disorder Act 1998 and continued by the Police Reform Act 2002.

It reflects a belief in a shift from central government control to local level control of anti-social behaviour, sometimes referred to as 'community governance'. It involves the notion that communities, organizations and individual citizens should share responsibility for crime prevention measures.

Community Safety Partnerships are agents of this participatory governance. This idea that responsibility for crime control should be shared coincides with some writers' view that the traditional divisions between the state and civil society are becoming blurred (Cohen 1985).

However, others argue that a gulf exists between rhetoric and reality; central government may seem to have devolved responsibility to the local level but at the same time has retained control over the community safety agenda (Garland 2001).

Tensions between central government, local partnerships and citizens may undermine the notion of responsibilization.

Further Reading

Cohen, S. (1985). Visions of Social Control. Cambridge: Polity Press.
Garland, D. (2001). The Culture of Control. Oxford University Press.

R

Restorative Justice

A criminal justice approach which aims to restore victims and members of the community, as far as possible, to the position they were in before the crime was committed.

> 'Restorative justice is a process whereby parties with a stake in a specific offence collectively resolve how to deal with the aftermath of the offence and its implications for the future'.
>
> (Marshall 1999)

It may take the form of

- Direct mediation where the victim and offender meet, face-to-face, in the presence of a mediator.
- Indirect mediation which involves non-face-to-face communication between the victim and offender via a mediator.
- Conferencing where the victim and offender and their supporters are brought together at a meeting arranged by a facilitator.

Further Reading

www.restorativejustice.org.uk

Retribution

See Theories of Sentencing.

Retributivism

A theory of punishment.

Influential in the late eighteenth century and early nineteenth century, retributivism was revived in the UK and US in the 1980s and 1990s.

It is often associated with German philosophers such as Kant and Hegel and maintains that justice requires that offenders be punished in order to pay their debt to society on just deserts and proportionality principles. Concern focuses on the just response to offending behaviour rather than the consequences or future effects of the punishment. The right to punish rests solely on the fact that the offender committed the crime; it can never be imposed merely as a means to promote some other good – for the individual or society.

The essence of this theory is that punishment should, and must, be imposed for its own sake. Retributivism therefore rejects utilitarianism which sees the justifications for punishment as being the protection of the greater good (society), deterrence and rehabilitation.

There a number of criticisms made of retributivist philosophy including that

- it could be seen as cruel and unjust; in that harming others does not restore justice;
- retribution for whom? If it is for society as a whole, surely, it is close to utilitarianism?
- the application of proportionality, influenced as it is by aggravating and mitigating factors, is difficult in practice,
- punishment may have knock-on effects beyond the offender (e.g., family);
- it is unduly based on intuition;
- it ignores factors such as remorse or mercy.

Further Reading

Easton, S. and Piper, C. (2005). Sentencing and Punishment (Chapter 2, 'Just Constraints? Sentencing Discretion and Retributivist Principles'). Oxford University Press.

Retrospectivity

Penalizing conduct that was lawful when committed.

In accordance with the <u>rule of law</u> there is a <u>presumption</u> against the retrospectivity of <u>criminal law</u> so that, unless a <u>statute</u> states otherwise, a person can only be prosecuted for activity committed after the <u>statute</u> comes into effect.

Reverse

See Appeal(s).

Right(s) of Audience

The right of a lawyer to represent a client in court.

Right Realism

See Criminological Theory.

Right to Silence

The right of a person arrested, charged or being tried for a criminal offence not to make a statement or give evidence.

In the past, suspects and defendants were reminded of this in a formal <u>caution</u> and juries were told not to assume guilt from failure to give evidence or answer questions.

Controversially, The Criminal Justice and Public Order Act 1994 curbed this right by allowing <u>adverse inferences</u> to be drawn from silence.

Thus the formal caution now reads 'You do not have to say anything but it may harm your defence if you do not mention, when questioned, something which you later rely on in court. Anything you do say may be given in evidence.'

Rigor Mortis (death)

A post-mortem process which aids the determination of the time of death.

It is associated with an increase in the lactic acid content of the muscles which become very stiff. This remains until decomposition commences which is usually 36–48 hours after death.

R

Risk Assessment

The process whereby offenders are assessed on key variables (risk factors) known to increase the risks posed by offenders (e.g., violent/sex offenders) based on the collection of data about them such as gender, personality, criminal history and record, social and economic circumstances, motivation, sexual preferences, associations, substance abuse and employment status.

The purpose is to predict future crime and manage offender risk. If offenders are considered likely to cause significant serious harm to members of the public, special <u>public protection sentences</u>, often <u>indeterminate</u>, may be imposed.

Standardized risk assessment tools have been developed to assist in the assessment of risk. They are divided into two main categories:

- Actuarial Instruments: which attach specific statistical weighting to different variables which assess the risk. They are based on the idea that if accuracy of prediction is crucial, it is best to find out how members of a group act through time. This involves longitudinal follow-up research of a particular group and
- Structured Clinical Guides: which invite clinicians to look at a number of variables which may apply to the assessment of a particular risk. They are based on the idea that much has been learnt through research about the factors which should be taken into account when making risk assessments of various groups, for example, offenders.

Different tools are used to assess different types of risk and these may vary according to age group (e.g., adult/youth).

Tools for assessment of violence and recidivism include, for example, The Offender Assessment System (OASys) and Young Offender Assessment Profile (ASSET) and The Level of Service Inventory Revised (LSI-R).

Further Reading

www.violence-risk.com/risk/instruments

Further Reading

Ward, R. and Davies, M. (2004). *Criminal Justice Act 2003: A Practitioner's Guide.* Jordan Publishing Ltd.

Risk Averse Society

A society which tries to evaluate all potential risks so as to eliminate them which is, of course, unrealistic.

Risk Factors

Individual or social factors which may be seen to increase the probability of anti-social or criminal behaviour.

Risk Management

The use of risk assessment to manage the criminal risk which an individual may pose in the future.

Risk of Sexual Harm Order (RSHO)

See Grooming.

Robbery (Theft Act 1968)

Theft accompanied by the use/threat of force (to the victim or another) either immediately before or at the time of the theft and in order to steal.

Rohypnol (Flunitrazepan)

The so-called date rape drug whose effects consist of rapid sleep inducement, sedation and muscle relaxation. It is tasteless, odourless and dissolves in alcohol which (along with coffee and carbonated drinks) accentuates its effects. Typically these begin 20–30 minutes after it is taken, peak at two hours and can last for up to 12 hours.

Detection is difficult but has been helped by the development of a preparation which colours safe drinks blue and clouds dark ones which contain the drug.

Routine Activity Theory

A subtheory of Rational Choice Theory concerned with crime prevention. It focuses on the characteristics of the crime rather than the characteristics of the offender and relates the pattern of offending to everyday patterns of social interaction.

During the 1960s–80s, for example, many women started to go out to work, which resulted in the routine of houses being unattended thereby increasing the opportunities for criminal activity (e.g., burglary).

The theory holds that

1) crime is normal and depends on the opportunities available.
2) For crime to occur three elements should be present:
   I. An available and suitable target.
   II. A motivated offender.
   III. Absence of a figure of authority to prevent the crime.
3) If a target is not protected enough and the potential reward is high enough, crime will happen.
4) Crime is relatively unaffected by social causes (e.g., poverty, unemployment); it just needs opportunity.

The latter aspect of this theory is controversial among those criminologists who believe in the social causes of crime but it could explain certain criminal activities quite convincingly such as petty and employee theft, corporate fraud, insider-dealing and intellectual property infringement.

Further Reading

Cohen, L. E. and Felson, M. (1979). Social Change and Crime Rate Trends: A Routine Activity Approach, American Sociological Review, vol. 44, 588–608.

Felson, M. (1997). Technology, Business, and Crime, in Business and Crime Prevention. Monsey, NY: Criminal Justice Press.

Felson, M. (1998). Crime and Everyday Life, Second Edition. Pine Forge Press.

Felson, M. and Clarke, R.V. (1998). Opportunity Makes the Thief, Police Research Series, Paper 98. Policing and Reducing Crime Unit, Research, Development and Statistics Directorate. Home Office [www.homeoffice.gov.uk/rds/prgpdfs/fprs98.pdf]

R

Rule of Law

The constitutional doctrine maintaining that

• government should be conducted according to law rather than arbitrary discretion,

- everyone is equal before the law,
- law should conform to certain standards (clarity and accessibility, proportionality and non-discriminatory),
- punishment should only be imposed after breach of the law has been clearly established and should generally be prospective rather than retrospective.

It is symbolized by the figure of Themis, the Greek goddess, who balances the scales of justice, blind-folded, above many court buildings (see Figure 4).

Figure 4   Scales of justice

R

Sanction

A punishment or <u>sentence</u> for a crime.

Sarah's Law

A campaign initiated by the press in 2000 in response to public anger at the murder of Sarah Payne. It was supported by her parents who were convinced that a paedophile had been responsible for their daughter's death. This was proved correct 17 months later when Roy Whiting was found guilty of the killing, and it was revealed that he already had a conviction for abducting and indecently assaulting an 8-year-old girl.

The campaign involved the publication of names and photographs of convicted <u>paedophiles</u> so as to pressurize the government to allow controlled access to the <u>Sex Offenders' Register</u>, so that parents with young children could know if a child sex-offender was living in their area.

The concept of Sarah's Law is similar to <u>Megan's Law</u>, which operates in the <u>USA</u> as a result of the murder victim Megan Kanka, who was <u>raped</u> and <u>murdered</u> by her neighbour in 1994. It was revealed, after his trial, that he was a convicted child rapist.

A pilot scheme giving parents access to information about paedophiles was introduced in selected counties in the UK in 2009.

Further Reading
Payne, S. (2004). A Mother's Story. Hodder and Stoughton.
Named, Shamed. News of the World, 23 July 2000.

Schizophrenia

A mental disorder characterized by delusions, hallucinations incoherence and social withdrawal.

It is estimated that about 1 per cent of the world's population suffers from this condition which is also associated with criminal behaviour.

Further Reading
Raine, A. (ed.) (2005). Schizophrenia and Crime; Causes and Cures. Nova Science Publishers.

Scotland Yard

See Metropolitan Police Service.

Secondary Victimization

The criminological explanation that describes how victims can be victimized by a primary criminal offence and subsequently revictimized by the response of the criminal justice system itself.

An inappropriate or insensitive reaction from the police investigating a rape, for example, can further traumatize the victim.

It is well described in the following quote:

> 'Secondary victimization is the re-traumatization of the sexual assault, abuse or rape victim. It is an indirect result of assault which occurs through the response of individuals and institutions to the victim. The types of victimization include victim blaming, inappropriate behaviour or language by medical personnel and by other organizations with access to the victim post assault'.
>
> (Campbell et al. 1999)

Further Reading

Williams, S. J. (1984). Secondary Victimization: Confronting Public Authorities Attitudes about Rape. Victimology: An International Journal, 9(1), 66–81.

Madigan, L. and Gamble, N. (1991). The Second Rape: Society's Continued Betrayal of the Victim. Lexington Books.

Campbell, R. and Raja, S. (1999). Secondary Victimization of Rape Victims: Insights from Mental Health Professionals Who Treat Survivors of Violence, Violence Vic. 14(3): 261–75.

Matsakis, A. (1996). I Can't Get Over It: A Handbook for Trauma Survivors. New Harbinger Publications.

Secretary of State for Justice

See Ministry of Justice.

Security Services

The government agency responsible for internal security and counter-terrorism in the UK.

It includes <u>MI5</u> whose role it is to protect the country from threats to national security. <u>MI6</u>, on the other hand, is the overseas intelligence agency of the UK which deals with threats from foreign governments and terrorist groups abroad.

Self-defence

A <u>defence</u> to many criminal offences when reasonable, proportionate force is used to defend oneself, family, another or (sometimes) property against actual or threatened violence.

Self-determination

See Autonomy.

Self-incrimination

<u>Evidence</u> by a <u>witness</u> that incriminates him/herself.

Generally a person is entitled not to give evidence which might incriminate him/herself in court.

Self-report Studies

A research methodology whereby members of the public are asked to report, in confidence, whether they have committed criminal offences.

They have been particularly useful in measuring youth offending and in tackling the problem of the dark figure in crime statistics. Their drawbacks, however, lie in the facts that participants are not representative of the general population (being adolescents mostly), may under or over exaggerate participation in criminal activity or lack knowledge of what actually constitutes criminal behaviour legally. Theoretically, cross-checking is possible through family, contacts, peer-groups, teachers, police or lie-detectors but in practice this is not always possible or effective.

Sentence(s)

A sanction or punishment imposed on a convicted offender, usually pronounced by the judge in open court.

Generally judges have wide sentencing discretion although mandatory sentences exist for some offences (e.g., murder).

Sentences maybe classified as:

- Custodial: e.g., imprisonment, youth custody.
- Financial: e.g., fines, compensation awards.
- Community based: e.g., community order.
- Discharge: e.g., absolute, conditional.

Sentences may also be *concurrent* (served at the same time as another sentence where an offender has been convicted of more than one offence) or *suspended* (does not take effect unless the offender commits another offence within a specified period of time).

Further Reading
www.homeoffice.gov.uk/justice/sentencing

Sentencing Theory

See Theories of Sentencing.

Sentence Discount(s)

The practice employed to persuade defendants to plead guilty and therefore avoid a criminal trial in return for a lighter sentence. Although courts have been reluctant to specify standard discounts, one-third would appear to be the norm for an early plea.

Additionally some defendants may receive enhanced discounts for additional co-operation with the authorities, for example, providing information or testifying against a co-accused(s).

Sentence Disparity

The imposition of different sentences for similar offences which clearly could lead to inconsistency and unfairness in particular cases.

Sentencing Guidelines

Guidelines issued to judges indicating the appropriate sentences they should impose on convicted offenders to ensure consistency and proportionality. Effectively, they operate as limits on judicial sentencing discretion.

These are issued by the Magistrates' Association, Court of Appeal, and the Sentencing Advisory Panel and Council.

Further Reading

www.sentencing-guidelines.gov.uk

Sentencing Advisory Panel (SAP)

The body, established by the Crime and Disorder Act 1998, to make proposals for sentencing guidelines for use in the criminal courts.

Its membership includes judges, law academics, civil servants and members of the CP, Parole Board and Probation Service.

In 2002–3 it published sentencing advice regarding offences of child pornography, causing death by dangerous driving, burglary, offensive weapons and murder.

Sentencing Guidelines Council (SGC)

The body, established by the Criminal Justice Act 2003, effectively to take over the Court of Appeal's role with regard to issuing sentencing guidelines. It acts on the advice of the Sentencing Advisory Panel.

It is chaired by the Lord Chief Justice and its members include judges and lay persons.

The Separation of Powers Doctrine

The constitutional law doctrine which requires the separation of legislative, executive and judicial powers of the state. In the UK these are carried out by Parliament, the Executive and the Judiciary respectively. Each of these bodies is expected to act as a check and a balance on the other to ensure accountability.

Serial Killer

A person who kills a number of persons, usually with a 'cooling off' period between each.

The manner of killing may be similar and victims may have something in common, for example, gender, age, race. Much information regarding serial killing has been obtained from the killers themselves – in the course of being caught, arrested, interviewed, incarcerated and counselled.

Researchers have identified characteristics often found in serial killers:

- feelings of inadequacy
- childhood abuse or humiliation
- low economic status
- retarded emotional development
- lack of human empathy
- rich, often violent, fantasy lives

A number of typologies have been advanced for serial killing, including

- Visionary: responding to voices, delusions or hallucinations, e.g., Peter Sutcliffe (Yorkshire Ripper).
- Missionary: driven to eradicate the world of particular persons/groups, e.g., prostitutes, ethnic groups, e.g., Bodkin Adams.
- Hedonistic: killing for pleasure, thrills or lust, e.g., Jeffrey Dahmer.
- Dominant: needing to exert power over life and death, e.g., Harold Shipman.

Serial killers seem to target women and strangers rather than relatives or acquaintances and are often sexually motivated.

Further Reading
Schechter, H. and Everitt, D. (2006). The A to Z Encyclopedia of Serial Killers. Pocket Books.

Serious Fraud Office (SFO)

The government department responsible for the detection, investigation and prosecution of serious, complex fraud cases.

It may act on its own initiative or on referrals from the police and regulatory bodies, for example, HM Revenue and Customs.

The key criteria for its investigation include

- Fraud in excess of £1 million
- Significant international or public interest dimension
- Specialized knowledge or financial expertise required

Notable investigations involved Severn Trent Water Ltd. which was fined £2 million for providing false leakage data and Balfron Pensioner Group which paid £2 million compensation after its conviction for fraud.

Serious Organized Crime Agency (SOCA)

An intelligence-led public body, sponsored by, but independent of, the Home Office, with law enforcement powers aimed at denying opportunities to organized criminals by frustrating criminal activity in the UK and abroad.

One of its responsibilities is dealing with financial information about the proceeds of crime in order to counter money laundering.

It acts as the UK point of contact for Interpol and Europol. It was set up in 2006 following the merger of a number of agencies including the National Crime Squad and the National Criminal Intelligence Service.

Further Reading

www.soca.gov.uk

Serotonin

See Neurotransmitter.

Sexual Abuse

Sexual attention towards a person which is forced, undesired or obtained by deception or emotional manipulation.

Where the person is under the age of consent, it is usually termed child sex abuse.

There are many types of sexual abuse, including

* Non-consensual, forced physical sexual behavior such as rape, sexual assault or incest.
* Sexual kissing, fondling, exposure of genitalia, and voyeurism.
* Exposing a child to pornography.
* Sexually suggestive statements towards a child.
* Misuse of a position of trust to gain otherwise unwanted sexual activity without physical force, e.g., sexual harassment in the workplace or clerical abuse.

It has been estimated that approximately 15–25 per cent of women and 5–15 per cent of men were sexually abused as children. Most offenders are thought to be acquainted with their victims; approximately 30 per cent are relatives of the child, most often fathers, uncles or cousins; around 60 per cent are other acquaintances, such as friends of the family, babysitters, or neighbours; strangers are the offenders in approximately 10 per cent of child sexual abuse cases. It was thought that most child sexual abuse is committed by men but there is increased evidence that women are involved in committing offenses. Most offenders who abuse children are paedophiles.

Further Reading

Laws, R. and O'Donohue, W. (1997). *Sexual Deviance: Theory, Assessment and Treatment.* Guildford Press.

www.napac.org.uk

www.survivors,gov.uk

S

Sexism

Oppressive attitudes and behaviours directed towards either sex which can lead to discrimination and stereotyping based on gender.

The study of sexism is a central feature of feminist criminology which defines it as prejudice accompanied by power.

More specifically, Sexism can have subtly different strands:

* the belief that one sex is superior to the other
* the belief that men and women are very different and this should be strongly reflected in society and the law

- the simple hatred of men (misandry) or women (misogyny)

Sexist beliefs are a species of essentialism, which holds that individuals can be understood (and often judged) based on the characteristics of the group to which they belong, in this case, their sex group (male or female).

Further Reading

Humphries, D. (2009). Women, Violence and the Media: Readings in Feminist Criminology. Northeastern University Press.

Gelsthorpe, L. and Morris, A. (1990). Feminist Perspectives in Criminology. McGrath-Hill Education.

Gelsthorpe, L. (1989). Sexism and the Female Offender. Cambridge Studies in Criminology. Gower.

Sex and Crime

This is a phrase which has a number of meanings but here it is taken to refer to the connexion between gender and crime.

In the context of crime, males have long out-numbered females: as offenders, law enforcers, policymakers and administrators in the criminal justice system, researchers and theorists.

It was not until feminist criminology developed in the 1970s that this gender bias was highlighted and there came to be more focus on females – as both victims and offenders.

Recorded statistics present an interesting perspective on male and female offending:

- 79% (approximately) of known offenders are male, peaking at 17 (15 for girls).
- 82–93% (approximately) of offenders convicted or cautioned for serious offences (e.g., violence, burglary, criminal damage, drugs) are male.
- 97% (approximately) of offenders convicted or cautioned for sex offences are male.
- 50% (approximately) of female offenders are convicted or cautioned for theft (30% males).
- Female offending and custodial sentencing is rising more rapidly than in males (which remains fairly static).
- Women represented about 5% of the prison population in 2008.

There has been much recent debate about the increase in female criminality, particularly violence and the growth of 'girl-gangs'. However, although the offending gap between the sexes seems to be narrowing, males still make up the majority of known offenders.

Further Reading

www.justice.gov.uk/publications/womencriminaljusticesystem

Sex Offences

These are crimes of a sexual nature, usually where consent is absent on the part of one person although some consensual activities may also be criminal, for example, sadomasochistic assaults.

The age of consent to sexual activity varies; it is 16 (heterosexual and homosexual) in the UK compared with other countries as seen in Table 5 below.

Table 5   Ages of consent

Age of consent	Country
18	Austria, Ireland, Belgium
17	Bosnia, Finland, Germany
16	Malta, Norway, Netherlands, Portugal, Russia, Switzerland
15	Czech Republic, Denmark, France, Greece, Poland, Romania, Slovakia, Slovenia, Sweden
14	Austria (some states), Bulgaria, Hungary, Italy, Serbia, Albania, Croatia, Lichenstein, Lithuania
13	Spain
12	Vatican City

Sex offending has become a major concern of the criminal justice system and there has been much legislative reform recently including the introduction of measures such as victim anonymity, video-link evidence, punitive sentences(sometimes indeterminate for the public's protection) and the sex offender register.

The categorization of sex offences has changed over the years as some activities have been de-criminalized (e.g., adult consensual homosexuality in private) while others have been criminalized (e.g., marital and male rape).

Some of the most important reforms have been contained in the Sex Offences Act 2003 which is considered under the offence of rape and related offences.

The investigation and prosecution of sexual offences poses unique and serious problems for the criminal justice system. These include

- under-reporting of offences
- evidence unavailability or deficiency
- medical examination difficulties
- vulnerability of witnesses
- secondary victimization
- oppressive examination by lawyers in court proceedings
- intoxication issues
- unsympathetic attitudes by agencies involved
- low conviction rates

Further Reading

Thomas, T. (2005). Sex Crime: Sex Offending and Society. Willan Publishing.
R v Brown 1994 AC 212
www.stopitnow.org.uk

Sex Offences Prevention Order

The civil measure introduced by the Sex Offenders Act 2003 to deal primarily with offenders not on the Sex Offenders' Register because their offences preceded its introduction.

The Order may be granted by a court:

(i) on the application of the <u>police</u> if they have reasonable cause to believe that a person (known to have convictions that would put them on the register if it were retrospective) is acting suspiciously as if intent on reoffending and it is necessary to protect the public from serious harm or

(ii) where it convicts a person of a listed offence (not exclusively sex offences).

The effect of the order is to place restrictions on the person and subject them to the <u>sex offenders register</u> notification requirements.

The order is available for any person over the age of 10 years but guidelines indicate that applications in respect of young persons under 18 years should be considered only exceptionally.

Further Reading
Criminal Justice Act 2003 s 104-113, 325-7, Schedules 3, 5.

Sex Offenders Register

The register of persons (names and addresses) convicted and sentenced for a range of <u>sex offences</u> set up in 1997 and now governed by the Sex Offences Act 2003. It is maintained by the police and based upon <u>risk assessment</u> principles.

Inspired by the perceived need to protect vulnerable children from the attention of <u>paedophiles</u>, it now also encompasses adult victims.

Registered offenders are required to notify the <u>police</u> every time they change their name or address and report in person annually.

The period of registration ranges from

• indefinitely (persons sentenced to imprisonment for life or 30 months or more)
• 10 years (persons sentenced to 6–30 months)
• 7 years (persons sentenced to 6 months)
• 5 years (persons sentenced to less than 6 months)

S

The major criticism of the system is that it is not freely accessible to members of the public and is not retrospective, therefore omitting an estimated 110,000 offenders who committed offences before its introduction.

As a result of <u>Sarah's Law</u>, controlled discretionary disclosure of sex register information is now permitted by the police and pilot schemes are running to allow increased access for the public.

The <u>Sex Offences Prevention Order</u> has been introduced to address the issue of retrospectivity.

Further Reading
The Sex Offences Act 2003 s 80–96
Plotnikoff, J. and Woolfson, R. (2000). Where are They Now? An Evaluation of Sex Offender Registration in England and Wales, Police Research Series Paper 126.

Sex Role Theory

The theory which concerns the ways in which, through <u>socialization</u>, boys and girls learn what is expected of them in relation to their gender.

Further Reading

Walklate, S. (2004). Gender, Crime and Criminal Justice. Willan Publishing.

Sex Tourist(ism)

A person who travels abroad for the purpose of having sexual relations with young persons in countries with less rigorous laws or law enforcement agencies.

Since 1997 <u>prosecutions</u> are possible in the UK for <u>sex offences</u> committed abroad, and <u>Foreign Travel Orders</u> were introduced in 2003.

Further Reading

Sex Offences Act 2003 s 72, 114–9, 122

Shaming

The publication of criminals' details on press and police websites or at public meetings or via leaflet distribution.

Data protection and human rights laws place restrictions on what is published and for how long. Guidelines also provide criteria for publication decisions which include consideration of <u>proportionality</u> and the potential adverse consequences for both the criminal and his/her family.

Sharia Law

The law operating in the Islamic legal system which derives from the teachings of the Koran and from Sunna (the practices of the prophet Mohammed) as well as rulings from Islamic scholars.

It is more than a legal system and is, effectively, a moral code for living, followed as a matter of personal conscience by most Muslims. However, it can also be adopted and formally enforced through courts dealing not only with criminal matters but also inheritance, banking and commercial issues.

Controversially, it has been suggested by some members of the <u>judiciary</u> and the clergy that it could play a role in parts of the UK legal system

Further Reading

www.islamic-sharia.org

Short Sharp Shock

The phrase, often heard in politicians' rhetoric, meaning punishment that is speedy and severe. The term appeared in the 1970s in the context of adopting a policy of harsh imprisonment as being the best crime deterrent measure, for young offenders in particular, in order to 'shock' them out of a potential life of crime.

Silcott, Winston

The <u>miscarriage of justice</u> victim whose conviction for the murder of P. C. Blakelock during the Broadwater Farm riots of 1985 was quashed in 1991.

Further Reading

James, S. (ed.) (1999). A Chronology of Injustice. New Beacon Books.

Silence

See Right to Silence.

Silks

See Queen's Counsel.

Situational Offences

Crimes where the <u>actus reus</u> consists of an event or circumstance connected to the <u>defendant</u>; there is no need to prove any act or omission by the <u>defendant</u>.

The classic case illustration of this type of liability is *Larsonneur* in which the <u>defendant</u> was convicted of the offence of being in the UK when permission to enter had been refused. This was despite the fact that the only reason for her presence was that she had been brought to the UK by the police against her will. The court's reasoning was that it was she to whom the <u>actus reus</u> (being in the UK without permission) happened and not because of anything she did.

Common examples of such offences are having possession of controlled drugs or weapons.

Further Reading

R v Larsonneur (1933) 24 Cr. App Rep 74
Misuse of Drugs Act 1971 s 5(2)

Social Altruism

See Altruism.

Social Ecology

The study of 'criminal places', deriving from the Greek word meaning household or living place.

Certain neighbourhoods are seen as high crime areas gaining unsavoury reputations. This theory examines the movement of persons and their concentrations in particular locations.

The <u>Chicago School</u> was influential in this context; high-density neighbourhoods with crowded housing and weak supervision of young persons increased the congregation of groups in the streets and public places leading to increased opportunities for criminal activity. Economic inequalities tend to produce an <u>underclass</u> of the poor who remain in the inner cities while the more successful move out to the suburbs.

S

In cities where there are concentrations of immigrants and diverse ethnic groupings these problems may intensify, for example, Los Angeles in the 1990s.

Social Disorganization Theory

See Criminological Theories.

Social Exclusion

The term used to describe people or areas which are excluded or alienated from mainstream social groupings and activities because of problems such as <u>criminality</u>, unemployment, low income, poor housing, ill-health, family breakdown or high-crime environments.

The government is trying to tackle social exclusion as a whole rather than focusing on areas individually. <u>The Social Exclusion Task Force</u> has this aim.

The Social Exclusion Task Force

The body responsible for co-ordinating the government's drive against <u>social exclusion</u> by supporting the most disadvantaged members of society within government and the public service.

Further Reading

www.cabinetoffice.gov.uk/social_exclusion_task-force

The Social Exclusion Unit

The body replaced by the <u>Social Exclusion Task Force </u>in 2006.

Further Reading

Young, J. (1999). The Exclusive Society; Social Exclusion, Crime and Difference in Late Modernity. Sage Publications Ltd.

Young, J. (1998). From Inclusive to Exclusive Society, in Ruggiero et al. (eds). The New European Criminology: Crime and Social Order in Europe. Routledge. [Digital Printing, 2005].

Young, J. (2007). The Vertigo of Late Modernity. Sage Publications Ltd.

S

Social Identity Theory

See Black Sheep Effect.

Social Inclusion

The term used to describe an approach which aims to ensure that marginalized individuals or groups are involved in civic and political decision-making and activities which affect their lives, so allowing them to participate more fully in society.

It is the inverse of <u>social exclusion</u>.

There is now an <u>Inclusion Institute</u> at the University of Central Lancashire.

Further Reading
www.socialinclusion.org.uk

Social Interactionism

A criminological approach which stresses that crime needs to be understood as a product of personal interaction among members of society.

Social Support Theory

See Altruism.

Socialization

The process of learning to be a member of a society which involves acquiring skills, values and beliefs compatible with social co-existence.

Sociopath

See Psychopath(y).

Soft Policing

A style of policing which involves community-based methods and citizen participation with increased focus on prevention and proactive approaches.

It is to be contrasted with the strong-armed, militaristic hard style which tends to be more reactive involving greater use of guns, CS gas and <u>surveillance</u> techniques.

Solicitor

See Legal Profession.

Special Branch

The police special units responsible for national security and protection of VIPS, intelligence and counter-terrorism.

The Metropolitan Police Special Branch and Anti-terrorism Branch are now amalgamated as the Counter Terrorism Command.

Specific Intent (Crime)

See Intention.

Spent Conviction [Rehabilitation of Offenders Act 1974]

An offender who has served a <u>sentence</u> of imprisonment (not exceeding 2.5 years) and has not reoffended within a specified 'rehabilitation' period is said to have a spent conviction and does not have to reveal the fact of it to (e.g., to most prospective employers) after a prescribed number of years, depending on the seriousness of the offence.

This does not apply to employment connected with children, the elderly or the sick. Sentences of imprisonment for more than 2.5 years are never spent, for example, life imprisonment and sex offenders convicted after 1997 who will remain on the Sex Offender Register.

Spree-killer

Also known as a rampage killer, this is a person who kills a number of victims in a short time in multiple locations, without a cooling-off period and frequently followed by suicide.

Notable spree-killings in the UK were the Hungerford (1987) and Dunblane (1996) Massacres.

Square of Crime

A concept in Left Realist Criminology which explains crime in the context of the relationship between the offender, victim, the state and the wider society in order to understand not only the action but also the reaction to crime.

No explanation which does not include these four factors is seen as satisfactory.

This model seeks to explain the crime rate as a consequence of the interaction between crime control agencies, the offender, the victim and the public (four sides of a square).

Thus for example:

- it is the relationship between the police and the public which determines the efficacy of policing,
- it is the relationship between the offender and victim which determines the impact of the crime,
- it is the relationship between the state and offender which is a determinate of recidivism.

Also these relationships and interactions vary with particular crimes.

Thus it emphasizes the fact that crime involves a relationship in which the impact of criminalization depends, among other things, upon the response of criminal justice agencies; an unsympathetic or inappropriate response may result in secondary victimization.

Stalking [Protection from Harassment Act 1997]

Persistent threatening behaviour by one person towards another, causing fear of violence or distress.

Standard of Proof

The degree of proof required to establish a fact(s).

In criminal law the standard of proof is on the prosecution to establish the guilt of the defendant beyond *reasonable doubt*.

Exceptionally, the lower standard (*balance of probability*) applies where criminal defences need to be established (e.g., insanity, diminished responsibility).

State Terrorism

State- sponsored and promoted political violence, usually ideologically inspired.

Further Reading

www.security.homeoffice.gov.uk

Stare Decisis

See Precedent.

Statement of Compatibility

See Human Rights Act 1998.

Statistics (Crime)

The systematic collection and arrangement of quantitative data which is then used to measure and analyse the rate, distribution, patterns and trends in crime and victimization.

Court records have been kept from medieval times and crimes known to the police have been published in England and Wales since 1857.

The main sources of crime data are

- Criminal Statistics, England and Wales
  Published annually by the Home Office and other government departments, these are based on offences recorded by the police according to the National Crime Recording Standard (NCRS).
- The British Crime Survey (BCS)
  Initiated in 1982, this victimization survey is now conducted annually to complement police statistics. It surveys a random sample of private households about their experiences of crime in the previous year, using questionnaires.
  This is seen as providing a more reliable picture of crime as it is independent and covers unreported crime, victim information and fear of crime perceptions. It also helps to identify persons or areas most at risk from different types of crime and, as such, aids crime-prevention programmes.
- Local Surveys
  Funded mainly by local authorities in inner city areas, these aim to discover information about victimization experienced by marginalized groups such as the young, elderly, poor, homeless and mentally-ill who are not surveyed by the BCS.

S

- Voluntary Private Surveys
  These aim to discover more about offending in local, domestic, commercial and institutional contexts.
- International Surveys
  A response to the growing globalization of crime, these collect information from different countries at the same time. They include the International Crime Victim Survey (2000), the International Crime Business Survey (2005) and Eurobarometer which is a public opinion crime-related cross-Europe survey.
- Self-report Studies
  Samples of the public are asked to report, in confidence, whether they have engaged in anti-social and/or criminal activity or been a <u>victim</u> of such. These have been used particularly to measure <u>juvenile</u> offending and experience.
  For example, underage binge-drinking (2005).

Crime statistics are an important influence on criminal justice research, policy and practice but they also need to be viewed with some caution for the following reasons:

- Sometimes they are given too much significance and are open to varying interpretation.
- The problem of the <u>dark figure.</u>
- Moral panics may be created by media manipulation or selective use of crime figures.
- Lack of public trust or understanding of figures.

Further Reading

Maguire, M. (2007). Crime Data and Statistics, in M. Maguire et al. The Oxford Handbook of Criminology. Oxford University Press.

Coleman, C. et al. (1996). Understanding Crime Data: Haunted by the Dark Figure. Open University Press.

www.crimestatistics.org.uk

Status Zero

The term used to describe a social group which is not in education, employment or training, may have learning difficulties, low qualifications and skills and tends to live in care or social housing.

Various government schemes (e.g., New Start) have been introduced to help this group and reduce the likelihood of its members degenerating into criminal lifestyles.

Statute

An <u>Act of Parliament</u>.

Statutory Interpretation

See Presumptions.

Stereotype

Originating as a name for a printing duplication process, it is now taken as referring to a rather conventional, over-simplified image or opinion conforming to a set type.

In the criminal context this often translates into a fixed, often exaggerated and negative impression of a particular individual or group based on preconceived, generalized and, maybe, distorted ideas (folk-devils).

Stigma

A mark of disgrace or criminality which may come to be associated with an individual as a result of conviction or labelling by the criminal justice system.

It is argued by some criminologists that such stigmatization may have the effect of consolidating criminal behaviour rather than deterring it and discouraging reintegration of offenders into society.

Avoidance of stigmatization underlies many policies of diversion.

Stigmatization

See Stigma.

Strain Theory

See Criminological Theories.

Street Bail

See Bail.

Street Crime

Crimes associated with the street, for example, robbery, drug-dealing and prostitution.

Strict Liability

Liability for a crime which is imposed without the necessity of proving mens rea in respect of one or more elements of the crime. These crimes are sometimes called regulatory offences and, effectively, are committed without proof of fault on the part of the defendant.

For example, selling liquor to a minor or selling contaminated food.

Structuralism

The theory that humans do not have ultimate freedom but are created and influenced by cultural systems.

Subculture

A minority subgroup within a dominant culture that has its own norms, values and beliefs which differentiates it from the majority which may regard it as subversive.

These emerge when individuals find themselves marginalized and isolated from mainstream culture and so group together for mutual support.

Subcultures may be based on any number of factors including age, race, religion, ideology, class, location, gender, politics, fashion, music and lifestyle. Distinctive subcultures have appeared throughout time such as Mods and Rockers, Punks and Goths.

As the Internet expanded in the 1990s, its forums fostered new subcultures, some of which are seen as worrying. Teenage suicides, for example, have been associated with 'Emo' (emotional) culture which started in the 1980s as a musical genre and developed into a lifestyle supported by the Internet.

In criminology, subculture theories (e.g., Strain Theory) developed to explain juvenile working-class delinquency.

Subjective Test

See Objective Test.

Subordinate Legislation

See Delegated Legislation.

Suicide Pact [Homicide Act 1957]

Although suicide is not a crime since 1961, killing in pursuance of a suicide pact is a form of manslaughter.

A suicide pact is where two or more persons agree that one shall kill the other(s) and then commit suicide himself/herself. A survivor of the suicide pact commits manslaughter.

Super Id

See Freud.

Summary Offence(s)

The least serious criminal offences, tried in the Magistrates' Courts.

Summing Up

The judge's speech at the end of a trial in which he/she explains to the jury its role, relevant points of law and summarizes the trial evidence.

The jury then retires to consider its verdict.

Summons

A formal court document requiring an individual to appear in court on a specified date and time.

Supervision/Supervisory Sentences

Non-custodial sentencing measures, often community based.

The terminology surrounding these has been changed several times since 2001. Under the Criminal Justice Act 2003 (effective 2005) the separate orders were subsumed under the generic term Community Orders.

Supervision (6–3 years) requires an offender to maintain contact with a supervisory officer, and failure to do so may result in resentencing, usually imprisonment.

Unpaid work (60–240 hours) requires the offender to undertake unpaid work in the community; typically this is in group projects such as painting, land reclamation, building or working in charity shops or other voluntary organizations.

Supervision differs as between adults and juveniles and post-custody supervision is also available.

Supervisory Jurisdiction

See Jurisdiction.

Supreme Court

The new court which has replaced the House of Lords in its judicial capacity as the final Court of Appeal for criminal cases in England, Wales and Northern Ireland. It opened in October 2009 and is situated opposite the Houses of Parliament.

Further Reading

The Constitutional Reform Act 2005
www.supremecourt.gov.uk

Surveillance

Close observation or monitoring of individuals/groups, usually for investigative or supervisory purposes and often over a prolonged period of time.

Surveillance devices include the use of CCTV, communications interception, criminal records checks, electronic tagging, biometric passports and the proposed identity card system.

Financial (e.g., cash machine withdrawals) and vehicle (e.g., speed cameras) surveillance is also common.

Ostensibly, these have been introduced to deter and reduce crime, but there is growing concern that they may be becoming too intrusive and a threat to personal privacy. The 1990s saw a dramatic increase in the use of CCTV cameras in streets, shopping centres, offices and prisons.

UK telecom providers are, since 2007, required to keep log calls (landlines and mobiles) which can be accessed by other organizations including the police, government departments and local authorities. This has been extended to Internet use so that government departments can be granted access to emails and web-browsing activity without a warrant or the subject's knowledge.

Employers can, likewise, monitor telephone and Internet activity in the workplace.

S

Oyster cards make it possible to track commuter journeys and Automatic Plate Recognition (ANPR) technology is now available via mobile phones.

Identity chips are being considered as part of new road-pricing schemes based on roadside radio receivers but they would also allow cars' movements to be recorded.

Airlines are also required to provide 'passenger name records' (PNR) and under the terrorism legislation the public are now liable to prosecution for failure to disclose any terrorist suspicion that they may have.

Further Reading

Lyon, D. (2007). Surveillance Studies; An Overview. Polity Books.
www.surveillance-and-society.org

Suspect

A person suspected of a criminal <u>offence</u> who may be arrested, detained and later prosecuted in a criminal court.

S

Tag/Tagging

See Electronic Monitoring.

Tariff

The judicial fixing of an appropriate, proportionate <u>sentence</u> on an informal scale of possible measures. The tariff prescribes a range of sentences for a particular offence and the <u>judge</u> fixes the precise <u>sentence</u> within that range after considering the nature and gravity of the offence and any <u>aggravating</u> or <u>mitigating</u> factors relevant to the <u>offender</u>.

For example, while the maximum sentence for <u>rape</u> is life-imprisonment, a <u>sentence</u> of 2–4 years might be appropriate for a non-violent rape where mitigating factors exist.

It also refers to the minimum period that a person serving an indefinite prison sentence must serve before they become eligible for <u>parole</u>.

The determination of the tariff by the <u>Home Secretary</u> was contested in connexion with the <u>Bulger Case</u> and it is now the responsibility of the <u>trial judge</u> to fix it.

A whole life <u>tariff</u> is where a prisoner is ordered to remain in <u>prison</u> until their death unless there were very exceptional circumstances. Release can only be ordered by the courts if the prisoner has made good progress after 25 years (minimum) in <u>prison</u> or on compassionate grounds (e.g., age/infirmity.)

Whole life tariffs have been recommended for <u>murders</u>

- of two or more persons or a child involving abduction, sadistic, sexual conduct or substantial planning or premeditation or
- a repeat murder.

It may also be applied to other offences where the court considers it is sufficiently serious, for example, <u>treason</u>.

There have been concerns that the whole life tariff contravenes <u>human rights</u> but the <u>Court of Appeal</u> ruled that it does not amount to inhumane and degrading treatment and therefore does not breach the <u>ECHR</u> (Art. 3).

The issue has also been considered by the <u>ECHR</u>.

Further Reading
R v Bieber [2008] 3 WLR 249
Kafkanis v Cyprus 2008 [Application 21906/04]

Telephone Tapping

The interception of telecommunications, which requires <u>the warrant</u> of the <u>Home Secretary</u>.

Terrorism

The use or threat of violence (often indiscriminate) to individuals or the public in general, for political, religious or ideological ends.
Terrorism which is funded by states is called 'state-sponsored terrorism'.
UK legislation has extended the powers of the police and security services to investigate terrorist activities within or outside the UK.
It could, perhaps, be noted that the label 'terrorist' varies with political expediency and one man's terrorist maybe another man's freedom-fighter depending on time and place.
Nelson Mandela, for example, became the President of South Africa despite serving 25 years' imprisonment for activities perceived as terrorism by the South African government of the time.

Further Reading

Furendi, F. (2007). *Invitation to Terror: The Expanding Empire of the Unknown*. Continuum International Publishing Group.
www.terrorism.com
www.security.homeoffice.gov.uk

Testimony

Witness statements given in court, usually orally and on oath, as evidence of the truth of particular facts.

Testosterone

The male sex hormone, popularly associated with aggressive, anti-social behaviour in crimes such as murder, assault and battery and sex offences.
Some studies have found raised levels of testosterone in male offenders and the fact that it peaks during puberty and the early twenties correlates age-wise with the highest crime rates.
In the twentieth century this link was used to justify chemical castration of sex offenders in countries, for example, Denmark (1920), Germany (1933), Norway (1934) and Sweden (1944).
It was never, however, proved that such treatments reduced levels of sexual aggression.
More recently, drug therapy has been offered to aggressive sex offenders as an alternative sentence and there is evidence that it is effective in some cases.

Further Reading

Bosely, S. (2007). What's Chemical Castration? *The Guardian* 14 June.

Theft [Theft Act 1968]

The criminal offence of appropriating (taking) the property of another, dishonestly and with the intention of permanently depriving the other of it.
It is a triable-either-way offence.

Theories of Sentencing/Punishment

The purpose(s) that a sentencer/policymaker seeks to achieve by imposing or creating criminal sanctions.

Several, sometimes conflicting theories, are evident in criminal justice systems and the balance between them may shift from time to time according to prevailing social values and attitudes.

Essentially theories of punishment fall into two main categories: utilitarian and retributive. The utilitarian theory seeks to punish offenders in order to deter future wrongdoing while retributive theory seeks to punish offenders because they deserve it.

The main theories are

- Retribution
  Historically, one of the oldest and most prominent aims, retribution is closely associated with morality and religion. It supports the infliction of punishment on an offender in the belief that he should atone for his crimes (sins) – 'an eye for an eye'. It is based on the premise that there is a relationship between the degree of punishment and the wrong done to society, that is, the penalty should fit the crime, sometimes referred to as 'just deserts'.

  Exemplary long-term custodial sentences and high fines are examples of retributive sentences.

- Deterrence
  Based on Benthamite principles of man as a rational creature who will calculate pain or pleasure as being the likely outcome of his actions; deterrence was, for many years, the most widely held aim of sentencing.

  The aim is both to deter the repetition of crime by the offender (specific deterrence) but also to deter potential offenders (general deterrence).

  Capital punishment, driving disqualification, extended custodial sentences and prescribed minimum sentences aim at maximizing the deterrent effect.

- Reform and Rehabilitation
  These reflect the dual humanitarian aims of
  1. reforming offenders' characters and criminal dispositions so that they can resist temptation or, even better, no longer experience temptation.
  2. assisting offenders to re-establish themselves in society after serving their sentences.

  In the 1960's these aims were evident in most penal systems but today there is less consensus as to their efficacy.

  Community and suspended sentences as well as therapy programmes are seen as having potential for reform and rehabilitation.

- Public Satisfaction
  An important influence on penal policy is, undoubtedly, public opinion; judges take into account the likely public reaction to excessive leniency or severity of sentences.

T

Criminal sanctions may be seen as society's condemnation of unacceptable conduct. Exemplary custodial sentences and high fines could be seen to serve this purpose.

- Social Defence
  It is sometimes suggested that sentencing policy should allow measures to be applied to persons *likely* to commit offences even before they are actually convicted so as to maximize public protection.

  Although controversial, this principle can be identified as underlying measures such as binding over to keep the peace and imprisonment for public protection (IPP).

- Incapacitation
  The idea is to remove the offender's ability to commit further crime. This can be achieved in a number of ways, physical and geographical.

  Capital punishment, castration or amputation of hands or licence cancellation might fall into the first method while extended prison sentences and curfews might satisfy the second.

- Justice and Equality
  Equality of punishment is fundamental to justice and judges therefore seek to impose proportionate and consistent sentences for similar offences.

  They are assisted in this by sentencing guidelines.

Further Reading

Walker, N. (2010). Crime and Punishment in Britain. Hart Publishing.

Valier, C. (2002). Theories of Crime and Punishment. Longman.

Three Strikes Policy

The punitive penal policy, originating in the US in the mid-1990s, requiring that anyone with two convictions for serious crimes be given a mandatory sentence save in exceptional circumstances; hence the phrase 'three strikes and you are out'.

This has proved controversial and critics argue that it is disproportionate, costly, inefficient and unfair.

There are a huge number of prisoners in US prisons serving life sentences for relatively minor crimes under this policy (e.g., 3000 in California).

At times, criminal justice agencies have tried to circumvent its application by making charges for lesser offences which do not carry a mandatory sentence and the judiciary are rigorously using the statutory discretion provided to them to avoid mandatory sentences if it appears 'unjust in all the circumstances'.

Further Reading

The Crime (Sentences) Act 1997.

Walsh, J. (2007). Three Strikes Laws. Greenwood Press.

Totality Principle

The principle that sentencers must have regard to the total length of a sentence imposed so as to ensure that the sentence properly reflects the nature and seriousness of the offending.

Thus, for example, an offender being sentenced for several offences should not simply receive the normal sentence multiplied by the number of offences for which he/she was convicted.

At first sight this would seem sensible but there is the problem that a multiple offender, convicted on separate occasions, would likely be treated more harshly than one convicted of several offences at one time.

Transferred Mens Rea/Fault

To establish criminal liability it must be proved that the defendant committed the actus reus of the offence while at the same time having the requisite mens rea, that is, the criminal act and criminal state of mind must coincide.

The concept of transferred mens rea applies where a criminal act directed towards one person or item results, in fact, in damage to another person or item.

For example, D intentionally aims a blow at B but misses and strikes C instead. In this situation the mens rea in respect of B is transferred to C so as to make D liable.

In the classic case of *Latimer (1886)* the defendant aimed a blow at a person whom he was quarrelling with in a pub but hit and seriously injured the victim instead. He was convicted of unlawful and malicious wounding of the victim; he had the actus reus of the crime and his mens rea was transferred towards the actual rather than anticipated victim.

This principle only applies where the anticipated and actual offences are of the same kind.

Where the defendant would have a defence against the anticipated victim, this will also be transferred in respect of the actual victim; were D to aim a blow at B in self-defence but strike C instead, he would be able to raise this defence against a charge of assaulting C.

Transnational Crime

Crimes committed across a number of jurisdictions (countries).

Globalization and rapid technological advances have undermined the exclusivity of national boundaries and have greatly affected organized crime, in particular money laundering, drugs and human trafficking, prostitution, kidnapping and hostage taking as well as terrorism.

This, in turn, has led to increased international intelligence-sharing and co-operation to tackle it.

In the UK the creation of the Serious and Organized Crime Agency in 2006 brought together various law-enforcement bodies and tried to secure greater co-operation between the police and Security Services.

Further Reading

Edwards, A. and Gill, P. (eds) (2003). Transnational Organized Crime: Perspectives on Global Security, Hart Publishing.

www.soca.gov.uk

Transportation

The practice of sending convicted criminals abroad as a punishment.

It emerged in the sixteenth and seventeenth centuries along with the development of capitalism when productive labour came to be seen as an important resource replacing harsh physical penalties (e.g., execution and corporal punishment).

At this time there was much land in the colonies that needed to be worked and transportation was introduced to facilitate this.

Initially offered as a commutation of capital punishment, by the early eighteenth century it was regularly used as a specific sentence for even quite minor offences.

America and then Australia were the focus of transportation policy and the growing prosperity in the colonies led to its decline in the mid-nineteenth century.

Treason [Treason Acts 1351, 1795]

Criminal conduct against the sovereign or the state which includes

- plotting the death or serious injury of the sovereign, spouse or heir;
- attempting to prevent the succession of the heir to the throne;
- levying war against the sovereign or government;
- aiding the enemies of the sovereign.

The penalty for treason is life imprisonment (formerly the death penalty).

Triable-either-way Offence (T-e-W)

A criminal offence that may be tried in either the Magistrates' Court or the Crown Court at the discretion of the magistrates and the option of the defendant. Theft falls into this category.

Trial

The hearing of a criminal prosecution in a court after a defendant has pleaded not guilty to the offence charged.

The ECHR declares that everyone is entitled to a fair and public hearing and the presumption of innocence. [Arts 5, 6].

The trial will usually follow the police investigation and the CPS decision to bring the prosecution.

Pre-trial disclosure of evidence is required of both the prosecution and defence to enable the trial to proceed efficiently and fairly.

There are substantial differences between Magistrates' and Crown Court trials. The principal distinction is that cases in the Crown Court are tried before a professional judge, usually sitting with a jury, whereas cases in the Magistrates' Court are tried by lay magistrates (JPs) and/or a district judge.

Typically Crown Court trial costs about ten times more than a trial before magistrates. The English trial process, being adversarial, is essentially a public and oral contest between the parties via their lawyers. The prosecution, as the complainant, has to establish the guilt of the defendant and the defendant has the choice of answering the prosecution case or remaining silent and, at the end, the court decides the issue of guilt.

An overview of <u>Crown Court</u> <u>trial</u> procedure is provided below:

- The <u>Indictment</u>: which specifies the actual offence(s) with which the <u>defendant</u> is charged and its particulars (e.g., date, place, nature of the case).
- <u>Prosecution</u> Opening Statement: in which the prosecution lawyer explains in simple, clear language what the case is about and how the prosecution will try to prove its case.
- Examination in Chief: whereby the prosecution calls and questions its own witnesses.
- <u>Cross-examination</u>: whereby the defence can try to undermine the evidence given by the prosecution witnesses.
- Defence Opening Statement.
- Defence Evidence in Chief.
- Cross-examination by the Prosecution.
- Prosecution Closing Speech: which summarizes the key aspects of evidence supporting guilt.
- Defence Closing Speech: which summarizes the weaknesses of the prosecution case and the reasons why it has not made out its case beyond reasonable doubt.
  Closing speeches are often critical stages in the whole trial process; advocates can speak directly to the <u>jury</u> and the speech by the defence may well decide the case.
- The <u>Sentence</u>: which is determined by the <u>judge</u> alone although the <u>defence</u> may make a speech in favour of <u>mitigating factors</u>.

Further Reading

McConville, M. and Wilson, G. (2002). The Handbook of the Criminal Justice Process. Oxford University Press.

Twin Studies

Studies used by <u>biological criminologists</u> to support <u>geneticism</u>; if crime is influenced by genetic factors one would expect to find more criminality in identical <u>(monozygotic)</u> twins than in fraternal <u>(dizygotic)</u> twins or ordinary siblings. This is because fraternal twin occur where two separate eggs are fertilized at the same time and as a result share about 50 per cent of the same genes. The rarer identical twins, which result from the fertilization of a single egg, share all of the same genes. Researchers have found that there are greater similarities in criminal convictions among identical twins than among fraternal ones.

The most comprehensive study was of Danish twins (3568 pairs) which found that 525 of identical twins had the same level of recorded criminality as compared with only 22 per cent in fraternal twins (Christiansen 1977). These findings persisted even where twins were separated at birth and raised in different environments.

Criticisms have been made of these studies including the facts that

- they were overly dependant on official crime statistics,
- the processes for the classification of twins were unreliable,
- the difficulties of controlling for the mutual behavioural influences of twins on each other and other environmental effects.

Typology

A system by which persons/things are classified into particular categories or types that have traits in common.

For example, Von Hentig's victim typology identified categories of persons prone to become crime victims owing to their social and/or psychological state (young, old, female, minority group, immigrant, depressed, mentally defective, lonely, bereaved).

T

Ultra Vires ('beyond powers')

A ground of judicial review challenging a public body with exceeding or abusing its powers. If successful, the court will render the act or decision invalid.

Underclass

The poorest or most disadvantaged class of persons in any given society which would include the long-term unemployed, homeless, chronically sick or disabled and criminals.

Unreported Crime

See Dark Figure.

Utilitarianism

The philosophy which holds that the value of something is determined by its usefulness (utility). It is particularly associated with Jeremy Bentham who identified the utilitarian goal for society; all action or policies should be judged in terms of their utility in promoting the greatest happiness for the greatest number of persons.

Vagrancy

A crime created in 1349 after the Black Death had wiped out about half of the population of England resulting in a chronic labour shortage and consequent rise in wages. The Vagrancy Laws made it an offence to give money to any person who was unemployed despite being of sound mind and body. These fell into disuse when the labour market recovered but were revived in the sixteenth century as a means of encouraging employment and reducing theft of goods carried by road.

Validity

The extent to which a conclusion or transaction is credible and, if appropriate, legal.

Verdict

A finding of guilty or not guilty after a criminal trial.
    After a guilty verdict, the convicted defendant will usually be sentenced.

Vetting

The practice of preliminary investigation of the suitability of potential jurors or witnesses before a trial on grounds of, for example, criminal record, political affiliation or national security.

Vicarious Liability

The term used to describe situations where one person is liable for the wrongs of another, usually because of the particular relationship between them.
    The most common example is an employer's liability for his employee.
    Vicarious criminal liability is imposed by statute on an employer where his/her employee sells unfit food or delivers goods under a false trade description. Likewise the registered owner of a vehicle is liable for parking penalties even if he was not actually at fault.
    The main purposes of this form of liability is to provide incentives for high standards and to ensure there are defendants to pay any costs incurred by the unlawful activity.

Victim

A person against whom a crime is committed.

Further Reading
Goodey, J. (2004). Victims and Victimology: Research, Policy and Practice. Longman.
Spalek, B. Crime Victims: Theory, Policy and Practice. Willan Publishing.

Victims' Charter

The <u>Home Office</u> Charter, first published in 1990 which set out expected standards for the <u>police</u> and other <u>criminal justice agencies</u> to achieve in their dealings with crime victims.

Further Reading
The Howard Journal of Criminal Justice (2002). vol. 38(4), 384–96.
www.homeoffice.gov.uk/documents/victims-charter

Victims' Commissioner

The independent commissioner responsible for the promotion of the interests and support for victims, witnesses and families.

Sara, the mother of murdered schoolgirl Sarah Payne who campaigned for <u>Sarah's Law</u> was appointed the first commissioner in 2009.

Victims of Crime Code of Practice

A Code, in force since 2006, which sets minimum standards of service which victims can expect from <u>criminal justice agencies</u>.

These include rights to

- Information about decisions relating to their case(s) within specified time scales (including arrests and court hearings).
- Measures to render trials less intimidating.
- Consultation regarding sentencing and conditions attached to offenders' release and release dates.
- Information about the <u>Criminal Injuries Compensation Authority</u> and eligibility for compensations claims.
- <u>Victim Support</u> information.
- A dedicated family liaison officer for bereaved relatives.

Further Reading
www.homeoffice.gov.uk

V

Victim Impact Statements

Statements, usually written, provided by victims or their relatives explaining the impact (physical, emotional, financial) of an offence on themselves and the family.

This is then taken into account by <u>criminal justice agencies</u>, especially the judiciary. It is usually given at the sentencing stage of a <u>trial</u> and also, perhaps at subsequent <u>parole</u> hearings.

They originated in US in the 1980s after the campaign by the mother of one of the victims of the Charles Manson <u>cult</u> murders resulting in her being heard at the <u>parole</u> hearing of her daughter's killer.

Their advantages are seen as

- giving victims a voice in <u>court</u> and therefore elevating their status in the <u>criminal justice system</u>;
- aiding recovery from the effects of crime;
- personalizing the crime by confronting offenders with the results of their crime, hopefully aiding remorse and <u>rehabilitation</u>;
- informing the <u>court</u> of factors relevant to <u>sentence</u>.

One of the most influential impact statements heard recently was the statement of the sister of the 'honour killing' victim, Tulay Goren, during the trial of her father in the <u>Old Bailey</u> in December 2009 when he was sentenced to 22 years for her <u>murder</u>.

Further Reading

www.telegraph.co.uk/Tulay-Goren-honour-killing-sisters-victim-impact-statement

Victimless Crime(s)

<u>Offences</u> sometimes characterized as involving no harm to anyone except, perhaps, to the (willing) participants themselves.

Gambling, prostitution, <u>suicide</u>, drug-taking, sadomasochism and <u>corporate crime</u> have, at times, been put in this category.

This is a controversial area which raises the issue as to whether the law should <u>decriminalize</u> these activities because they only concern private morality and self-autonomy, in the absence of proof of actual harm to others.

<u>Criminalization</u> of these activities, it is argued, not only creates new classes of criminals but also

- leads them to commit further offences in support of their habits and
- encourages <u>organized crime</u>, law enforcement corruption and <u>blackmail</u> and diversion from health and treatment programmes and policies.

Victimization

The process of making a person the <u>victim</u> of crime, that is, subjecting them to the effects of criminal behaviour directly from the criminal himself/herself or less directly by the experience of the workings of the <u>criminal justice system</u> itself (secondary victimization).

It is thought that some individuals maybe more susceptible to being a victim of crime than others because of their gender, domestic circumstances, age, vulnerability, associations or high risk lifestyles or locations.

However other criminologists see offenders as victims because of their individual pathology or social factors.

Victimology

The study of <u>victims</u> of crime which includes the interrelationship between offenders and their victims and with the <u>criminal justice system</u>, the media

V

and other social institutions. It also looks at the consequences of crime such as physical, psychological and emotional reactions.

Early studies relied heavily on criminal justice statistics and case data but modern researchers conduct victim surveys which include not only questions about victimization experiences but also try to elicit information about the victims' view of the response of criminal justice agencies towards them.

Further Reading

Walklate, S. (2007). Handbook of Victims and Victimology. Willan Publishing.
www.victimology.ni

Victims' Advisory Panel (VIP)

A statutory, non-departmental public body set up in 2003 to enable victims of crime to have their say regarding the reform of the criminal justice system and developments in services and support for victims.

It includes members who themselves have been victims or are family members or carers or supporters of victims.

Victim Support

An independent, government-funded organization, established in the 1970s, working to help victims and witnesses of crime by providing free, confidential support and practical assistance via national and local support schemes.

In a wider sense the term could be taken to mean the measures introduced to improve the treatment of victims in the criminal justice system including

- The Criminal Injuries Compensation Scheme
- Compensation orders awarded against offenders in criminal courts
- Women's aid refuges, rape crisis centres and child line services
- Victim identity protection
- Victim-offender mediation
- Vulnerable persons' protections
- Witness care units

Further Reading

www.victimsupport.com

Victim Surveys

Research tools involving the questioning of victims about their personal victimization experiences.

Vigilante

Someone who, effectively, takes the law into their own hands and punishes others for perceived anti-social activity.

It is a form of self-help, sometimes adopted by groups or communities where there is a lack of confidence in official law enforcement especially when there may have been a moral panic whipped up by the media. The protests and violent attacks directed at suspected paedophiles in a number of UK cities after the newspaper campaign for Sarah's Law was launched in 2000 is a clear example.

Vigilantism is controversial as it may result in violence or criminal behaviour on the part of the vigilantes such as breaches of the peace.

Voire Dire

A phrase deriving from old French ('to speak the truth') referring to a preliminary investigation into the competence or suitability of prospective jurors or witnesses; a way of challenging and removing a juror from a jury in a particular case.

Voyeurism

The practice of spying on persons engaged in private, often intimate, relations.

Derived from the French word 'to look', it is a criminal offence in the UK if non-consensual.

It has been claimed that some individuals who engage in such activities are prone to violence, especially sex offences.

Further Reading
The Sex Offences Act 2003 s 67

Vulnerable Persons/Victims

Persons under 17 years and those with mental or physical disabilities who receive special consideration in the criminal justice system, especially in relation to the application of procedural and evidential rules during trial proceedings.

This might include opportunities to give evidence behind a screen or via video-link.

V

Waiver

The act of refraining from asserting a legal right, benefit or claim.

War Crimes

Violations of the law and customs of war constituting criminal offences, defined by the Nuremberg Charter 1946 as including

- War Crimes
  For example, murder, ill-treatment or transportation of civilians or prisoners of war, hostage taking, plunder or destruction of populations (genocide) or property beyond the necessity of war.
- Crimes against Humanity
  For example, murder, extermination, enslavement, deportation, torture, rape and other inhumane acts against civilians before or during war and persecution on racial, religious or political grounds (connected with war crimes).
  These are not usually isolated events but part of concerted government or state policies or a toleration of such practices.
- Crimes against Peace
  For example, planning or waging a war of aggression in violation of international treaties.

The International Criminal Court (ICC) has jurisdiction to prosecute individuals for war crimes committed after its establishment in 2002.
   The War Crimes Act 1991 was passed to give UK courts jurisdiction to try World War II war criminals, irrespective of their nationality.

Further Reading
War Crimes, Genocide and Crimes Against Humanity Journal
www.war-crimes.org

Ward, Judith

The victim of a serious miscarriage of justice who was convicted and served 17 years for the murder of 12 soldiers and their families in an army coach bombing in 1972. Her conviction was eventually quashed for substantial non-disclosure of evidence to the defence at her trial and acknowledged police frame-up.

Further Reading
Ward, J. (1995). Ambushed: My Story. Vermilion (Ebury) Publishing.

Warrant

A document authorizing some action, for example, an arrest or search of premises.

Welfare/Welfare Model

A model of criminal justice which focuses on why an offender committed an offence and how best to adjust his/her behaviour rather than focusing on the penalty for the offence (justice model).

A brief historical look at the youth justice system in England and Wales reveals the tensions between the welfare and justice models.

In the context of juvenile crime the prevailing view in the 1980s was that criminal justice interventions had little impact on future offending patterns (and could even be counter-productive) and that policy should, as far as possible, focus on diverting young offenders from the criminal justice system.

By the early 1990s, however, public concerns about the level of juvenile crime led to a reversal of this welfare approach and a move towards a 'just deserts' policy which shifted the emphasis to the nature and seriousness of the offence rather than the offender.

The abduction and murder of Jamie Bulger in 1993 by two 10 years old boys escalated this trend and within a year new legislation was introduced which provided for stiffer sentences for young offenders and represented a much more punitive response than the earlier welfare approach.

In 1996 the Audit Commission severely criticized the effectiveness of the youth justice system. Its report recommended that emphasis should shift towards proactive, preventative work with young people at risk of offending. This return to the welfare model was put on a statutory basis in 1998.

While more recent legislation retains welfare principles to an extent, these are seen as rather subordinate to the central aim of preventing offending.

Further Reading

Criminal Justice Act 1991
Children and Young Persons Act 1993
Criminal Justice and Public Order Act 1994
Crime and Disorder Act 1998
Misspent Youth Report 1996: Audit Commission
Arthur, R. (2009). Demise of Welfare Considerations in the Youth Justice System: The Criminal Justice and Immigration Act 2008. Family Law, 38, 1117–20.

White Collar Crime

Crime committed, usually by professional persons or corporations, for financial gain and often in the workplace. It would include fraud, tax evasion, insider-dealing, unfair competition, forgery and computer crime.

Traditionally this type of crime has not been systematically prosecuted because of its complexity, expense and financial vested interests. Recently, however, public awareness of the scale and cost of such activities has increased the rate of prosecutions.

Further Reading

Nelken, D. (1994). White Collar Crime. Hart Publishing.

White Paper

A government paper, presented to <u>Parliament</u>, regarding proposed <u>legislation</u> and often including a draft <u>Bill.</u>

Whistle-blower

A person, often an employee with inside knowledge, who reveals information in the public interest (which he may be contractually bound to keep confidential) in order to put a stop to illegal activity or wrongdoing.

The term derives from the practice of English policemen of blowing their whistles when they observed the commission of a crime in order to alert law enforcement officers and/or the public.

To counteract the reprisals (e.g., bullying, intimidation, suspension and dismissals) that these informants often encountered, the Public Interest Disclosure Act was passed in 1998. It protects genuine disclosures of information or suspicions regarding criminal and civil wrongs, <u>miscarriages of justice</u>, cover-ups and health, safety or environmental concerns.

Witch Hunt

A search for witches or evidence of witchcraft often involving popular hysteria, witchcraft trials and even lynching.

The classic witch-hunting period in Europe was from about 1480–1700 during which there were many thousands of executions.

The modern use of the term is often in connection with (<u>moral panics</u>) about perceived threats or wrongdoers rather than witches (e.g., communists, Satanists).

Witness

A person who gives evidence in court, usually on <u>oath</u> or <u>affirmation</u>.

Witness Care Units

Units set up to improve communication of information to witnesses during criminal justice processes involving staff from both the <u>police</u> and <u>CPS</u>.

Witness Service

The Service, run by <u>Victim Support</u>, which covers all courts in England and Wales and provides information and support for <u>witnesses</u> throughout their <u>pre-trial</u> and court experience.

It encourages victim reporting, testifying and co-operation in criminal <u>prosecutions</u>.

Wolfenden Report

The report produced by the Wolfenden Committee on Homosexual Offences and Prostitution in 1957 which recommended that the law should not interfere in private behaviour on moral grounds unless it was necessary to prevent harm to individuals or the public generally.

It led to the decriminalization of adult, consensual homosexuality in private.

Further Reading

The Sex Offences Act 1967

Women Offender Reduction Programme

A programme which co-ordinates work across criminal justice agencies to ensure they respond more appropriately to the characteristics and needs of female offenders.

Wootton, Barbara

An academic supporter of strict liability in criminal law under which the requirement of proving mens rea may be dispensed with in order to ensure high standards of care and deterrence for the public's protection.

This deterrence-based reasoning is reflected in regulatory offences such as selling contaminated food for which a seller can be prosecuted even though he/she was not reckless or even careless.

Further Reading

Wootton, B. (1981). Crime and the Criminal Law. Cambridge University Press.

Wounding

A most serious non-fatal offence against the person comprising a breach of the skin; a bruise or ruptured blood vessel is not a wound.

Further Reading

Offences against the Person Act 1861 s 18, 20

Xenophobia

A fear or dislike of foreigners or strangers or of anything which is strange or foreign. In the context of crime it is linked to hate crime and racism.

XYY Syndrome (Klinefelter's Syndrome)

The chromosome disorder which has been associated with anti-social and criminal behaviour.

A normal female's sex chromosome is referred to as XX while a male's is XY. At conception, a sperm and egg form a single cell which develops into an embryo.

Rarely, an abnormal cell division may occur resulting in an embryo having an unusual number of sex chromosomes.

Research in the 1960s identified males with an extra Y complement and associated these XYY individuals with 'hyper masculinity' and a tendency towards violence. More recent research has thrown considerable doubt on this theory, particularly as only a very small number of men exhibit this chromosomal abnormality – about 1 per 1000.

Yob

The nineteenth-century slang word for an unruly or aggressive boy (spelt backwards).

Yorkshire Ripper

The colloquial name for the serial killer Peter Sutcliffe who was convicted in 1981 of the murder and mutilation of 13 women in Yorkshire between 1975 and 1980.

He is currently serving a sentence of life imprisonment in Broadmoor prison hospital.

Further Reading

Cross, R. (1981). The Yorkshire Ripper: The In-depth Study of a Mass Killer and His Methods. Harper Collins.

www.yorkshireripper.co.uk

Young Offender

An offender between the ages of 10 and 17 years who is prosecuted in the Youth Court.

Young Offender Assessment Profile (ASSET)

See National Offender Management Service.

Young Offender Institutions (YOIs)

Custodial institutions for young offenders (15–21 years) run by the Prison Service for example, Feltham in West London.

Their focus is on incarceration rather than rehabilitation and care (which are the concerns of secure training centres and local authority secure children's homes).

Young offender wings also exist in adult prisons.

YOIs were introduced by the Criminal Justice Act 1988, although special institutions (borstals) for young offenders have existed since the 1902.

Criticisms have been made that

- imprisonment is inappropriate for young persons;
- intimidatory atmospheres are common which inhibit rehabilitation work and often encourage the adoption of criminal lifestyles;

- education, social, physical and mental health needs of young inmates are not adequately addressed;
- there are inadequate resources and consequently poor conditions;
- violence, disorder and excessive restraints are all too common;
- suicide rates are, tragically, very high.

Further Reading

Young Offender Institution Rules 2000
Prison and Young Offender Institution (Amendment) Rules 2009

Youth Court

A <u>Magistrates' Court</u> trying offences allegedly committed by <u>young offenders</u>.

These magistrates are drawn from a youth panel whose members receive specialist training and sit as a mixed gender <u>bench</u>.

Proceedings are less formal than adult courts and are not usually held in public. Reporting restrictions apply and the media cannot identify <u>defendants</u> without the court's permission.

The aims are to segregate young offenders from adult offenders, minimize the chances of reoffending and to emphasize <u>rehabilitation</u> and <u>restorative justice</u>.

Youth Crime

Crime committed by <u>young offenders</u>.

Historical attitudes to this phenomenon are discussed under the <u>Youth Justice System</u> and the <u>Welfare Model</u>.

In the last decade or so, standardized <u>risk assessment</u> systems (e.g., <u>The Young Offender Assessment Profile (ASSET)</u>) have been adopted whereby attempts are made to identify factors associated with youth crime which are then targeted for intervention.

The main risk factors identified (Farrington 1996) are

- low income and poor accommodation, usually in declining inner cities,
- family instability and weak parental supervision,
- delinquent friendship groups or <u>gang</u> membership,
- drug and alcohol abuse.

This approach has been criticized on the grounds that

- such risk factors will be relative to time, place, ethnic grouping and life-styles;
- it places responsibility too strongly on young persons and their families and underrates situational and environmental factors;
- it may result in premature <u>labelling</u> (as potential offenders) of those who fall within the risk categories.

Y

Further Reading

Muncie, J. (2004). Youth Crime: A Critical Introduction. Sage Publications Ltd.

Youth Justice Board

The statutory Board established in 1998 to provide strategic direction, primarily aimed at preventing offending, to the reformed youth criminal justice system according to three guiding principles:

- Restoration (young offenders should make amends for their offending)
- Responsibility (young offenders and their parents should take responsibility for the prevention of offending)
- Re-integration (young offenders should be reintegrated into society to avoid social exclusion)

The Board operates through youth offending teams.

Further Reading

www.youth-justice-board.gov.uk

Youth Justice System

The distinctive part of the criminal justice system which deals with young persons.

It has its own institutions, personnel and sentencing structures.

Approaches to youth justice have varied enormously through time.

The nineteenth-century welfare model clearly demarcated between adult and juvenile criminal justice regimes; reformatory schools and borstals emphasized discipline, training and caring facilities for young persons.

Twentieth-century legislation continued this protective approach (e.g., Children and Young Persons' Act 1933) predicated on the idea that young offenders were likely to be victims of circumstances and deprivation. This trend continued after World War II as criminality came to be explained in sociological terms and continued into the 1960s.

The legal age of criminal responsibility was raised from 8 to 10 years and responsibility for young persons was transferred from the criminal justice system to local authorities. This approach gave way to the justice model which shifted the emphasis away from the background of offenders towards their behaviour.

The 1980s Conservative government tried to balance commitment to law and order with public expenditure. This led to the strategy of 'diversion' based on the premise that young persons grow out of crime and so should be diverted from custodial institutions wherever possible; at the same time parental responsibility was increasingly emphasised.

This approach was undermined by the moral panics of the 1990s and perceptions that youth crime was escalating; the murder of the toddler, James Bulger, by two 10-year olds was, perhaps, the last straw.

A wide range of punitive 'get tough' measures followed including longer custodial sentences, secure training centres, modelled on US 'boot camps' and de-juvenilization policies. New labour continued this with its 'tough on crime, tough on causes of crime' approach aimed at crime prevention and early intervention. The main measures introduced at this time were contained in the Crime and Disorder Act 1998 and Youth Justice and Criminal Evidence Act 1999 and included

- Removal of doli incapax
- Introduction of curfews, child safety orders, anti-social behaviour orders

Y

Table 6 Models of criminal justice

	Justice model	Welfare model	Restorative justice	Principled/human rights
Underlying principles/ philosophy	• Stable society crucial • Crime is an act against society (disturbs equilibrium between individuals & society, weakens the rule of law) • Young offender is threat to society (individually responsible) • Need to establish blame/guilt • Punishment is effective (imposes pain, deters crime, incapacitates) • Punishment is proportionate (fits the crime, just deserts) • Crime control characteristics • Emphasis on law / lawyers	• Youth crime is a fault / creation of adult society (an expression of social malaise) • Causes of crime are crucial • Young offender is a victim of society's neglect (not individually responsible) • Focus on offender not the offence • Punishment is ineffective • Prevention is crucial • Emphasis on informality and individualisation (flexible procedures) • Educate public opinion • Causes of crime are crucial	• Crime is an act against the community • Crime control lies in the relationship within the community • Victims central in the process • Accountability assumes responsibility • Focus is on individual and social dimensions • Less emphasis on law • Punishment alone is not effective • Catharsis and forgiveness • Reintegration of young offenders	• Rights-based • Uniform standards and treatment-based on inherent rights of children • Children as innocents in need of protection
Features	• Focus on Young Offenders • Formalism • Adversarial process • Due process • Custodial sentences	• Focus on young offenders' needs • Informal and discretionary • Inquisitorial process • Crime control rests with community • Early detection and treatment • Individualised disposal	• Focus on victim • Problem-solving strategies • Voluntary settlements outside judicial system • Reduced institutional disposals • Individualization	• Standard minimum rules for juvenile justice on ratification of international and European conventions and rules • Return of young offenders in family/ community
Success =	Just, deserved punishment	Rehabilitated young offenders	Satisfaction of all parties	
Countries	Finland, Germany, Hungary, Netherlands, Norway, Poland, Sweden, South (Canada, China, Russia, South Africa, US)	Austria, Belgium, France, Italy, Netherlands, Scotland (Australia, India, New Zealand, South Korea)	Belgium, France, Germany, Italy, Netherlands, United Kingdom (Australia, New Zealand)	Most countries (exception: USA)

Source: Moore, C. and McFarquhar, H. (2004).

- Restorative justice measures (e.g., reparation and referral orders)
- Youth Justice Board
- Youth Offending Teams
- Parenting Orders

There has been significant opposition to these measures and subsequent legislation shows signs of return to welfare ideas.

Further Reading

Table 6 below which summarizes aspects of criminal justice models in the context of youth justice.

Youth Offending Service

Multiagency teams, co-ordinated by local authorities and overseen by the Youth Justice Board, dealing with young offenders.

They were established by the Crime and Disorder Act 1998 to reduce the risk of juvenile recidivism and incarceration and to provide support and counselling. They supervise youngsters who have been given community sentences and can encourage meetings with their victims with a view to reparation and rehabilitation. They also try to engage them in positive community tasks and supervise their general activities, liaise with their schools and arrange therapy sessions for them where appropriate. They also write pre-sentencing reports.

These are crucial agencies whose aim is to ensure consistency in the Youth Justice System.

Y

Z z

Zemiology

Derived from the Greek word 'zemia' (harm), this is a contemporary criminological theory advocating a move away from study based on the legal definitions of crime towards the study of a much wider range of harms, including racism, sexism, economic exploitation, corporate corruption, pollution and homelessness.

It recognizes that there are greater threats to society far more serious than crime in its narrow legal sense.

Zero-tolerance

The term given to extreme intolerance of anti-social behaviour adopted in the US and Canada in the 1980s and in the UK in the 1990s.

This is reflected in very punitive criminal justice policies with the emphasis on crime reduction and hard-line punishments, even for first offenders.

Specifically zero-tolerance puts emphasis on

- fear of crime
- targeting crime hot-spots
- reducing crime opportunities
- toughness on crime (e.g., boot camps)
- strict, and often automatic, sentences (three strikes rules)
- refusal to ignore low-level criminality
- Short-term strategies at the expense of longer-term ones

This approach has given rise to many concerns, not least of which are its

- apparent simplistic 'quick fix' approach which fails to address the underlying causes of crime
- tendency to operate disproportionately on minority groups
- encouragement of heavy-handed police practices
- reduction of police discretion and criminalization of relatively minor activities
- heavy administrative burden and consequent drain on resources
- exaggerated success rate

Zone Theory

See Concentric Zone Theory.

Index